BAROMETER
OF
FEAR

BAROMETER OF

AN INSIDER'S ACCOUNT OF ROGUE TRADING AND THE GREATEST BANKING SCANDAL IN HISTORY

FEAR

ALEXIS STENFORS

ZED

Zed Books

LONDON

Barometer of Fear: An Insider's Account of Rogue Trading and the Greatest Banking Scandal in History was first published in 2017 by Zed Books Ltd, The Foundry, 17 Oval Way, London SE11 5RR, UK.

www.zedbooks.net

Typeset in Haarlemmer by seagulls.net
Index by John Barker
Cover design by Alice Marwick

A catalogue record for this book is available from the British Library.

ISBN 978-1-78360-929-1 hb
ISBN 978-1-78360-928-4 pb
ISBN 978-1-78360-930-7 pdf
ISBN 978-1-78360-931-4 epub
ISBN 978-1-78360-932-1 mobi

CONTENTS

ACKNOWLEDGEMENTS

Maria, I cannot thank you enough for your endless support, encouragement and optimism with this project ever since I scribbled down those first few sentences in February 2009. 'Skriv boken!' were two words that meant a lot to me during the writing process. It has been a rocky ride and, yes, I wish I had chosen a somewhat different path. Rebecca and Magdalena, thank you for being such wonderful daughters. I am so happy to have been given the opportunity to be a more present father since you were eight and six.

Ian Ryan, many thanks for getting me into the habit of taking mental and written notes of important events, and for enlightening me about the difference between law and morality. Ken Barlow, thank you for motivating me to explain things I take for granted. You have been a great editor and listener throughout this project. Judith Forshaw, thank you for the copyediting and your love of language.

I am also grateful to many of you on the trading floors across the world, whether still physically there or in memory alone.

ABBREVIATIONS

ACI	Association Cambiste Internationale
BBA	British Bankers' Association
BBAIRS	BBA Interest Rate Settlement
BIS	Bank for International Settlements
CDO	collateralised debt obligation
CDOR	Canadian Dollar Offered Rate
CDS	credit default swap
CEO	chief executive officer
CIA	Central Intelligence Agency
CIBOR	Copenhagen Interbank Offered Rate
CME	Chicago Mercantile Exchange
CPI	Consumer Price Index
CRS	cross-currency basis swap
ECB	European Central Bank
ERM	Exchange Rate Mechanism
EU	European Union
EURIBOR	Euro Interbank Offered Rate
FBI	Federal Bureau of Investigation
FCA	Financial Conduct Authority
FIBOR	Frankfurt Interbank Offered Rate
FRA	forward rate agreement
FSA	Financial Services Authority
FX	foreign exchange
GDP	gross domestic product
HELIBOR	Helsinki Interbank Offered Rate

ICMA	International Capital Market Association
IMM	International Monetary Market
IRS	interest rate swap
ISDA	International Swaps and Derivatives Association
KLIBOR	Kuala Lumpur Interbank Offered Rate
LIBOR	London Interbank Offered Rate
LIFFE	London International Financial Futures and Options Exchange
NIBOR	Norwegian Interbank Offered Rate
OIS	overnight index swap
OPEC	Organization of the Petroleum Exporting Countries
OTC	over the counter
PIBOR	Paris Interbank Offered Rate
PRA	Prudential Regulation Authority
SEC	Securities and Exchange Commission
SFO	Serious Fraud Office
SIMEX	Singapore International Monetary Exchange
STIBOR	Stockholm Interbank Offered Rate
STIRT	Short-term Interest Rate Trading
TAF	Term Auction Facility
TIBOR	Tokyo Interbank Offered Rate
TIFFE	Tokyo International Financial Futures Exchange

INTRODUCTION

'It's a misunderstanding'

'How can the FSA be sure you will not do this again?' This is the last question I can remember from my interview with the UK financial regulator on 24 August 2009. Whenever I reconstruct that day in my head, or the events that led up to my being compelled to attend the meeting in Canary Wharf, I try to recall what I answered. The easiest option would be, perhaps, to listen to the CD recordings of the interview. Signed and sealed copies are held by both the regulator and myself.

For some reason, though, I do not want to force myself into being reminded of that precise moment, or what led up to it. So no, I am not going to listen to the recordings.

I do, however, remember exactly what I was *thinking* when the last question was shot across the table (the phrasing of it made it quite clear that the hearing was approaching its end). The sky was unusually clear that day, and I looked briefly out of the window to my left. I never wanted to go through this again, would never put myself in a position where I *had* to go through this again. That, then, was my answer.

* * *

Six months earlier, after 15 years working in the foreign exchange and interest rate derivatives markets, I had been labelled a 'rogue trader'.

1

I had gone to India on holiday, and on the second day (it was 17 February 2009) I made a phone call to my manager at Merrill Lynch, who, as it happened, was also away from the office, telling him I wanted to talk. He said he was in a ski lift in Switzerland, and told me that he would call back in two or three hours. When he did, he initiated a conversation that would become the most difficult of my life.

I informed him that my trading books were overvalued and had been so since mid-January. I had hoped that this would only be temporary but the markets had continued to move against me.

'How much are we talking about?' he asked.

'It could be 100 million.'

'Why didn't you tell me?'

'I really don't know,' I replied. 'But now I feel ashamed. I want to apologise.'

Having opened the floodgates, the questioning began. I was interrogated about risk, volatility, hedging, 2008, liquidity, the credit crunch, Lehman Brothers, Merrill Lynch, other people's losses, price movements, my previous boss, Bank of America, bonuses, profits, honesty, 2009, management, pressure, smoothing of profit and loss, exhaustion.

Towards the end of our 45-minute conversation he asked: 'Could this be a momentary lapse of reason?'

'Yes,' I replied.

'This is obviously very serious,' he said. 'It could go all the way up to the FSA.'

'What do you mean by that?' I asked, having never had anything to do with the regulator, let alone met anyone from the Financial Services Authority.

2

'My job could be in danger. You're a good trader, and I just wish you'd told me earlier.'

I apologised again.

'How long will you be on holiday?' he asked, winding up the conversation.

'Until 2 March.'

'Let's talk about it when you come back. In the meantime, call me if anything new comes up and I'll do likewise,' he responded. Before hanging up, he told me to enjoy the rest of my holiday.

I had just admitted to mismarking my books by $100 million, and the conversation had ended with 'Enjoy your holiday!'

It didn't make sense.

At that moment, my confusion very quickly turned into suspicion, and suspicion turned into fear. I no longer trusted my boss. The fact that he wished me well made me certain he was hiding his real intentions, and I did not want to be judged within the four walls of a Merrill Lynch boardroom.

I desperately wanted an objective opinion on the situation, so decided to call an employment lawyer and explain everything in detail. When, a few hours later, my case was passed on to Ian Ryan, a partner and Head of Business Crime and Professional Discipline at Finers Stephens Innocent, I began to realise the scale of the problem. What, then, was the right thing to do? I made the decision to fly back to London in order to see him the next day. Back home, I also booked a session with a psychotherapist. Over the following months, there would be many sessions, both with the lawyer and with the psychotherapist.

It took about two weeks before the *New York Times* got hold of my mobile number. A media storm ensued, as well as investigations on both sides of the Atlantic.

In the end, it was claimed that my actions had resulted in the loss of $456 million for Merrill Lynch. It was a lot of money, but it did not involve criminality. The Irish Financial Regulator (Merrill Lynch had many trading entities, and many trades were done, presumably for tax reasons, in the name of Merrill Lynch International Bank Limited Dublin) fined the bank €2.75 million in October 2009. The regulator concluded that the bank had an inadequate month-end independent price verification process and had failed to put in place a well-defined and transparent line of supervisory responsibility. Moreover, there had been a failure to supervise my 'activity' and to manage effectively market risk limits in respect of my activities.[1] Effectively, they had shirked their responsibility to oversee what I was doing.

In March 2010, when the FSA had concluded its investigation, I was handed a five-year prohibition order. This was, in effect, a ban from working in the City of London. Considering the status of the FSA and of the City of London as a global financial centre, it basically meant being barred from working in the financial services industry anywhere in the world. The case was closed.

* * *

This book project started when I sent myself an email on 19 February 2009. The email contained everything I could remember of what had happened two days previously. I wrote it to myself out of fear and paranoia and not thinking much more about it. It finished in the middle of a sentence, in the middle of a word. Perhaps I got interrupted. Perhaps I needed a break. I can't remember.

Most likely, I wanted to decipher the words and short sentences I had written on page after page in the notepad from the hotel. Some of them simply read like this:

no market, no liquidity
Why hide?
46 min
1 min enjoy holiday 2 weeks
WHO TO TRUST?
Asgamar ('vultures' in Swedish)
If I thought this was this serious I had resigned
Pressure
Higher up
Apologise
WHAT TO DO?

Since I had been a teenager, I had been writing notes, diary entries and (both finished and unfinished) letters. This time, however, it was different. It was difficult to explain how I felt when I scribbled down those notes and what was truly going on inside my head when, three weeks later, my name suddenly appeared on the front pages of newspapers across the world. As I was still employed by the bank, I could not speak to journalists to put my version across. And as I was suspended pending an investigation, I was not allowed to speak to any colleagues, clients or competitors either. My world had shrunk drastically, and I knew nothing would ever be the same again. I felt that the media reporting was narrow and one-sided and writing became a way of letting off steam.

I also wanted to create a counterbalance on my Google history. I knew that my daughters, who were eight and six years old at the time, would one day look me up on the internet. When – not if – that happened, I wanted to be able to explain and tell the story from *my* perspective. They would forget that I had ever been a trader, but I wouldn't. Gradually, the purpose of the writing became less about taking notes and organising memories, and more about the search for some kind of understanding. I began reading what others had written about 'people like me' and the world I had worked in for 15 years. As I continued to receive numerous questions about myself, about trading, about banks and about the episode in 2009 – many of which were extremely difficult to answer – I began to structure these thoughts.

Therefore, the first purpose of this book is an attempt to describe *why*, when looking out of that window in Canary Wharf in August 2009, I felt that I would never want to go through it again. *Why* I would never put myself in a position where I had to go through it again. Where did that *fear* come from?

There was, however, another element that kept me moving forward during this episode. I had always wanted to do a PhD, and a lifelong dream had now been granted an unusual beginning. Despite everything that was going on around me (not to mention within myself), I managed to put together a research proposal and send it off to Costas Lapavitsas, a professor at SOAS, University of London. Reading it now, the proposal looks both unprofessional and non-academic. I had not set foot in a university for 15 years. My writing style had been heavily influenced by the trading floor lingo I had picked up over the years. Rather than a clearly constructed research plan, I sent across fragments and observations that I thought were important, and that had bothered me deeply for a while.

One such observation I introduced in the heading 'London Interbank Offered Rate (LIBOR[2]) manipulation'. Another was 'Foreign exchange (FX) order books'. Both of these outlined how the foreign exchange and money markets were systematically manipulated, how it was being covered up, and how it affected people all over the world. I was mostly concerned by the fact that 99.99 per cent of people were completely unaware of the fact that it was going on.

Costas, who agreed to become my supervisor, seemed to believe in my radical statement that LIBOR, contrary to what all academic textbooks said, was not a market *at all*. It was something different. I could not put my finger on precisely where the problem lay, but there *was* a problem. I had seen it with my own eyes. However, when I approached SOAS in April 2009 (only a month after the media storm), I could not foresee the enormous scandal that would unfold three years later.

My PhD was never intended to study financial markets as 'scandals'.[3] In 2011, however, when I realised that this was, in fact, exactly what they one day would be regarded as, I decided to keep my academic work strictly academic, and instead share some of the anecdotes later. The reason why I felt the need to compartmentalise my academic work, separate from my personal relationship with the financial markets, was as follows.

On a sunny afternoon during the summer of 2011, I met up with a former colleague and money market broker for a couple of beers in Borough Market, not far from London Bridge. He had sent me warm and encouraging text messages back in March 2009, at a time when I was feeling extremely isolated. I had not been allowed to reply to any of his messages, as he counted as a person Merrill Lynch had forbidden me from having any contact with during the investigations into my trading activities. Now, however, I had slowly begun to find my feet again and truly appreciated when ex-colleagues, ex-competitors, ex-clients and ex-brokers invited me out for a beer or two to chat about the good old days. Although it was nice to meet up again after more than two years, I also had a couple of questions relating to my PhD research that I thought he could shed some light on. I had traded LIBOR derivatives amounting to billions of dollars on a daily basis. He had acted as an intermediary, matching banks that wanted to buy with banks that wanted to sell.

He said he felt sorry for what I had gone through during 2009, and passed on regards from former competitors who occasionally claimed that they missed having me around, especially Tom Hayes, who had been the biggest player in the Japanese yen market and with whom I had traded more or less daily for a number of years.

Then, evidently unaware of the scale of what he had done, he brought up LIBOR manipulation in the Japanese yen market. He did not use the word 'manipulation', but I immediately understood what he was referring to. He casually, but also somewhat nervously, asked me whether I thought he had done anything wrong by being part of 'it'.

I remember that I replied: 'Yes, this could be very serious.'

I didn't ask more. I probably didn't want to know.

When I got back home to North London, I was still in shock. I felt sick, vomiting several times while trying to make sense of what I had learned.

The incident brought back very clear memories of my spontaneous reaction when Louise Story, a journalist from the *New York Times*, called me out of the blue in early March 2009. I was on my way to see Ian, my lawyer. When I came out of Great Portland Street tube station, I could see that someone had tried to call my mobile. The number began with +1 212. New York? I had no idea who it was, so I dialled the number.

I cannot remember what she said. But somehow she knew about my mismarking and wanted me to confirm it, and then comment and elaborate on a theory linking it to the senior management at Merrill Lynch.

'It's a misunderstanding,' I recall replying, and quickly hung up.

Although I never expanded on the words, I was referring to the whole situation, which to my mind was immensely complicated. I could not explain over the phone in a way she would understand. But at the time, I don't think I fully understood it either.

Ian's law firm was only a few minutes' walk from the tube station. The conversation had made me uneasy, so when I mentioned it to him he took control of the situation, went into another room and called the newspaper. I remember from our conversation afterwards that the journalist had claimed that I had a nickname in the market: 'The 900 Million Dollar Gorilla'. Ian asked me whether this was true. 'I've never heard it before,' I said.

'Thought so,' he replied. 'I told her she wasn't allowed to write that.'

It was, however, quite clear that she was going to write a story and that it could be on the front page of *The New York*

Times the next morning. We decided to let Merrill Lynch know about the upcoming article. I don't know if this was necessary, but it felt like the right thing to do at the time. I knew that I had done something wrong, and wanted to help put things right in any way possible.

The newspaper story with the headline 'Undisclosed Losses at Merrill Lynch Lead to a Trading Inquiry' went like this.[4] The day on which Lehman Brothers went bankrupt in September 2008, Bank of America agreed to buy Merrill Lynch, which otherwise would also have gone bankrupt. The acquisition was supposed to go through on 1 January 2009. However, during the last quarter of 2008, Merrill Lynch lost *another* $13.8 billion (there had been huge losses previously) on risky investments and complex derivatives, which forced Bank of America to seek a second rescue package from Washington, DC, i.e. the American taxpayers.

Bank of America's shareholders (who, in essence, had bought Merrill Lynch) did not know about the losses. Nor did they know that senior management at Merrill Lynch had decided to speed up the bonus payments ahead of the takeover. Rather than paying bankers and traders (and themselves) during the spring, which was the norm, the bonus payments would take place on New Year's Eve, only a few hours before Bank of America would formally take over the assets and liabilities of the 100-year-old investment bank.

As Brad Hintz, an analyst with Sanford C. Bernstein & Company, told the newspaper: 'There is a massive cultural disconnect in the trading area. You have Bank of America, where it would seem foreign to ride a motorcycle without wearing a helmet, and at Merrill, the legacy is still there, from the CDOs [collateralised debt obligations] and the risks they took on.'

The analyst was certainly right about the culture. I had taken an enormous amount of risk and had not been wearing a helmet.

'Of particular concern are the activities of a Merrill currency trader in London, Alexis Stenfors, whose trading has come under scrutiny by British regulators, according to people briefed on the investigation,' the *New York Times* wrote. Although the newspaper seemed to be right about Merrill Lynch, and more or less so about me too, I didn't feel that the story made sense. Who was the Bank of America executive who 'spoke on the condition that he not be named because of the delicate nature of the inquiry'? Why did the journalist write that risk officers had 'discovered irregularities' in my trading account during my holiday, making it sound like I was some kind of fugitive? What did I have to do with the Bank of America takeover of Merrill Lynch?

It was a misunderstanding.

But it got a lot worse. Within 48 hours, it seemed like every newspaper and TV channel had reported on the story. It spread like wildfire. *The Guardian*, *Financial Times*, *Wall Street Journal*, *Sydney Morning Herald*, Sky News. The *Evening Standard* rang the doorbell while I was making pancakes for my daughters. A picture of me, looking startled in my favourite long-sleeved shirt (emblazoned with the logo of Swedish rock band Kent), appeared on the front page the next day.[5] Someone told me that a local paper close to the Finnish town I grew up in even went on to claim that I had caused the global financial crisis. Later, Jon Snow, the anchor for Channel 4 News, analysed me on his blog.

'You're famous now!' a broker from Tradition texted.

Yes, but for the wrong reasons, I thought.

I desperately wanted to comment on some of the things that were being said. However, until Merrill Lynch (and Bank of America, of course) had concluded their investigation, I was still an employee and had to follow their rules. I was not allowed to talk. Even so, I am not sure that I would have been able to make myself feel *less* misunderstood. I was completely out of touch with reality after my years as a trader. It would take some time before I rediscovered the ability to reflect upon things.

I knew that my acquaintance, the former broker I met in Borough Market, had done something very serious. *If* LIBOR were to be manipulated, thousands of companies and millions of people would be affected. But equally, it was quite clear that he did not understand *how*. To him, LIBOR was just a number. An important number, yes, but important only for a few traders and brokers who traded derivatives linked to it. He had no idea what LIBOR really was and how extremely important it had become.

I was certain that he, one day, would feel very misunderstood.

Almost exactly a year later, in July 2012, the LIBOR scandal erupted.

* * *

When, on 3 August 2015, Tom Hayes was found guilty of LIBOR manipulation and sentenced to 14 years in prison,[6] I skimmed through an ever-growing list of articles about him. By now, the newspapers had stopped reporting on what LIBOR *was*. What until 2012 had been known to only a few traders and bankers was now general knowledge. *The Telegraph* provided a list of the most hilarious and outrageous quotes from the world's first LIBOR trial. 'Just give the cash desk a Mars bar and they'll set [LIBOR] wherever you want,' Tom had told a broker in 2006. 'Not even Mother Teresa wouldn't manipulate LIBOR if she was setting it and trading it,' he had said in an interview with the Serious Fraud Office (SFO).[7] Comments such as these did not look good in a newspaper, or in front of a jury, of course. But during 15 years on the trading floor I had heard much worse.

One quote forced me to pause and reflect. 'I used to dream about LIBORs,' Tom had told prosecutors. 'They were my bread and butter, you know. That was the thing. They were the instrument that underlined everything that I traded.'

I used to be woken up at 1.30 a.m. every morning by LIBORs. Brokers in Asia texted me 'run-throughs' of where the market expected LIBOR would be later that day when London woke up. I remembered how I, too, used to have dreams about LIBOR.

LIBOR is sometimes said to be the world's most important number. It is therefore not surprising that the 'LIBOR scandal', or the discovery that the number had been manipulated by banks, has also been coined the greatest banking scandal in history. From an academic perspective, the whole episode has put the integrity of arguably the most important 'price' in economics and finance into question. However, the real issue is not academic at all. LIBOR is used not only in more than $350 trillion worth of financial derivatives, but also in mortgages, bonds, and corporate and student loan contracts – as well as in valuation methods relating to accounting, tax, risk management and central bank policy. Although investigations, litigation processes and criminal proceedings are still ongoing, it is already safe to conclude that a vast number of people and institutions have been affected by the manipulation of LIBOR rates by banks. Benchmarks referencing interest rates are of crucial importance for society by virtue of being deeply rooted in the financial system as a whole. They affect not only central banks and other banks and financial institutions, but also corporations, investors and households. That is why the LIBOR manipulation has had consequences far beyond the few dozen traders and banks involved in setting the rate. If you have a mortgage, student loan or credit card, it is quite possible that you are exposed to LIBOR. And even if you manage all your finances under the mattress, it is probable that you have been affected *indirectly* by the manipulation.

LIBOR was not an isolated incident. Other benchmarks that were supposed to reflect how banks lend to each other were also manipulated, such as the Euro Interbank Offered Rate (EURIBOR) and the Tokyo Interbank Offered Rate (TIBOR). As was the lesser-known ISDAfix, a widely used reference rate for complex interest rate derivatives. Even the largest market on earth – the $5.1 trillion-a-day foreign exchange market – was found to have been subject to a conspiracy between banks.

It appears, then, as if banks have used their power to secretly abuse markets, manipulate benchmarks and defraud customers in virtually all the markets in which I had actively been a trader for 15 years. When people talked about a cultural and ethical crisis in the world of finance, I was definitively one of those who had 'been there'.

* * *

The second purpose of this book is to try to explain, through my eyes, what this world looked like. To a degree, it is an exploration into the sometimes seemingly arcane benchmarks and acronyms that few people had heard of before the scandals broke – and the markets for certain financial instruments that Warren Buffett famously referred to as 'weapons of financial mass destruction'.[8]

It is also about trading psychology, strategies and techniques in these markets that, despite being ethically and legally questionable, seem to have been passed down from one generation of traders to the next. It is about the banks creating, selling and trading all those financial instruments, and the culture of risk taking and money making in the City and on Wall Street. Most of all, however, it is about *perceptions* about these markets and the people working in them. No matter how convenient they are, perceptions can be deceptive.

From August 2007 onwards, everything I did as a trader came to focus on what the former Chairman of the Federal Reserve Alan Greenspan famously termed 'the barometer of fears of bank insolvency'.[9] Greenspan argued that LIBOR, when put in a specific context, was a kind of fear index related to banks.

He was right. The fear was measurable. And because it was measurable, fear could also be bought and sold. Which is what I did.

CHAPTER 1

THE BAROMETER OF FEAR

My first encounter with LIBOR came in August 1992. I had finished a semester at the University of Cologne as part of a university exchange programme, and was given the chance to extend my stay in Germany for five months by doing an internship.

I had just written an essay entitled 'Exchange-rate Risks and Hedging Strategies', and sent an application to the second-largest bank in Frankfurt: Dresdner Bank. They seemed to like that I was interested in derivatives and foreign exchange markets and invited me to an interview. A month later, I found myself in the back office for interest rate derivatives.

I rented a cheap room in the Bahnhofsviertel, just a few blocks from the central station and within walking distance from the bank. It struck me that the heroin addicts who inhabited the red light district and the park next to it did not seem to pay any attention to the swarms of bankers in dark suits who walked past them every morning. But the ignorance seemed mutual.

I was seated next to a gold trader who was approaching retirement and for some reason did not have a desk on the trading floor below. He was probably 40 years older than me and constantly made jokes in an amusing Düsseldorf dialect. I liked him. Somehow, he had access to the vault in the basement,

17

which held the bank's stock of gold bars. Once (he was probably eager to impress), he took me downstairs. It was huge and looked exactly as I'd imagined it would from watching films. He invited me to hold one of the bars. I can still remember how astonished I was by its weight.

I was fascinated by the buzz on the twenty-seventh floor, where the trading took place. I had never seen anything like it. Grown men (there were not many women around) in suits shouting down phone lines, shouting at each other, or doing both at the same time. But I was also intrigued by the large numbers on the time-stamped trade tickets that were passed to the back office throughout the day. They could be 10, 50 or 100 million deutschmarks (or dollars, pounds, francs …). And they all related to the newly invented derivative instruments: interest rate swaps, forward rate agreements, cross-currency basis swaps, caps, floors and so on.

The actual work I did, however, was not that exciting. When a deal was done on the twenty-seventh floor, the trader would scribble some details on a ticket the size of an A5 sheet of paper. Each ticket was numbered and had boxes that had to be filled in: Instrument, Counterparty, Buy/Sell, Benchmark, Maturity, Currency, Amount, Trade Date, Fixing Date, Settlement Date, Deal Rate.

We regularly took the elevator down one floor to pick up the tickets. I then had to check whether the trade details corresponded to the deal confirmations sent out to the counterparties, and whether the confirmations sent by the counterparties corresponded to the confirmations sent by the bank. They had to match. What mattered to us in the back office was that clients and banks received their trade confirmations promptly, and that the correct payments were made and received. Some clients were more important than others, we were told, and their deals needed to be processed faster. Some traders also appeared to be more important than others, and their trades had to be prioritised.

Everything else was just about numbers, and after having seen thousands of such trade tickets, the fascination with the big numbers gradually wore off. It was just a job, and equally monotonous as sorting and packaging tomatoes, which I had done throughout the whole summer in 1989. It was like a factory. A box filled with 10 kilograms of vegetables had been replaced by a box filled with 10 million deutschmarks' worth of financial derivatives written on a feather-light piece of paper.

Of all the things that were checked on the trade tickets, the 'Benchmark' was probably the one that received the least attention. The box simply contained a five-letter word in capital letters: LIBOR, FIBOR (Frankfurt Interbank Offered Rate), sometimes PIBOR (Paris Interbank Offered Rate).

The five-letter words referred to which interest rate would be referenced when the contract was settled at some point in the future. The rate would then ultimately determine whether the bank (or the client) had made or lost money – and how much – by having done the deal in the first place.

The interest rate was simply a number provided by Telerate, a market data and information provider that competed with Reuters. Every day, around lunchtime, page 3750 on Telerate would be updated with the new LIBOR interest rates for different currencies (US dollars, British pounds, Swiss francs, etc.) and for maturities ranging from one day to one year. Page 22000 would contain the FIBOR rates, page 20041 was dedicated to PIBOR, and so on.

The numbers looked a bit like *The Matrix*: a grid of orderly sequences of flickering green numbers filling up a black screen.

* * *

I have often said to people that I became a trader almost by accident, but that is only partially true. The fact is that I had been interested in foreign currencies, foreign languages and international affairs since I was a child. I quite liked maths, and went on to study at the Stockholm School of Economics. In that sense, trading was undoubtedly a job where I would be able to make use of my skills, while also having the opportunity to analyse international trends and events on a daily basis.

However, when I returned to Sweden to finish my master's degree in December 1992, there were not many jobs around in finance (or at all, to be honest). Sweden was recovering from a devastating banking crisis and the situation in Finland, my home country, was even worse. The Soviet Union, Finland's biggest trading partner, had collapsed and a long era of austerity had arrived. Everyone, it seemed, had a hiring freeze, not least the banks, which were either bankrupt, had been nationalised, or were afraid of going bankrupt or being nationalised.

The only ad that I found on the noticeboard outside the Student Union matching my educational background was from Midland Montagu. It was a British bank with a tiny office in Stockholm, and they were looking for money market trainees. I applied, stating in my letter dated 17 June 1993 (freely translated): 'Starting as a money market trainee would not only be a great challenge, but also provide me with great pleasure and stimulation. Even though I lack rigorous work experience, I am somewhat familiar with, and particularly have a burning interest in, money markets and economics.'

From then on, things moved quickly. I got an interview, and they offered me a job – not as a trader but as a sales person. At the time, I didn't really know the difference between the two, but I happily accepted anyway. The client base consisted of insurance companies, pension funds and large Swedish multinationals making cars, refrigerators, phones or flat-pack furniture. I would be given a list of (the least lucrative) clients and I had to try to convince them to buy or sell T-bills (treasury bills), government bonds and mortgage bonds.

The basic idea behind these products was rather simple. Imagine you decide to lend £1,000 to a friend for a year, and that your friend promises to pay back the whole amount plus £100 in interest. You have now entered into a standard loan contract where you run the risk that your friend might not be able to pay the money back. A T-bill, however, would work as follows. Your friend announces that they want to borrow £1,000 and would be prepared to pay it back with £100 in interest. They issue a piece of paper stating that £1,100 will be paid to whoever happens to own that paper in a year's time. From your perspective, this is a slightly better proposition. Should you, in a couple of months' time, begin to doubt your friend's ability to pay the whole amount, you could try to sell the paper to someone else (perhaps even an enemy). Your friend might like the T-bill idea too, because, in theory, money could be borrowed from almost anyone. In reality, however, only large institutions are able to raise money this way.

T-bills are securities that expire within a year and are issued by governments, whereas bonds refer to papers with longer maturities. Mortgage bonds are securities issued by institutions involved in mortgage lending. Considering the small size of the country, the Swedish fixed-income market (the common name for these products) was enormous. The government had borrowed a lot for an extended period of time and therefore had accumulated substantial debts. These debts could be traded in the market as securities, and this is precisely what we did.

The dealing room was minuscule compared with the one I had seen in Frankfurt, containing no more than 15 or 20 seats. In fact, it looked more like a gentlemen's club than a bank: high ceilings, expensive oak floors, chandeliers and only a discreet sign outside revealing the nature of the business conducted by Midland Montagu on Birger Jarlsgatan in Stockholm.

My training programme, which took place on day 2 and day 3 of my employment, looked like this:

Tuesday
09.30 IT
10.30 Credit and Risk
13.00 Finance Department
14.00 Back Office
15.00 Equity Department
16.00 Management

Wednesday
09.30 Human Resources
10.30 Corporate Banking

On day 4 (having successfully completed my training course in less than 48 hours), the time was ripe to learn how to become a trader. It turned out that just a few weeks before I joined,

Swedbank (a large Swedish bank) had poached every trader but one from Midland Montagu. The situation was a bit uncertain to say the least, and the junior trader who had decided to stay was catapulted into the position of acting chief dealer. The sales person with whom I was supposed to work suddenly became assistant trader. This was neither the time nor the place for me to be trained as a sales person looking after clients. The pecking order was made clear to me. A sales person could be sacrificed for a trader, but never the other way round.

The chief economist took charge of the training. An odd choice perhaps, but he was very respected in the dealing room and also happened to know the ins and outs of trading. It was old school. The junior economist, who was the other new recruit alongside myself, and I were told to stay in the dealing room for an hour after work one evening. The session was about learning how to master the technique of using two ears, two hands and two telephones to call two banks at the same time.

The chief dealer might have to buy 500 million T-bills from the other market makers to cover a client trade. As the dozen or so banks and brokerage firms quoting Swedish T-bills did so only in tickets of 50 million, we would need to deal with ten of them. The task therefore required five people. The chief dealer would tell the five traders to call out on, say, the 'December T-bill' (a debt obligation issued by the Swedish government maturing in December). We would then each press the speed dial to the two banks that were designated to us and ask for a two-way price on the December T-bill. One by one, the banks would quote a price at which they would buy (a 'bid') and at which they would sell (an 'offer') 50 million. One by one, these prices would be shouted across the dealing room to the chief dealer, who would then decide what to do and would shout back 'Mine!', 'Yours!' or 'Thanks, but nothing there!' We would then immediately repeat 'Mine!', 'Yours!' or 'Thanks, but nothing there!' to the person on the other line.

Clients were referred to as market or price '*takers*', referring to how they approached the market place. We and our competitors, on the other hand, were market or price '*makers*', as we quoted the prices they could trade at. One of the key requirements to becoming a member of the market-making club was that you always had to quote two-way prices to the other club members: a bid and an offer at the same time. A gentlemen's agreement also dictated that you had only a few seconds to decide what to do. Otherwise, the person on the other line would shout 'Risk!' This meant that you could no longer deal based on the stated price and would need to ask again. If, however, you had dealt on a price, you had the right to ask the same bank for another price before they hung up. In this case, the unwritten rule stated that you should ask: 'Next price, please?'

It reminded me of the games we used to play after school when I was a child, where a series of strict rules were solemnly announced ahead of play by the older and more experienced children. As a beginner you would never ask why and how these rules had been invented, or by whom. And when a new player arrived, you recited the rule book as if it were the most natural thing in the world. You did not break the unwritten rules, nor did you ask why they existed.

A 'call-out' was very quick, exciting, loud and sometimes quite chaotic. A large client trade or a choppy market resulted in a large number of trade tickets with different banks in different amounts and at different prices. This invariably meant even more market movement. As soon as we hung up the phone to the other banks, they were already calling us on the other lines because their traders had been commanded to press their speed dials to demand prices from *us*.

An attack led to retaliation, and sometimes it felt like we were foot soldiers repeatedly sent out on missions to shoot at each other. I don't remember if I ever got to meet the two traders who were responsible for picking up the phone at Aragon and Aros, the two brokerage firms behind the enemy line designated to me. However, after thousands of phone calls, hostility was gradually complemented by sympathy and mutual respect. Our loyalty was shared between the bank we worked for, the market we traded in, and the rules of the game. And just as your closest colleague was not always your best friend, your fiercest competitor was not always your worst enemy.

Sometimes call-outs were made for no particular reason, or simply to check the barometer. A string of low prices would indicate that banks were keener to sell than to buy. High prices hinted the opposite. Call-outs were also made to hear the voice of a competing trader. Did he or she sound relaxed, stressed or perhaps nervous about something? Or to listen to the noise levels in the other dealing rooms across the city. What were they up to?

As a result, clients had to be given nicknames in case an incoming caller might accidentally snap up some confidential information. A large construction company might be renamed 'The Screw' or a car manufacturer 'The Shark' (perhaps refer-ring to the copious amounts of hair gel the customer used). These codenames were then changed regularly in order to protect trade secrets and clients' identities. Traders, too, were given nicknames. Paradoxically, such nicknames later came to be used in order to reveal, rather than protect, identities that were supposed to remain secret.

A trader's 'book' would consist of all the trades a trader had in his or her portfolio. A trader's 'position' was then a general term for how sensitive this book was to different price movements in the market. This sensitivity would normally be expressed in the amount made or lost if the market moved by one basis point (0.01 per cent). A 'long position' meant that money would be made if prices in the market went up, and a 'short position' was the opposite. The chief dealer had an assistant keeping track of the positions. It was, of course, necessary to know whether you had accidentally bought too little or too much. You did not want to find out that 50 million T-bills were missing when the market closed for the day. Who knew how much they would cost tomorrow?

When the market was volatile, mistakes happened rather frequently. Simply the *fear* of a possible mistake could lead to irritation and heated conversations. As all phone conversations were recorded, junior traders were often sent out to listen to the tapes of each individual call. It goes without saying that, with the phones bugged, you tried to keep your private life relatively private when you were in the dealing room. Beyond this, nosiness and gossip outside the dealing room were generally frowned upon. Perhaps the collective feeling of constantly being observed led traders to accept and tolerate each other's vulnerabilities. Although the dealing room banter could be raw and unfiltered, it was supposed to be kept secret from 'others'. This naturally strengthened the feeling of 'us versus them',

'them' being pretty much everyone who wasn't a trader (or maybe a sales person or broker).

* * *

My life as a trader was shaped to some extent by the transformation of the banks I worked for. Midland Montagu became Midland Bank Stockholm Branch and we moved to a new dealing room. Soon afterwards, new business cards had to be printed as we adopted the HSBC brand. Within two years, we had developed from a boutique merchant bank into an integral part of an ambitious global banking giant. We, as the tentacle in the Nordic region, would now serve clients not only by quoting prices in bills and bonds, but also in FX and interest rate derivative instruments. Tomas was brought in from Hong Kong to run the dealing room, and extra expertise was flown in from London. A small army of traders and sales people was hired, mostly from Nordbanken, which had been nationalised following the Swedish banking crisis.

I became part of the treasury desk, sitting bang in the middle of the trading floor. Surrounded by the bond and FX spot traders and their respective sales forces, our job was to take care of the funding of the operation as well as to trade a range of money market instruments. Uffe and Toby were experienced FX swap traders and took charge of the risk-taking activities, whereas Erik sorted out the funding of the bank. My job was to look out for arbitrage opportunities in the FX, money and derivatives markets. Basically, it was about mathematically working out – and, as the market moved, continuously recalculating – how to borrow at the lowest possible rate or to lend at the highest. It had taken some time for the derivatives market to establish itself in Scandinavia. Senior traders still talked about the 'yuppie tax', a financial transaction tax; although it had since been abolished, this had completely wiped out the derivatives market during the late 1980s. But the derivatives market was now booming again. Since the Nordic countries had introduced their own LIBORs (Stockholm Interbank Offered Rate (STIBOR), Helsinki Interbank Offered Rate (HELIBOR), Norwegian Interbank Offered Rate (NIBOR) and Copenhagen Interbank Offered Rate (CIBOR)), I now had the opportunity to trade the instruments I had only seen on paper in Frankfurt a couple of years before.

As was the case for most other short-term interest rate traders, understanding and trying to accurately predict the various LIBORs were central parts of the job. They had become the key benchmarks for instruments used to hedge and speculate in the money markets. Corporations, pension funds and insurance companies had real hedging requirements that were met by quoting them appropriate LIBOR-indexed derivatives. The instruments therefore served their original purpose, namely as tools to eliminate risk – or at least to reduce it. Banks, on the other hand (but also some treasury departments of large multinational corporations), preferred to use them for speculative purposes. For instance, if traders believed that the market was underestimating the probability that the central bank would raise the interest rate soon, they would simply buy a forward rate agreement (FRA). A FRA was a derivative contract that enabled you to protect yourself from, or profit from, interest rate movements in the future. If, for instance, the central bank took people by surprise and raised the interest rate, the price of the FRA would rise in line with the now higher interest rate and a profit could be booked. Or vice versa.

The structure of the FX and derivatives market seemed much more sophisticated and internationally oriented than that for Swedish bonds and T-bills. Instead of old-fashioned telephones, we used Reuters Dealing 2000-2 to communicate and trade with other banks. It was high-tech at the time, a kind of two-person electronic chatroom that predated the internet. Each trading desk at each bank had a four-letter identifying code, and you simply needed to type the code and hit the send button on the custom-made keyboard and then a beeping sound would signal an incoming call at the other end. We opted for 'MIST', referring to Midland Stockholm, but also because it was memorable and sounded cool.

You could call four banks in one go, meaning that you could trade more, and faster. A young FX spot trader sitting opposite me was even able to use two machines at the same time, enabling her to talk to eight competitors simultaneously. I was impressed and became determined to learn her skill. In the end, I did.

Then, one night, I got a call from a person claiming to be a headhunter. He asked me whether I wanted to move to London and work for Citibank. Initially I thought it was a prank call. Citibank had the biggest and most professional FX operation in the world, and the trading floor in London was the heart of it. I was young and inexperienced.

But it was for real. I flew to London, had interviews, and they offered me the job. When I asked my girlfriend Maria whether she wanted to come along, she simply asked: 'What shall I bring?'

'Bring everything,' I answered.

* * *

At Citibank, I joined the Short-term Interest Rate Trading (STIRT) desk, where we acted as market makers in a range of FX and interest rate derivative instruments in all currencies that were not classified as 'emerging markets'. Upon arrival, I was given responsibility for the small Finnish trading book and acted as a back-up trader in the Nordic currencies, the Japanese yen and the Canadian dollar. I was also, like everybody else, trading US dollars. Nobody else wanted the Finnish book, as it had never been a money-spinner. The sales people in our Nordic bank branches demanded quick and competitive prices, and unless you were on top of the game, it was going to end in tears. I remember a senior trader looking at me gleefully when it was announced that I had formally taken over the hopeless task. But it suited me perfectly. I got along well with the sales people, and they had impressive client lists covering most of the large domestic corporations and institutions.

Apart from not having to cross any cultural or language barriers, it also turned out that we had a clever desk setup. At the time, being able to trade a range of different financial instruments on a STIRT desk such as ours was a rather novel invention. Apart from Chemical Bank (which later became Chase Manhattan and then JPMorgan Chase) and maybe a few others, virtually all major banks still separated their FX trading desks from their interest rate derivatives activities. The Nordic banks did likewise. To me, this separation did not make any sense. FX swaps (which I traded) were contracts with which you bought one currency against another, and simultaneously did the opposite on a predetermined date and at a predetermined price in the future. For instance, you could buy $100 million against Japanese yen now and agree to sell them back in a year's time. The FX swap price was the difference between the future price (the FX forward price) and the current price (the FX spot price). Theoretically, however, the FX swap price could also be seen as the difference in interest rates in two currencies. Imagine you bought a car for $10,000 and simultaneously agreed to sell it back to the car dealer at $9,000 a year later. This could be seen as having bought and sold a car. However, it could also be seen as having borrowed a car and simultaneously lent money for one year. As FX swaps involved money in one currency versus money in another currency, the prices simply captured the cost of borrowing in one currency versus lending in another.

If the price differed from this theoretical price, someone would jump in to do *arbitrage*, effectively buying one thing cheaply and selling the same thing expensively at the same time. We and a few other banks were in a perfect position to benefit from such opportunities in the FX and interest rate markets, and this edge could also be turned into more competitive prices quoted to the sales people and their clients.

* * *

As my formative trading years had been spent in Scandinavia during the early 1990s, the Scandinavian banking crisis and the crisis of the European Exchange Rate Mechanism (ERM) had had a strong and lasting impact on me. Everyone I worked with had stories to tell, each one more remarkable than the last. Experienced traders often said that your early trading years were important, that they shaped the way you looked at the world – for instance, whether you became an eternal optimist (a bull) or an eternal pessimist (a bear). The person who influenced me the most as a trader was my boss at HSBC Stockholm. Uffe was certainly not the most technical person

I knew – he had scribbled 'Ctrl+Alt+Del' on a yellow Post-it note to remind himself what to do if his computer crashed in the middle of a hectic trading day. He called it the 'all-to-hell button', and the keyboard sequence was pressed very often. Despite this, Uffe had the rare ability to read the market like an open book. He could sense when things were about to go wrong, almost 'feel' when other traders were beginning to become afraid. An instinct that was quicker than any other person or computer algorithm. I was very lucky to be seated next to him and Toby, a close colleague who joined him from Nordbanken. Sources claimed that he had made over 1 billion Swedish kronor for his bank by trading foreign exchange in 1992 – a staggering amount of money back then, but also in today's money. It was the same year when speculators had begun to doubt the sustainability of the fixed exchange rate regime, and then successfully bet against it. George Soros had famously 'kicked the pound out of the ERM'. Sweden had also been among the victims, having been forced to raise interest rates to an astonishing 500 per cent. Rumours, however, also suggested that Uffe had assisted the central bank during the crisis, by 'policing' the market and informing the policy makers of who was betting against their currency. He was an active trade union member (a rarity among foreign exchange traders) and apparently his bonus during that remarkable trading year had been precisely zero. I didn't know if these rumours were true, and I didn't care. I liked Uffe. He was a bear and so was I. Financial crises were inevitable and always around the corner when people least expected them. Stock markets would crash. Currencies would collapse. Interest rates would soar.

* * *

My attention shifted more and more from the Nordic countries to Japan. There were two reasons for this. First, the Japanese yen and the Canadian dollar happened to be part of the 'Scandi' desk at Citibank in London. I still don't know how the two currencies, which were so vastly different, had ended up with us, but the desk setup required me to follow what was going on in both Japan and Canada. Second, and more importantly, Japan was heading towards a financial crisis.

Up until 1995, whenever a Japanese bank was in trouble, the government had intervened by arranging the merger of an insolvent bank with a sound bank. With this framework, the Japanese banking sector was perceived to be safe by financial market participants. In August 1995, however, the government let Hyogo Bank default. The bank had $37 billion worth of assets and it was the first bank failure in Japanese history. Suddenly, the perception of Japanese banks changed.[1] Others became reluctant to lend to them. The Japanese banks were massive, and a number of them had previously embarked upon ambitious expansion programmes abroad. As they typically did not have retail networks outside Japan providing them with deposits, much of their foreign currency borrowing was done in the interbank market. In the Japanese yen market, this was not much of a problem, as Bank of Japan, the central bank, ultimately was able to provide liquidity. However, they also needed foreign currency, and US dollars in particular. Bank of Japan could not print US dollars, only the Federal Reserve could.

So the Japanese banks came to us in the interbank market. Lending directly to them was out of the question. The credit lines had been either filled up or withdrawn. And it seemed like every single foreign bank was in the same situation. As the

Japanese banks struggled to borrow dollars directly, they turned to the FX swap market instead. By entering into agreements to buy US dollars against yen *now*, and simultaneously to do the opposite at a predetermined date *in the future*, they effectively 'borrowed' US dollars that they needed and 'lent' Japanese yen (which they had or could obtain).

With Japanese traders now rushing to the FX swap market, for the first time I realised that this market could deviate quite substantially from what theory said. Basically, the banking crisis in Japan seemed to have messed up the mathematical equation. Theory said that the US dollar LIBOR should reflect the interest rate level at which banks were lending US dollars to each other. This might have been the case for most banks, but it certainly did not apply to the Japanese banks. They had to pay a significant premium to access the US dollar money market, and this premium was reflected in the FX swap prices we quoted day in, day out.

I was instructed to watch out for a range of four-letter codes calling on the Reuters Dealing 2000-2 machines: SUMG (the dealing code for the FX swap desk at Sumitomo Bank in Tokyo), TMFT (Tokyo-Mitsubishi), IBJK (Industrial Bank of Japan), SNWT (Sanwa Bank), and so on. Whenever one of them called on the machine, they had only one purpose in mind: to trade on the price I quoted. And as a market maker, I had to quote them a two-way price almost immediately. If I let the phone ring (or in this case the machine beep) for half a minute or so, I would automatically break one of the many unwritten rules in FX trading.

After having clicked on one of the incoming calls, the first three lines of a conversation could look like this:

3M USD/JPY 100
-140/-138
-140

The trader at the other bank first asks me to quote a three-month FX swap price for $100 million against Japanese yen. I then quote -140/-138 (a bid and an offer). The trader deals at -140. Within seconds, the remaining parts of the transaction are agreed and confirmed, such as the FX spot rate used to work out exactly how many US dollars and Japanese yen will be shipped back and forth (or, put differently, the actual interest rates at which we have borrowed from and lent to each other), as well as the payment dates and bank details. The short conversation finally ends like this (depending on 'fat fingers' and the keyboard shortcuts used):

#THANKS AND BYE
#TXBBIIB
#END LOCAL#

Given the state of the Japanese financial system at the time, the Japanese banks needed to get hold of US dollars and so were constantly looking for bids in the FX swap market. The more they traded (or were expected to trade), the lower the bids became. They became easy to 'read'. Rather quickly, a two-tier market evolved. Non-Japanese banks faced no funding issues, so their market continued to function smoothly. Japanese banks, however, had to pay an additional premium in the FX and money markets. This extra cost later became known as the 'Japan premium' in academic journal articles and economics textbooks.

Japan also happened to have a unique derivatives market, with not one but *two* money market benchmarks: LIBOR and TIBOR. LIBOR was set in London, mainly by non-Japanese banks. TIBOR, however, was set in Tokyo and its panel was mainly composed of Japanese banks. Some derivatives were indexed to LIBOR, others to TIBOR, with some clients preferring LIBOR, others TIBOR. Before the crisis, it did not really matter which one you used, as they tended to be almost exactly the same every day. Now, this symmetry was distorted as the Japanese banks had to pay a premium to access funding. The 'TIBOR–LIBOR spread' (the difference between the two benchmarks) turned into a kind of barometer of fear in relation to the Japanese banking system. It was possible to put a number on this fear, and this number went up and down. More than this, bets could be put on this number.

After a series of bank capital injections by the Japanese government, the Japan premium more or less disappeared around March 1999. The market slowly began to return to normal. However, the atmosphere on the STIRT desk was now different. The launch of the euro meant that a massive business could be built around a brand new currency. Still, this did not compensate for the fact that a number of currencies had disappeared from the face of the earth. If you had been a specialist in one of the major currencies, such as the deutschmark, the French franc or the Italian lira, you would probably fit in. If your career had been built around the Austrian schilling or the Portuguese escudo, on the other hand, your future was much more uncertain. However, the birth of the euro had been preceded by financial crises not only in Japan but also in South Korea, Russia, Malaysia, Indonesia,

Thailand and the Philippines. The newly formed 'emerging markets' desks needed experienced traders and currency experts in a range of markets. A brilliant Dutch guilder trader sitting opposite me became a Malaysian ringgit expert almost overnight. I remember talking to him about 'the old KLIBOR', after he had informed me that Kuala Lumpur actually had its own LIBOR. The Finnish markka faced the same euro destiny, but it had not been my main book for several years now. My key focus was on Japanese yen, US dollars and the other Nordic currencies.

Some of the derivatives traders I used to hang out with after work decided to return to Citibank Sydney. I also felt that it was time for a change and asked whether I could be transferred to New York for a couple of years. My manager was supportive of the idea and plans were drawn up. Over lunch at Christopher's in Covent Garden in October 1999, however, he told me that the situation had changed. I could either wait a few years, hoping for a posting to New York, or I could become chief dealer in Tokyo *now*. Although I was hesitant about getting management responsibility, I was truly excited by the prospect. For as long as I could remember, I had been interested in foreign languages and cultures. I had visited Japan once and loved it. Two weeks later Maria and I were looking at apartments in Tokyo.

* * *

During the following eight years, many things happened. I became a father, I returned to London, I joined Crédit Agricole Indosuez and I lost my father. The financial markets became much more sophisticated, bigger, more competitive, perhaps more ruthless. And as the derivatives markets expanded, the importance of LIBOR grew exponentially.

Every day arrived with a precise timetable for economic data releases. It could be the UK inflation number, the US unemployment rate, the Japanese retail sales figures or the Australian GDP (gross domestic product). These numbers would have an impact on how central banks shaped their assessments about the economic outlook. This, in turn, would influence their monetary policy strategy. At the end of the day, it was about predicting if, when and by how much the central banks would change the official interest rate in the future, because this would affect LIBOR by roughly the same magnitude. We watched every step the central banks took, scrutinised every word they said – anything that could provide a clue to the future direction of LIBOR.

The interest in LIBOR, however, was mutual. Just as much as it mattered to traders, it mattered to central bankers. This is why. Assume that the UK inflation rate falls, and the Bank of England therefore decides to lower the base rate (the official interest rate used for lending to other banks) to meet its inflation target of 2 per cent. The interest rate cut is supposed to be transmitted immediately to the interbank money market rate (where banks lend to each other). Unless people think that the Bank of England will change its mind and reverse the rate cut the following day (or week or month), banks will probably decide to lower the one-week rate, the one-month rate, the three-month rate, and perhaps even interest rates with longer maturities. Then, as banks compete with each other for customer business, they lower the interest rates they charge for variable rate loans, overdrafts, and so on. Rates offered to savers are also lowered and mortgages might get a touch cheaper. As the lower interest rates gradually filter through to the real economy, inflation begins to creep up towards the Bank of England inflation target of 2 per cent.[2] This process, the 'monetary transmission mechanism', can be seen as the channel through which a specific interbank money market rate – the three-month rate, say – is generated. The central bank does not determine the three-month interbank money market rate. The banks do. However, the central bank has considerable power to influence it.

How do banks know what the Bank of England base rate is? The answer is simple: it is on the front page of the Bank of England website. Whenever it is changed, a press release is sent out and press conferences held. The Bank of England even announces a calendar with exact dates when they might consider changing the base rate. Over the years, this process has become increasingly open and transparent. How do central banks know what the three-month interbank money market rate is? This is more complicated, because trades between banks are secret. Instead, LIBOR is used as a gauge for this interbank rate.

During the years prior to August 2007, changes – or expected changes – in the official central bank rates filtered through smoothly to LIBOR, lending support to the assumption that a central bank rate change leads to a proportional change in interbank money market rates. Central bankers, having grown accustomed to a seemingly transparent and well-functioning money market more or less without credit and liquidity issues, could rely on the first stage of the monetary transmission mechanism. As LIBOR could be relied upon, focus could be put on the channels affecting the real economy, and on new methods to minimise monetary policy surprises and to increase transparency.

In the old days, central bankers often flexed their muscles by taking the markets by surprise. As a trader, it was difficult to figure out when they were meeting, what they were saying, what they were thinking. A radical shift was now taking place, spurred by influential academics arguing that transparency was a good thing. Step by step, central banks began to lay their cards on the table. Their meeting schedules were announced up to a year in advance, meaning that surprises were unlikely to happen in between. The minutes from the meetings were published, helping traders understand what they were saying. The identities of the people attending the meetings were revealed, making it easier to grasp the composition of their monetary policy committees. Who was a 'hawk' (advocating higher interest rates) and who was a 'dove' (preferring lower interest rates)? How hawkish were the hawks and how dovish were the doves? Some central banks even went so far as to publish their own interest rate projections and the probabilities of this actually materialising.

And, as central banks gradually became more and more open, the attention paid to these meeting dates became intense. For a STIRT trader like myself, the meetings became exciting 'events'. Everyone had an opinion about what would happen, and bets were placed in the financial markets accordingly. Generally, there was a consensus about the direction of the next interest rate move by the central bank. However, if they were going to hike rates, it could happen now or they could wait until the next meeting. If everyone shouted 'Unchanged!' after the newsflash appeared on our screens, the rest of the trading day became an anti-climax. Those who had put bets on nothing happening could book some profits and those aiming for some action had to lick their wounds. An unexpected rate move resulted in chaos, with traders trying to make sense of it all. Larger profits or losses were booked on such days. On some rare occasions, traders also disagreed on the magnitude of the potential rate change. 'Fifty!', referring to an unusually large 50 basis point change in the official central bank rate, could result in tears of joy and despair across the dealing rooms.

During the final minute before the anticipated press release, my heart rate would increase. Hearing nothing but my own heartbeat, fuelled by numerous cups of triple espresso and cans of Red Bull, it could be unbearable. My hands would be too soaked in sweat to control the mouse, so I would go to the bathroom and wash them with extra soap. I would then obsessively tidy up my desk to make sure everything was in the right place: the computer screens, the two telephone sets, the broker microphones, the calculator and the blotter showing the trades I had done so far that day. I made sure I had a few extra blank sheets printed out in case the afternoon turned out to be messy. I would mentally prepare a list of banks to call once the announcement had been released, and what kind of prices I would ask them for. Because I knew that once the bright red newsflash appeared, there would be no time to read the full press release by the central bank, let alone the whole 50-page monetary policy report. Within a second, my switchboard and Reuters Dealing machine would light up like Christmas trees with incoming calls. It was the ultimate adrenaline rush.

* * *

The fact that there was an important theoretical difference between the interest rate at which banks traded with the central bank and the interest rate at which banks traded with each other was gradually ignored.

This difference, the 'money market risk premium', has two components – in effect, taking account of the fact that central banks can print money endlessly (which private banks cannot) and that central banks are annexed to the state and therefore are unlikely to go bust (whereas private banks can default). The first component is *liquidity risk*.[3] Liquidity is normally referred to as the ease and speed with which an asset can be turned into cash. For instance, a painting by Picasso is relatively liquid, as Sotheby's or Christie's would probably be able to sell it easily and quickly should you want to put one up for auction. The artwork by your cousin who just finished art school, however, is likely to be illiquid. That is not to say it is worthless – simply that, in order to get a decent price for the painting, it would take longer and be more difficult to find a buyer for a relatively unknown talent. The same principle applies to the money markets, and can take two forms.

Market liquidity risk is the fear of not being able to borrow back the money once you have lent it (or sell back the painting once you have bought it). It is also the fear of causing the market to panic after having borrowed only a fraction of what you need (imagine desperately having to sell 100 Picasso paintings). It could also be the fear that a temporary rise in the interest rate turns out to be long lasting – that, for some reason, the market becomes too slow to return to some kind of normality. A common way to quantify the market liquidity risk is to look at the bid–offer spread (i.e. the difference between the price quoted for the sale [bid] and purchase [offer]) of the 'thing' that is being bought and sold relative to the price of that thing. Anyone who has tried to resell a used car will have discovered that the bid–offer spread of used cars is relatively wide. Unless you are an expert in the business, buying a used car from one dealership will most likely result in a sizeable loss if you change your mind and go to another dealership looking to sell it the next day. The same goes for foreign currencies you buy at airports or in popular tourist destinations. Doing exactly the opposite transaction at exactly the same time is generally an extremely expensive exercise – perhaps not in total money lost, but definitely in relation to the amount you are exchanging. In this respect, the various financial instruments in the money, FX and derivatives markets between banks and between banks and large corporations tend to be very liquid and the bid–offer spreads are tight.

Funding liquidity risk, on the other hand, represents something different. It is the ease with which a bank can obtain funding from others. It represents the fear that the lenders will suddenly require some kind of collateral (that you might not have). The fear that it will become more costly or impossible to roll over short-term borrowing. Or, in the absolute worst-case scenario, the fear that depositors will begin to queue up in front of the ATM to withdraw funds because they think you are about to go bankrupt.

Even though it might be useful to distinguish funding liquidity risk from market liquidity risk, it can be very difficult to separate them as they can be highly interconnected. If there are problems with funding liquidity, often there are also issues with market liquidity. However, the reverse does not need to be the case. If the market dries up – ahead of the release of important economic data or a central bank policy announcement, for instance – the market can be regarded as illiquid temporarily, but without having any real impact on funding liquidity. Even the most liquid markets tend to be 'dead' during the World Cup final – this is not to suggest that concerns should be raised regarding the health of the financial system during those 90 minutes. Funding liquidity issues, however, do tend to automatically affect market liquidity. For decades, recurring year-end cash squeezes have been common even in liquid currencies such as the US dollar and the Swiss franc. This type of liquidity risk can happen regularly, even quarterly or monthly, but they need not be serious for the financial system as a whole. If the events are well anticipated (which they sometimes are), central banks can simply inject ample amounts of liquidity to maintain financial stability.

However, when events are *not* anticipated, fear in the money markets can quickly emerge. And these fears are invariably reflected in LIBOR. For instance, on 29 November 1999, the one-month US dollar LIBOR jumped 86 basis points because of fears surrounding the so-called 'millennium bug'. Considering that the Federal Reserve often tended to cut or raise interest rates in 25 basis points at a time, and rarely changed them more than a few times per year, 86 basis points represented a remarkably large move. Banks had spent billions on system upgrades and contingency plans relating to the Y2K software problem. What would happen if we arrived in the office after the New Year's celebrations to find that the date was 1 January 1900, rather than 1 January 2000? A collapse of the banking system and a return to the Stone Age, it was thought. Therefore, banks borrowed money as a precaution and LIBOR shot up.

Soon after I had returned from Tokyo to London and joined Crédit Agricole Indosuez, two planes flew into the World

Trade Center in New York. As George W. Bush reportedly headed to Camp David, banks hoarded cash. However, as the Federal Reserve cut rates as a response, the three-month US dollar LIBOR fell 75 basis points within ten days. The effect of 9/11 lasted for months and years. The fear of sudden events that could cause a meltdown of the financial system became incorporated into trading. But the trading did not stop. Rather, traders grew accustomed to how to react to crisis situations, and elaborate trading strategies, often involving LIBOR derivatives, were crafted to take advantage of them. Hurricane Katrina, the London 7/7 bombings and many more became market-moving 'events', as they created uncertainty, panic and ultimately mispricing of LIBOR-indexed derivatives.

Importantly, both market and liquidity risk can change without having any impact on the perceived *credit risk* of the banks, the second component of the money market risk premium. However, liquidity issues can also be closely related to credit issues. If the perceived credit risk of a bank is high, the bank should find it more difficult to borrow money. Therefore, it would have to pay a higher rate to compensate for this and LIBOR should go up. The bank might then find itself actively seeking to raise cash, and at the same time trying to reduce lending, as a precautionary measure. However, traders not active in the Japanese yen market (or having no memory of the banking crisis almost a decade earlier) became used to very small deviations of LIBOR from what could be regarded as the risk-free interest rate. Banks did not go bust, and they were not expected to do so any time soon. Access to liquidity was easy, and central banks became increasingly transparent and predictable in what they were doing. Overall, LIBOR (and its equivalent benchmarks elsewhere) seemed to be working as intended. Although the market had become more sophisticated, many traders and banks believed that the new normal would last forever. A situation in which banks would have to pay a considerable premium above the current and expected future central bank rates to access liquidity was seen as unthinkable. A situation in which European banks would have to pay a premium to access US dollars was seen as impossible. As long as the banks' risk management systems showed that there was no risk, there was an illusion that no risk could exist.

* * *

When I received a phone call from the Merrill Lynch office on 9 August 2007, I was in the middle of chopping wood in the Swedish countryside. Although I trusted my assistant who covered for me whenever I took a few days off, I always had my mobile with me just in case.

It can sometimes be difficult to connect to a trader when you are 'off'. The buzz in the dealing room is contagious, and traders often become hyper without any particular reason. Sometimes, when you are not there, you almost have to pump yourself up to get a certain level of heartbeat in order to have a meaningful conversation. But this time it was different. I repeatedly had to ask him to calm down as he kept on stuttering about FX swaps, dollars, prices people had dealt at – without making any sense at all. He kept repeating that things were 'crazy' and 'completely mad' out there. There was not much I could do about it from a woodshed more than 1,000 miles away, so I asked him instead whether our trading positions were OK.

'It's difficult to say,' he said, 'but I think we're OK.'

During our phone conversation, it became clear to me that something quite extraordinary was happening in the financial markets. Something I had never seen or heard of before. At the time, there was nothing in what he said that made me worried about my position, let alone the global financial system. However, it prompted me to buy an earlier Ryanair flight back to London. I had to see it with my own eyes. I needed to get back into the game.

As a trader, you regularly have to change your opinion. The market changes every second and new information constantly feeds your brain. Often, you have to accept that you were wrong, take the loss, forgive yourself and move on. However, some trading ideas might be more long term. They can become fundamental to how you see the market, and such convictions can stay with you not for days or weeks but for years. They become part of your 'trading style' and shape the person you are as a trader. I had several trading styles, certainly, but one of them was that I normally thought that short-term interest rates would go up rather than down. Having been trained in the aftermath of the Scandinavian banking crisis, and then having experienced the Japanese banking crisis, I always had an underlying fear that another banking crisis loomed around the corner. Consequently, I tended to ensure that my long-term trading position took that into account. This view often deviated from the market consensus and was sometimes both irrational and foolish.

I did not, of course, predict the global financial crisis. I did, however, ensure that my trading book would generate money should the global financial system tip over into disaster. I also happened to be working for a bank that had a reputation

47

for taking risks, and for encouraging traders to do so too. I generally took a lot of risk, and risk taking as a banking activity had increased exponentially since I had become a trader. The net outcome was that my trading positions were enormous. Overall, I had put bets on LIBORs, on the barometers of fear. Bets that a vicious storm would come in.

The world did not end on 9 August 2007. But my trading positions were definitively more than just 'OK'. They were magnificent.

* * *

A little over a year later – on Monday 15 September 2008, to be precise – I went to work as normal. Having exited Farringdon tube station, I walked through Smithfield market towards King Edward Street. It was about 6.30 a.m., and trading in the biggest meat market in the country was about to finish for the day. Trucks had already been loaded with fresh meat and the cleaners had begun to spray the surrounding area, as they always did at this time of day. The blood had to be cleaned up before the commuters arrived.

When entering the Merrill Lynch Financial Centre, I took the escalator, ordered a triple espresso from the in-house Starbucks and went into the dealing room. This was not going to be a normal day. People often talk about the financial markets being '24/7' or 'around the clock', but this is not entirely true. Traders rarely go into the dealing room at the weekend. When the lights go off in San Francisco on Friday, the market does not properly open until Wellington wakes up on Monday morning. The day before, on Sunday 14 September, I had been called into the office. The reason was Lehman Brothers. People no longer feared that the US investment bank might go under. We now *knew* they were going under.

When I got into the dealing room, it was as if someone had died. But this was not a sudden or unexpected death; rather, it was a slow and painful process that had reached an inevitable outcome. No matter how fierce the competition between Merrill Lynch, Lehman Brothers, Morgan Stanley, Goldman Sachs and Bear Stearns had been, there remained a sense of respect and togetherness among the US investment banks. Everything would change from that day on. With Lehman Brothers declared bankrupt, Merrill Lynch would not have survived another day had Bank of America not stepped in and rescued us at the very last minute. Surprisingly, perhaps, the traders in the dealing room did not seem thankful.

Even today, central bankers, regulators and other policy makers talk about measures that ought to be taken to avoid another 'Lehman moment'. What they refer to is a situation in which the entire global financial system is on the brink of total collapse – when you stare into the abyss and realise that the world is about the re-enter the Stone Age. The trigger, but hardly the cause, was the demise of the US sub-prime mortgage market during the first half of 2007, which had a snowball effect. At first, some asset-backed securities markets that hardly anyone had heard of ran into trouble. The virus then spread to markets that had traditionally been seen as relatively safe. The crisis kept on coming closer to traders such as myself, and soon substantial losses were reported by names we were familiar with: the UBS hedge fund Dillon Read, two hedge funds run by Bear Stearns, and the US home loan lender Countrywide.[4] The money market began to dry up and did so quickly. Then, when the German bank IKB reported that they had rollover problems, we knew that the crisis had spread from the US across the Atlantic. More and more hedge funds reported losses, forcing them to sell assets to raise cash and to post more collateral to their brokers. Everyone, it seemed, needed to borrow money. Nobody, however, dared lend any. On 9 August 2007, the French bank BNP Paribas announced that they were to freeze redemptions for three investment funds, citing its inability to value complex structured products. Although an analyst had claimed to Bloomberg that it wasn't 'too significant' (considering how large the bank was) and that it was 'more of an image problem', I was not so optimistic. BNP was a 'proper' bank. IKB was not a player, and many had never heard of Countrywide. Everyone, however, had heard of BNP. They had always been part of the trading community and had made markets in everything: FX, bonds and derivatives. They were active in major currencies and in emerging markets. They had branches everywhere and were also French. The French banks were famous for hiring the best programmers and mathematicians. If they did not know how to value their books, who did?

The central banks reacted fairly quickly by pumping money into the banking systems. The European Central Bank (ECB) injected €95 billion and the Federal Reserve $24 billion. A week later, the Federal Reserve went a bit further by broadening the type of collateral they accepted for lending to the banks. They also lowered the 'discount window' (the level at which banks were allowed to borrow from them) by 50 basis points and increased the lending horizon to 30 days. However, the measure was not deemed a success. The 7,000 or so banks that were based in the US and could borrow at the discount window from the Federal Reserve were reluctant to do so because of the stigma associated with it. Using the discount window would signal desperation and hence a lack of creditworthiness in the eyes of the rest of the market. Nobody wanted to look as if they were in trouble. From that standpoint it was indeed an 'image problem'.

The problems refused to go away. October and November 2007 saw a series of write-downs of sub-prime and other mortgage-related assets. The total losses kept being revised upwards. When the Federal Reserve realised that the interest rate cuts announced during the autumn were not filtering through to the money markets, it introduced the Term Auction Facility (TAF), an arrangement whereby US-based banks could borrow from the Federal Reserve *without* using the discount window.

Similar market movements were observed in other currencies, with central banks across the developed world resorting to comparable measures. Central banks found themselves in a difficult position as the symmetry of the monetary transmission mechanism had broken down. Price stability through inflation targeting had gradually become more important than financial stability as a central bank goal. However, the former goal no longer applied. Having become more transparent themselves, central banks now had to rely on information and signals provided by the banks and the markets. The key indicator, the 'LIBOR–OIS spread', provided evidence of severe stress in a range of currencies and markets. The overnight index swap (OIS) was a derivative instrument that was indexed to the 'risk-free' central bank interest rate. The idea was to reduce the LIBOR–OIS spreads towards levels seen before the crisis broke out. From August 2007, the LIBOR–OIS spread became the focal point for everything we did as traders. This is also why, in 2009, the former Chairman of the Federal Reserve, Alan Greenspan, famously described the LIBOR–OIS spread as 'the barometer of fears of bank insolvency'.[5] It was precisely that: a kind of fear index relating to banks. This fear had soared since 9 August 2007.

From a personal perspective, the global financial crisis also acted as a trigger point in revealing the wider implications of LIBOR.

The STIRT desks at the banks had not been particularly glamorous before 2007. We traded a range of instruments that were important, but not interesting and complex enough to represent the forefront of financial innovation. The turnover in OISs, FRAs, IRSs (interest rate swaps), CRSs (cross-currency basis swaps) and FX swaps, among others, was enormous. However, options, long-end interest rate swaps and structured products enjoyed considerably more prestige. The crisis turned everything upside down. Suddenly, the spotlight fell on us. Options traders needed to know the direction of LIBOR in order to price customer deals and value their books correctly. So did the bond and long-end swap traders. FX traders needed to know where they could fund the currencies they had sold, and the same applied to the cross-currency basis swap traders. As everything we did had a direct link to the interbank money market and LIBOR, the STIRT desks evolved from being merely profit centres to a place people turned to in order to get some 'market colour'.

Which bank was rumoured to be in the worst shape?

Which bank seemed most desperate to borrow?

Which bank had been ordered to throw in the towel and temporarily suspend their market-making activity?

Which bank had refused to deal with which other bank for fear of insolvency?

All of these aspects, coupled with continuous reliable and less reliable information flows in the dealing room and in the corridors about how *our* bank was coping, forced senior management to take notice. As interest in LIBOR and the markets closely connected to it grew, it did not take long before central bankers joined in on the conversations. I had spoken to numerous central bankers before, probably representing a dozen countries. The discussion topics had generally related to the technicalities of new derivative instruments, overall market liquidity, and the arrival (or departure) of new banks and large clients in the market. Naturally, they were interested in whether the market in their currency was functioning well. As a trader, it was like being called into the principal's office to provide an update of what was happening in the school playground. A phone call from a central bank gave me an immense sense of pride, a feeling that what I did for a living was important. Now, central banks seemed interested in only one thing: LIBOR.

In a way, this sudden change was not surprising; until August 2007, LIBOR had more or less appeared to work as intended, namely as a largely harmonious outcome of the central bank on the one hand, and various market participants on the other. Seen from this perspective, our job had been to implement their policy: to ensure that the first stage of the monetary transmission mechanism worked as intended. They obviously wanted to get this mechanism working again.

However, it was the phrasing of the questions I got from the central banks that surprised me. One senior central banker was under the illusion that LIBOR had to be correct because how could a price on a Reuters screen be wrong? A central banker representing another country believed that their LIBOR was traded on the stock exchange. A third, and very senior, central banker seemed to know roughly how the process worked, but privately said that the soaring LIBOR–OIS spreads were a good thing as they acted to dampen inflationary pressures in their economy.

I was shocked by how little they seemed to know about the benchmark rate they now wanted to get under control. But in truth, I was not wholly surprised. For years I had thought that central banks were much less powerful than the public was led to believe. 'Central banks are put at a constant disadvantage versus the market when it comes to implementing monetary policy,' I scribbled down on a piece of paper in early 2009. 'The LIBOR problem has implications as it delays information to policy makers who are supposed to steer LIBOR. This probably led to a very long delay in the rate-setting process after the credit crunch started in 2007,' I then went on to write as I tried to formulate a research question for my PhD application.

There was nothing wrong with the way central bankers saw the market, in theory. LIBOR *should* reflect the rate at which banks lent to each other, so the idea that the LIBOR–OIS spread was a kind of barometer of fear of bank insolvency was logical. The standard technique they then seemed to be using was to measure this fear in detail by quantifying each of the components that made up the LIBOR–OIS spread. By assuming that LIBOR was a perfect reflection of the money market, and taking the OIS market prices as representing the risk-free interest rate for a given maturity (i.e. the final payment date of the financial contract), it simply became a task of allocating the difference between the two variables into the appropriate credit and/or liquidity components making up the spread. In fact, if a measure for credit risk could be agreed upon, the remaining component could be regarded as liquidity risk. This was the approach taken by the Bank of England[6] in an indicative decomposition of LIBOR. Following this approach, liquidity risk (effectively the fear of not being able to get hold of cash), rather than credit risk (the fear of default), was shown to have been the main driver behind the widening LIBOR–OIS spreads since the beginning of the global financial crisis. Central bank action, aimed at reducing this spread through extensive liquidity injections, confirmed this thought process. Similar studies were done by other central banks, showing the same results and all pointing to the same conclusions.

But something was not quite right. I had become confused by what seemed to be unreasonably low LIBOR quotes by some banks that quite obviously could not raise funding in the interbank market. After all, the benchmark was also supposed to reflect this. But it didn't. Something told me that LIBOR understated the problem quite substantially and that the whole process was flawed, from start to finish.

'You can almost argue that LIBOR is but a fictive number upon which many decisions are made, and that it makes economic sense for banks to manipulate it,' I wrote in a Word document at some point during the crisis.

I never thought I would be proved right, though.

CHAPTER 2

'WHY DID YOU DO IT?'

My first bonus as a trader seemed large to me at the time, but was not as extraordinary as people might expect. 'You can buy a new sofa,' my boss said to me encouragingly. And that was exactly what I did with the money. It was second-hand, greyish blue and very comfortable. A year or two later, in 1995, I carried the sofa outside in the middle of a winter's night and left it in a nearby park. It was way too large to be shipped from Stockholm to London. While the snow was falling, I sat on the sofa one last time, thinking about the future. I couldn't wait to leave.

The next morning the sofa was gone, and so was I.

A few years after that, I suddenly got paid eight times my yearly salary as a bonus. This time, I strode excitedly through Regent's Park to Resurrection Records, my favourite record shop in Camden Town. I wanted to celebrate and pictured myself carrying home bags full of CDs. In the end, however, I could not find anything I really wanted. I remember holding a copy of *The Head on the Door* by The Cure in my hands (an album I loved but only had on vinyl), but then putting it back when I realised I didn't really need it. I returned home with only two or three CDs. A few days later, I flew back to Finland, went into Merita Bank, and asked if I could pay back my student loan. The bonus had allowed me to write off all my debt in one go. I was now free of 'debt', and also free of 'guilt', as my native langue does not distinguish between the two words in English.

Earlier, I had made a triumphant phone call to my father to inform him of the good news. However, I think he was more in shock than happy for me.

'I hope you won't change,' he said, apparently worried I might become obsessed by money.

'Of course not. Why would I?'

Throughout the next ten years, I was convinced I hadn't changed. That I was the same old down-to-earth Alexis I had been before my 'glory days' as a trader. But maybe I was wrong.

* * *

I loved my father, and ever since I was a boy he had acted as a kind of inner voice – not by telling me what to do, but by listening and asking me the right questions. If I faced a difficult problem I would call him, or sometimes just imagine that we were sitting down to have a conversation. The topic could be anything – from mathematical equations and difficult bosses to the latest asthma medicine or how to get babies to fall asleep on aeroplanes. In February 2009, in the midst of everything that was going on, I was overcome by a desperate urge to call him. I felt way out of my depth and needed his advice. But although I still had two of his numbers on my mobile phone, I knew there would be no answer.

I would probably have started the conversation along the lines of 'I have some bad news' – similar to the words he had used when he called me during the late spring of 2004. We both cried, but otherwise did not say much. As he was a Professor of Medicine, I knew he had no illusions about the seriousness of his illness. What he did not know already, he could find out by asking one of his colleagues who were experts in the field. I naturally wanted to see him as much as possible, but as we lived 18 hours away from each other it was not that easy. However, I remained optimistic, or perhaps in denial. Everything, I told myself, would be fine. But during the autumn his condition deteriorated. I decided to call my brother, who was also a doctor, and he gave me the medical version of the truth I did not want to hear. The dark reality then began to sink in.

2004 had started off as a very good trading year for me at Crédit Agricole Indosuez. But my thoughts had started to drift elsewhere. To succeed, I needed to be 100 per cent focused, which no longer seemed possible. My trading performance suffered. I say this with hindsight; at the time I felt that I was giving everything. Nonetheless, after having talked to my brother, I decided to ask my manager about taking time off to spend with my father.

Such a request was untypical for me; this was due to an experience I had had at Citibank back in late 2000, when Maria was having a very difficult pregnancy with our first child. The doctor at the hospital in Tokyo informed us that the chances of the unborn baby surviving were slim. As a result, Maria decided to fly back to her home town in Sweden to give birth, and I, having already used up my holiday allowance for the year, asked if I could use my forthcoming allowance for 2001 to take time off to be with her. My manager in New York, however, was against such a plan, as the trading budgets had to be decided during the week I wanted to be off. 'Can't she be induced instead?' he asked, as if we hadn't thought it through rationally. I can't recall how I responded, but I remember feeling like I had been handed an ultimatum. In the end, I ignored his instructions, flew to Sweden, and, thankfully, the birth went well. My relationship with my manager, however, was no longer the same.

* * *

'No,' was the curt answer I got when I asked the manager at Crédit Agricole Indosuez whether I could take time off to see my father in 2004. 'Who's going to take care of your trading books when you are away?' Market making had to be prioritised, and there was nobody around who could step into my shoes at such short notice. I am not sure why, despite the fury I felt inside, I meekly obeyed. Was I afraid of letting my manager, or the bank, down? I told myself that my father would live until Christmas at the very least, and then I could travel to Finland without having to ask for permission. Perhaps my brother's diagnosis was too negative. In the middle of the night on 10 December I was woken by a phone call. It was my mother calling to tell me that my father had passed away. The next day I decided that I was going to leave Crédit Agricole Indosuez.

I wasn't angry with the bank at the time. Rather, I was angry with my manager, so angry that for many years I kept telling myself I would never be able to forgive him. To me, that moment captured the complete lack of empathy that sometimes got the upper hand in the dealing room environment within which I worked. It was as if the job I loved, and truly believed served a positive purpose, came with an undetectable virus. It was impossible to know in advance who had been infected and who, if any, were immune to it. In fact, it was impossible to know if you had caught it yourself.

I had interviews with Barclays, Lehman Brothers and ABN AMRO. But when Merrill Lynch came along, I immediately knew that they were right for me. The desk chief dealer seemed highly intelligent and was a good listener. The most senior manager wanted to get things done, but also had a good sense of humour. The dealing room looked fabulous. Everything was just 'professional'. It was love at first sight.

Four years later, in October 2008, I decided that I was going to leave Merrill Lynch. But this time it was different. I was not only going to leave the bank, but also the industry. I was tired of everything that was going on. Most market makers I knew specialised in one or two currencies. I did five. Most traders I knew specialised in one, two or three types of derivatives. I did six or seven. I was working too much, trading too much, all without any time to catch my breath. Having cancelled or cut short at least ten attempts at taking a short break since the financial crisis had erupted, I was now physically and mentally exhausted. Perversely, though, I retained a strange kind of loyalty towards the bank. Merrill Lynch was bleeding money, but some of us were being pushed (or allowing ourselves to be pushed) even harder to make up for the disaster seemingly caused in other areas of the bank. Despite my best intentions, I told myself I couldn't leave. Not now.

I still regret that I didn't stick to my decision to leave I made in October 2008.

* * *

In early January 2009, I was promoted into a position running a small trading group. I was never asked whether I was interested in the job; I was simply expected to accept the challenge of becoming the leader of a team that included one person who was about to be fired, a second person who wanted to leave, and a third person who was openly unhappy. The financial crisis was the worst in generations and impacted millions, perhaps billions, of people. Although traders were by no means ruined (instead, many of their banks were), many had begun to feel demoralised. Motivating such a group, not to mention myself, to work harder, to make more money, felt like an impossible task. When the discussion gravitated towards trading budgets, I optimistically said to my manager that I would try to make $150 million in 2009. He burst out laughing.

'I expect much more than that.'

A common trading budget for a market maker was something between $3 million and $10 million. This was roughly what I was expected to make when I joined the bank. In the major currencies such as euros, dollars and yen, the budgets were somewhat higher. Because I had done well, my budget had increased exponentially. However, I had never heard of a market maker having to aim for $250 million, perhaps even a half a *billion* US dollars when the other team members were included. To have any chance of achieving this, I would have to put on the biggest bets I had ever laid down, seen or heard about in the markets in which I traded. It would have to be done in the middle of the worst financial crisis in generations, in an extremely illiquid and volatile market. Not only that, my bets would have to turn out to be the *right* bets.

Something inside me must have screamed that it was an impossible task. The bank was underestimating how difficult the markets were. They were also overestimating my ability to perform miracles. But I avoided such thoughts. I had to keep my act together – especially now, given that we were in the middle of the financial crisis. I convinced myself that it was the right thing to do, and in doing so made a spectacular error of judgement.

Because of the level of risk I took on behalf of Merrill Lynch, even the tiniest price move came to have an enormous impact on the reported value of my trading book. During my early years as a trader, $10,000 could easily turn a good day into a bad one or vice versa. Later, the crucial number became $100,000, and then $1,000,000. Simply put, a large amount of risk is more likely to result in large gains or losses than a small amount of risk. I took a lot of risk.

The trading books were 'marked to market': that is, they were valued according to where the market was – or was perceived to be – immediately after the market closed. Following the financial crisis, this process had become increasingly difficult. First, prices in the market moved around a lot. LIBOR-indexed cross-currency basis swaps, for instance, used to be remarkably stable before the crisis. Now, prices in them could move more in one hour than they used to in a whole year. Second, markets became less liquid and the bid–offer spreads often ballooned. For some FX swap prices, two or three basis points (0.02–0.03 per cent) had been standard. Now they could be 10, 25 or 50. Moreover, indicative prices on Reuters and Bloomberg screens, or on those provided by interdealer brokers, could be highly unreliable. Sometimes, the prices had not been updated for weeks. There was simply no market out there. Third, the credit situation had worsened. Prices quoted in the market involving a substantial amount of credit risk were often not tradeable for banks that were perceived to be at risk. Fourth, some markets that had acted, at least theoretically, as a backbone to almost everything I traded – the actual money market – had disappeared. LIBOR, EURIBOR, NIBOR, STIBOR and TIBOR had become highly unpredictable and often, I thought, made no sense whatsoever.

Tens of thousands of trades had to be valued according to hundreds of 'mid-market' inputs, the average between the bid and the offer price in the market at around 4 p.m. It was not possible to close the trades at the mid-market point, because these were only hypothetical prices. However, it was not possible to eliminate them at the prevailing bid or offer prices either, because any such attempts would have caused the market price to move. It would either have scared the market away, or have prompted other players to anticipate that I was afraid.

Some prices were straightforward. Futures exchanges, for instance, were highly transparent as they showed where buying and selling actually took place. But this was the exception rather than the norm. Most of my trades were 'over the counter' (OTC) and therefore followed a convention which stated that whatever numbers were out there were 'correct'. It did not matter whether it was possible to trade on the prices or not. It did not matter whether I believed that the various LIBOR benchmarks were dubious. They had to be treated as if they were objective and correct.

During the third week of January 2009, when the market stabilised somewhat, I began to doubt some of my valuations. However, the doubts were not serious enough to raise concerns or for me to discuss them with management. Rather, I saw them as being at the 'optimistic', rather than the 'conservative', end of the scale. Some valuations were perfectly 'objective and correct', whereas others were not.

I wanted to focus on reducing my risk, a gargantuan task considering that the financial crisis was far from over. What was worse, to achieve my budget I now had to take on *more*, not less, risk. My mismarking episode ultimately boiled down to this: I took matters into my own hands and ignored the dealing room compliance handbook I had signed when joining the bank. Even though the regulator later said that Merrill Lynch had failed to 'supervise the trader's activity' and had an 'inadequate month-end independent price verification process', the fault was, of course, mine. Regardless of what my opinions were, my valuations ought to have been correct.

* * *

I never saw trading in the FX, money or derivatives markets as a socially useless activity, or something that might be considered as 'wrong' more generally. However, I never saw it as a means to become rich either. It was just something I had been tremendously interested in for a very long time. As a child, I was fascinated by the fact that coins from other countries had different people and landscapes on them. I was given a few coins here and there, and I exchanged a few using my pocket money or the occasional monetary gift. I kept track of my 'positions' in a tiny little unused bank book. The earliest record I have is from 1975, when I was just five years old:

Colombia	20 centavos
USA	6 cents
Canada	2 dollars 41 cents
Norway	23 kroner 66 øre
Belgium	1 franc
Spain	121 pesetas
Hungary	10 filler
France	30 centimes
Finland	2 markka 75 penni
Sweden	62 öre

Switzerland	6 francs 55 centimes
Austria	2 Schilling 50 Groschen
Denmark	2 kroner 15 øre
West Germany	80 Pfennig

It looks like the currency reserve of Lilliput's central bank. I was heavily loaded with Canadian dollars at the time, thanks to my grandparents' trip to see relatives who had emigrated to North America in the early 1900s. I had quite a few pesetas as well, but I also knew how little they were worth. So, years later, when I found myself being interviewed for the internship at Dresdner Bank in 1992, I could talk quite passionately about currencies and how different FX hedging strategies could help the bank's customers. It felt natural.

Rather early on, though, I learned to accept that the rules of trading did not always apply to the rest of society or vice versa. Despite this, conventions within the dealing room felt logical and everybody seemed to accept them, so I never thought to question these social norms. In the absence of outside regulation, the banks simply wrote the rules themselves, which were then accepted by the rest of the market as well. The environment might not have been pleasant, fair or honest all the time – but even so I did not think of trading as immoral.

* * *

During the 1939–40 Winter War between Finland and the Soviet Union, the Finnish army had a sniper called Simo Häyhä. Having killed 505 soldiers in fewer than 100 days, he came to be nicknamed 'White Death' by the Red Army. Some 40 years later, when Häyhä was asked whether he had any regrets about killing all those people, the former sniper answered: 'I only did my duty, and what I was told to do, as well as I could.'[1] Traders who showed no compassion for wounded competitors were sometimes also nicknamed 'snipers'. Individuals who do their duty, what they are told to do, and as well as they can, are often considered perfect employees – no matter what their job description is.

I was once told by a senior manager to fire a Japanese employee in my team who had served the bank for two decades. The trader in question had done nothing wrong and had generated a stable revenue stream every year. But the trajectory was not steep enough for senior management and the trader had to go. I remember expressing unease about the assignment, not least because of the Japanese tradition of lifelong employment.

'Don't worry,' I was told. 'We can always suggest a cleaning job in Hokkaido.'

I understood. Giving the trader the option of moving to another island of Japan would mean that the bank, technically speaking, still required the employee's services. However, given that it would mean being humiliated in front of family and friends, the trader would never exercise that option.

I did my duty.

Afterwards, some colleagues jokingly began to call me 'The Axeman'. I hated the nickname, but thankfully did not have to perform any more such executions. Money probably does have a tendency to drive out morality.[2] However, where do you draw the line between the morals of society and the morals of the market? Where do you draw the line between the morals of the bank and the morals you hold yourself? Should any such line be drawn at all?

* * *

Over time, the financial crisis made me feel more and more disillusioned. I began to feel uneasy about Merrill Lynch, particularly in the run-up to the takeover by Bank of America. I began to feel uncomfortable with the market as a whole – not only with LIBOR but also with the erosion of a range of trading principles. The camaraderie and mutual respect that I felt had once existed in the market had been replaced by a ruthless, backstabbing mentality. This was probably due to the desperation traders and banks felt about having to make money – or not lose it. Part of my disillusionment was reflected in how I felt physically. I tried to address this by going to see the company nurse, and also my GP. Prescription drugs could ease some of the pain I felt in my ribs, stomach and right arm, but in reality my attempts to deal with the situation were half-hearted. Subconsciously, I think I was keen to be taken off the pitch, but in reality I was shouting: 'I want to play, I want to play!'

I should have told my manager sooner. But I did not trust him. I should have alerted the FSA to the concerns I had about myself, about the bank, about the industry and about the market. But communication with the regulator was supposed to be done at the bank, not trader, level. I should have been more persistent when talking to central bankers. But they did not seem to understand. I should, perhaps, have contacted the media. But a confidentiality agreement prevented me from doing so. I should have resigned. But the loyalty I felt – however misguided – was too strong. On Friday 13 February 2009, which was to be my last day as a trader, I left the office to go on holiday with no concerns.

* * *

'When I make this phone call, it will be the end of my banking career,' I told Maria before I dialled my manager four days later.

'It's the right thing to do,' she said. 'You've got us.'

I realised I had made a huge mistake and needed to act immediately. I also knew that, no matter how horrible the next chapter in my life would be, there was no going back. I did not *want* to go back. The manner in which my manager had responded led me to contact a lawyer, well knowing that this was exactly the thing I was *not* supposed to do. De facto, it meant that I had betrayed the bank, and it was going to be me versus them. I was under no illusion that the blame would fall on me once the internal investigation had been concluded and passed on to the regulators. At the time, few would argue that the management, the bank, the market or the financial system had anything to do with the problems I had caused. Judging from the emails, voicemails and text messages I got during this period, though, the scale of what I had done took colleagues and people in the market by surprise. I was told that someone higher up at Merrill Lynch said that mismarking amounting to $40 million or $50 million would be 'OK' given my strong reputation. Others warned that my trading book was being plundered, or dumped in the market, while I was away. They knew how incredibly difficult, and expensive, it would be to close such an enormous trading book. Quite a few also expressed sympathy and argued that I had been made a scapegoat for a rotten banking system. I think they wanted to avoid the unpleasant thought that I actually had done something wrong. The strange thing was that, even though my reputation was in tatters, I felt surprisingly confident that I had made the right decision.

'If you are dealing with a regulator, the best approach is always to co-operate, if you can,' Ian, my lawyer, told me emotionlessly later the same day. Even though he supported and defended me throughout the case, it never occurred to me that I could have opted for a different route – one that emphasised the guilt of *others*. Yes, the situation was complex and there were many misunderstandings to be cleared up, but arguing for complete innocence was nonsensical. And regardless of the outcome, I still had to deal with my own sense of guilt. I felt guilt towards Merrill Lynch. I felt it towards colleagues and other traders, brokers and clients in the market. I felt guilt towards Maria and my children who had to live through the aftermath of my actions. It was my fault that some neighbours and parents in the schoolyard suddenly began to avoid us. Without me, journalists would not have harassed relatives and old school friends. Beyond this, there was a seemingly endless list of people I had never met who argued that I also owed *them* an apology.

After a year of discussing morality with a lawyer, two years with a psychotherapist, and several more years talking about it with people I have met since, I am not sure whether I have come any closer to a definitive answer to the question 'Why did you do it?' Perhaps getting an answer was always less important than *seeking* an answer.

CHAPTER 3

SUPERHEROES AND BEAUTY PAGEANTS

For a derivatives trader such as myself, being able to accurately predict future LIBORs was as difficult as trying to solve a Rubik's Cube for the first time.

There were so many things that had to be taken into account when working out what the next move by the central bankers was going to be, and how many of these potential decisions had already been anticipated by the market (and by how much). Central bankers were mostly concerned about ensuring that the inflation rate reached a certain target. However, this target was set at some point in the future. A number of important variables could influence it, such as the employment rate, retail sales, household consumption or the exchange rate. Moreover – and especially during times of financial instability – liquidity risk and credit risk also mattered, as well as how these risks developed over time.

Because you could not look into the future, LIBOR was a puzzle that could never be solved completely. Anything might happen right up until LIBOR was published around noon. Some days you might get very close, or even be spot on. But then, after lunch, the matrix would have been rearranged and you had to start all over again.

In 2008, I was actively trading derivatives linked to eight IBORs: the Japanese yen TIBOR, the Japanese yen LIBOR, the US dollar LIBOR, the Swiss franc LIBOR, the euro EURIBOR, the Norwegian NIBOR, the Swedish STIBOR and the Danish CIBOR. Each benchmark had around ten different maturities: for example, for the one-week LIBOR, banks supposedly lent to each other for one week; on the one-month LIBOR, banks lent to each other for one month, and so on. Most derivatives contracts were indexed against the three-month LIBOR, but there was also substantial activity in the one-month, six-month and in some currencies even the 12-month LIBOR. With eight benchmarks and, say, four maturities, it meant keeping an eye on around 32 different LIBOR fixings per day. Almost all my trading related to financial instruments maturing within three years, approximately 750 business days, from now. That meant potentially being exposed to up to 24,000 future LIBOR fixings at each moment in time. In reality, it was much fewer – probably a few thousand. However, if I changed my opinion about these future LIBORs every day, every hour or sometimes every minute or second (which I often did), it meant having to process millions of LIBOR opinions every single year. For me, it was one of the most stimulating parts of the job.

It should therefore not come as a surprise that the future LIBOR became a popular conversation topic when I met up with traders at other banks, but also with brokers, hedge funds and multinational corporations that were active in the same markets as I was. LIBOR was something we had in common. Not everyone shared my taste in indie and Goth music, and not everyone was interested in football statistics. But everyone could at least have a decent conversation about LIBOR. It often became a route into discussions about the inflation rate, the voting intention of central bankers, the market psychology, and unqualified gossip about who was buying and who was selling, or who was hiring and who was firing.

* * *

'I used to dream about LIBORs,' Tom Hayes said in an interview with the SFO in 2013.

I remember that I also used to have dreams about LIBORs and sometimes even nightmares. For better or for worse, however, I cannot recall any of them. I also used to think about LIBORs when going out for a run. There is a place between two houses in the Swedish countryside that, for some reason, still makes me think about the LIBOR fixing for the next International Monetary Market (IMM) date. Of all the potential three-month LIBORs in the future, there are certain dates that are especially significant: the so-called IMM dates. These are standardised dates each quarter when a large proportion of derivatives contracts are settled.

A market maker at a competing bank once called me up after having paid a visit to IKEA. He had found no free parking slots on a Sunday morning. The surprisingly strong demand for flat-packed furniture on a Sunday morning, he argued excitedly, surely meant that the retail sales figure would go up next month. This, in turn, would lead to higher prices and thus meant that the risk of inflation had increased overall. He wanted to share this anecdotal evidence with me, as it obviously had a direct impact on the future NIBOR; this was because the central bank watched the level of inflation like a hawk. He also told me that he had traded some derivatives on Monday morning, based on this information he had gathered.

Other conversations were more mathematical. Some of us would argue for hours about the likely LIBOR on the next IMM date. If a dinner party ended up with a discussion about the next IMM LIBOR fixing, you knew that it had become a guaranteed conversation killer for non-traders. You truly had to be a nerd to be interested.

For a trader not working for a LIBOR panel bank, or not seated physically close to one of the LIBOR submitters (the traders or other bank staff on the cash or treasury desk responsible for inputting the numbers) – both of which were true in my case – the benchmark also became a daily source of irritation. The LIBOR fixing sometimes appeared to be deliberately skewed in one direction or the other. Of course, quite often my opinion was biased depending on the position or view I had. It tends to be more common to question the referee's decision if it goes against the team you support. However, my risk taking had increased substantially over the years, and my attention to the various LIBOR fixings had grown accordingly. Every single basis point mattered immensely. Often, even half or a quarter of a basis point could make or ruin a day. In the major currencies, such as US dollars, euros and yen, even an eighth or a sixteenth would be significant. The bigger my bets were, the more nervous I became of the outcome.

I can't remember precisely when I started to become irritated about the LIBOR fixings, or in relation to which currency, but it must have been around 1999. Later, probably around 2001, I had discussions with an important client about the inaccuracy of LIBOR. He was a very active trader, but also a fascinating person to talk to. We often had opposing views about the future LIBOR. However, I had never met anyone with the same passionate interest in that five-letter word, nor anyone who shared my view that the ultimate fixing was sometimes highly questionable. Although I do not recall what was said, we did talk about the fact that LIBOR sometimes could be 'wrong'.

I became increasingly frustrated by this incorrectness, which somehow seemed to have become systematic, often around IMM dates – this was particularly true with regard to NIBOR. The market was relatively small, and you could count the number of NIBOR banks on your fingers. I had grown into a rather big fish in the small Norwegian derivatives pond, and I was placing massive bets on the NIBOR rate. The problem was that when I 'wanted' a high NIBOR, it sometimes – and for no apparent reason – fell on the day when the relevant fixing took place and then rose back again the day after. But by then it was too late. The opposite often happened when I was betting on a low NIBOR; a group of panel banks then managed to push it higher.

I decided to call the trader with whom I had spoken in 2001 and ask him whether he had had the same experience.

'Occasionally,' he said, without any particular passion.

But on an IMM date a few months later, he phoned me to ask whether I had seen that day's NIBOR fixing.

'Yes, of course,' I replied.

'It's an outrage!' he shouted back, correctly pointing out that it had dropped several basis points from the day before – seemingly out of the blue and without any reason.

I decided to call a trader at one of the Norwegian panel banks to ask what was going on.

'The thing is,' he said indifferently, 'the large fixing banks skew the fixing depending on their FRA positions.'

'So what can you do about it?' I asked.

'Nothing, but I'll give you a hint. The small panel banks don't carry any risk up until the fixing. If you call them a few minutes before the fixing and sell them a fraction of the position you have, they won't have time to get out of it before they submit their NIBOR quotes. They will set them high.'

He was explaining that the larger panel banks had an incentive to skew the fixing in one direction or the other, and that they did so systematically. There was nothing in it for the smaller banks, however, as they did not take much risk. Small panel banks were invariably also small market makers, which meant that they had less client flow as well as a less aggressive risk-taking culture. All in all, there was less reason for them to skew the fixings as they had smaller positions. Thus, his suggestion was that I should sell some of my positions to them just before fixing. A gentlemen's agreement stipulated that all market makers, and the panel banks especially, were required to quote bids and offers in FRAs until shortly before they expired, after which the fixing took place. By selling to them if I were 'long' (or buying from them if I were 'short'), the smaller banks would end up long (or short) as well. By leaving it until the very last minute, they would not be able to pass on the FRAs to anyone else in the market, ultimately leaving them with a similar position to mine – albeit on a smaller scale. If they were greedy, they would try to manipulate the fixing in their own favour, which obviously would suit me too. They would be playing on my team, so to speak.

I did not like it. It was basically like forcing someone, against their will, to become an accomplice. The fixing process was just a game that was played among the panel banks, and the rules had now been explained to me. I could not change the rules.

However, it was obvious that I had been taking far too much risk in the run-up to the NIBOR fixing dates. I had to be more diligent and did some calculations back and forth. In the end, I came up with a number showing the maximum derivatives exposure I could have ahead of any specific NIBOR fixing.

I cannot remember how I worked it out, but the number was 27 billion Norwegian kroner, or about $3 billion. If I had more than that, it was almost certain that a majority of the panel banks would want the opposite fixing from the one that would suit my trading book. Despite the phenomenally large amount, the number of banks involved was small. Every player had significant power to influence the market. But some also had the power to influence the NIBOR fixing. There was no doubt that the NIBOR fixing banks would take advantage of the situation. I would be slaughtered.

* * *

When Barclays was fined £59.5 million by the FSA and $360 million by US regulators in June 2012, I read the released transcripts with a mix of academic curiosity and outright anger. At the time, I was still trying to come to terms with my own guilt from my case in 2009. I knew there was a problem with the LIBOR 'system', but for some reason I repressed the thought that human beings other than myself were at fault. Having lost patience with my endless monologues about LIBOR, TIBOR, STIBOR, NIBOR and EURIBOR, Maria said to me: 'You keep on assuming you're the only person in the market who's done something wrong. You've been so busy carrying around your own guilt that you can't see how the system has manipulated everybody. Stop assuming that you are the bad guy all the time. Accept that everybody is guilty.'

According to the FSA, Barclays had made 'submissions which formed part of the LIBOR and EURIBOR setting process that took into account requests from Barclays' interest rate derivatives traders. These trades were motivated by profit and sought to benefit Barclays' trading positions.'[1]

This statement echoed a sentence in my PhD proposal from April 2009, where I claimed: 'Setting a LIBOR that creates a profit for the underlying derivatives makes economic sense.' I had tried to sound cynical but objective about the market. At the time, though, it had never occurred to me that LIBOR would ever become a 'scandal'.

The revelations caused public outrage in the UK. Marcus Agius resigned from his position as Chairman of Barclays, as did Chief Executive Bob Diamond and Chief Operating Officer Jerry del Missier. The media appeared keen to recite the potentially incriminating and often outrageous conversations between the individuals whom the regulators had decided to keep anonymous – and in each case I instinctively tried to work out who they were referring to. Who were 'Trader A', 'Trader B' and 'Trader C'? Did I know 'Broker D'? All of them had been active in exactly the same markets as me. All of them had been working for banks and interdealer brokerage firms that I had traded with on a daily basis for years.

Maria was tired of my naivety, and thought I should have the mental strength to see reality for what it was, or at least what it had become. Effectively, she wanted me to stop acting like I was the only black sheep in the industry when clearly this was far from the case.

True, I no longer needed the same kind of survival mechanism as I had when working in the industry or even throughout my case in 2009. Still, I wasn't totally convinced by Maria's argument that I wasn't uniquely culpable. I did not want revenge. I did not want to know who had rigged LIBORs against me. Somehow, I found it easier to come to terms with my own mistakes without them. Still, I have to admit that I also felt a great deal of anger, and that some of this anger was purely personal. I had spent 15 years trying to predict the various LIBORs. But an *ability to predict* LIBOR is not the same as a *privilege to determine* LIBOR. These banks traded trillions of LIBOR derivatives, pretending that they were trying to predict LIBOR like anyone else while secretly rigging it in their favour. How could I have been fooled by so many for such a long time? I made a conscious decision not to get involved in actively trying to figure out the identities of the LIBOR manipulators. Instead, I would stick to my original plan and focus on the academic work. A personal narrative could wait.

A key element of the problem, as I saw it, had to do with the design of the LIBOR fixing mechanism itself. This mechanism was quite simple, and was almost precisely the same as it had been three decades ago. Other financial centres had copied the methodology, so CIBOR, TIBOR, EURIBOR and all the others looked very similar. It worked like this. A LIBOR 'submitter' (a trader or other bank person at the cash desk or treasury) submitted their LIBOR quotes from a bank terminal, and the other panel banks did the same without being able to see the other banks' quotes. The LIBOR rule book stated that each bank should submit a quote according to the following question: 'At what rate could you borrow funds, were you to do so by asking for and then accepting interbank offers in a reasonable market size just prior to 11 a.m.?' A designated calculation agent (such as Reuters) then collected the quotes from the individual LIBOR panel banks. During a short period, the calculation agent audited and checked the quotes for obvious errors and then conducted the 'trimming' – the omission of the highest and lowest quotes (the number of which depended on the panel size). Thereafter, the arithmetic mean was calculated, rounded to a specified number of decimals and finally published at a certain time midday.[2]

One of the problems was that the rule book was not binding. The LIBOR panel banks did not have to commit to their quotes in any way, nor was there a way of checking whether they had actually traded at a specific price just before 11 a.m., or whether they had traded at all. Trades were kept secret. Instead, the banks were supposed to submit their *perceptions* about the rate at which they could borrow, and the other benchmarks were phrased similarly. For instance, STIBOR banks were supposed to submit quotes at a rate they 'claimed' they could lend to each other. CIBOR banks submitted rates according to the rate at which banks were 'prepared to' lend, and TIBOR banks[3] what they 'deemed to be' prevailing market rates, 'assuming' transactions between banks. The integrity of the whole process therefore rested upon the assumption (and trust) that the banks were revealing the truth, or at least what they believed to be the truth. The rule book and the lack of transparency gave the banks a tremendous *opportunity* to deceive right from the start.

While the LIBOR fixing mechanism gave the banks an opportunity to deceive, the seemingly ever-growing derivatives market provided them with an extremely strong *incentive* to do so. Every single derivatives contract remained in the trading book until the final LIBOR fixing had taken place, after which payments were made and the deals disappeared. Banks, being profit maximising and by far the most frequent users of financial instruments indexed to LIBOR, naturally had an interest in the outcome of the LIBOR fixing being favourable to them. The bigger the stakes, the stronger the incentive to be right. Or to *get* it right.

To illustrate this, let us assume that each panel bank submits a quote according to the LIBOR rule book above. The highest and the lowest are omitted, and the average of the remaining quotes becomes the LIBOR fixing. If there is nothing stopping the banks from lying, all of them could submit quotes that would favour their respective LIBOR-indexed derivatives portfolios. If a bank prefers a high fixing, the bank would submit a relatively high quote. If another bank prefers a low fixing, that bank would submit a relatively low quote. The only banks not submitting deceptive quotes would be those without any derivatives whatsoever. This, however, is highly unlikely given that all banks (and especially LIBOR banks, as it turns out) have enormous amounts of LIBOR-indexed derivatives in their portfolios.

Think about match fixing in sports. All players have the opportunity to influence the outcome of the game. All players also have an incentive to win the game (because of prestige, money or whatever). The crucial difference between the final score of the game and the LIBOR fixing was the following. The former normally has a referee determining what can be regarded as a fair and objective result. In the latter, some of the players acted as referees.

* * *

Before the LIBOR scandal broke, the trimming process was widely regarded as an effective prevention method against systematic manipulation.[4] The logic went like this. Since banks did not know whether the *other* banks wanted high or low LIBORs, it was not rational for a bank to submit, say, an unreasonably high quote because it knew that this quote would end up as an outlier and therefore would not count towards the LIBOR fixing. A manipulative strategy was doomed to fail. Paradoxically, the Japanese banking crisis of the late 1990s showed that this trimming mechanism worked properly as a deterrent even under 'stress'. At the time, Japanese banks had to face a premium on their borrowing costs in Japanese yen. As the yen LIBOR and the yen TIBOR were interbank money market benchmarks for yen deposits, they not only should have reflected the current and expected future official rate of the Bank of Japan, but also should have incorporated credit and liquidity risk. However, the TIBOR was set in Tokyo and its panel largely consisted of Japanese banks, whereas the London-based LIBOR panel included mainly European and American banks. During the crisis, the quotes by the few large Japanese banks that were part of the LIBOR panel in London were consistently higher than the others, and therefore they were omitted from the calculation of the LIBOR average. This left the London-based yen LIBOR fixing largely in the hands of non-Japanese banks without funding issues. The Tokyo-based yen TIBOR, however, had more Japanese than foreign banks. The outcome was that the difference between TIBOR and LIBOR for Japanese yen, or the TIBOR–LIBOR spread, widened sharply during this period – exactly as it 'should' have done.

It was thought that no bank *wanted* to be an outlier. But if a bank ended up as one, there would be a scientific reason for it. Likewise, if a group of banks ended up as outliers, something must be structurally different with these banks. Other explanations, for instance that they simply agreed to rig the result, were not seen as plausible. Moreover, the larger the panel, the larger the number of quotes that were omitted. The US dollar LIBOR, for instance, had 16 banks and the highest four and lowest four were omitted. This meant that you needed at least five outliers in the same direction in order to influence the fixing. Why would five banks competing fiercely with each other in the financial markets suddenly decide to become collaborators?

Well, it turned out that one way to get around the trimming process was simply to make a phone call to a friend at one of the other LIBOR banks. For instance, on 26 October 2006, a Barclays trader received an email from a trader at another bank who wanted a low three-month US dollar LIBOR: 'If it comes in unchanged I'm a dead man.'

The Barclays trader then replied that he would 'have a chat'.

Later that day, after the LIBOR fixing, the other trader thanked the Barclays trader: 'Dude. I owe you big time! Come over one day after work and I'm opening a bottle of Bollinger.'[5]

When UBS, on 19 December 2012, agreed to pay the UK, US and Swiss authorities £940 million for its involvement,[6] the LIBOR scandal reached a whole new dimension. According to the FSA, a least 2,000 requests to manipulate LIBOR had been documented, and at least 45 individuals (including traders, managers and senior managers) were involved in, or aware of, these manipulative practices.[7]

When the press release came out, I was standing outside the Hertz car rental at Nyköping airport in Sweden. I downloaded the 40-page Final Notice from the FSA website, sat down in the passenger seat and read it during the 90-minute trip to our cottage. For me, this was a tipping point. I was furious. Not in a million years had I imagined how widespread the manipulation had been. And the worst thing was that it had all been played out in front of my eyes. It involved people I knew: traders I had dealt with on a daily basis and brokers I had chatted with dozens of times every day for years. If I had been able to get hold of a database of my old trades, I could literally have used the regulator's transcripts to trace when, where and by how much I had been deceived. Even though I was no longer a trader and should not care, I was still bitterly disappointed with what they had done to the game. When we finally arrived, the snow was unusually deep for December.

'I'll go and chop some wood,' I said to Maria.

* * *

The next bank in line was RBS, which had been rescued during the height of the financial crisis and which was now largely owned by UK taxpayers. On 6 February 2013, the bank was fined £390 million by regulators for its involvement in the LIBOR scandal.[8] Others followed: Rabobank on 29 October 2013 (£660 million), Lloyds Bank on 28 July 2014 (£226 million) and Deutsche Bank on 23 April 2015 ($2.5 billion). The following conversation had taken place on 26 June 2009,[9] showing that this was not a matter of just one or two banks:

Broker A: Alright okay, alright listen, we've had a couple of words with them. You want them lower, right?

Trader B [LIBOR Bank 1]: Yeah.

Broker A: Alright okay, alright, no we've okay just confirming it. We've, so far we've spoke to [LIBOR Bank 2], [LIBOR Bank 3], [LIBOR Bank 4], who else did I speak to? [LIBOR Bank 5]. There's a couple of other people that the boys have a spoke to but as team we've basically said we want a bit lower [Japanese yen LIBOR] so we'll see where they come in alright?

Trader B: Cheers.

Broker A: No worries mate.

The conversation above reveals the level of complicity. This was not about a few traders, submitters or brokers. It was much more systematic. At the same time, however, the dialogue illustrates the almost casual approach to skewing numbers that ultimately would have an impact on contracts amounting to billions – whichever currency it involved. The laid-back attitude in other transcripts, where sushi lunches or steak sandwiches were mentioned as favours in return for helping to tweak these numbers, understandably caused public outrage. Manipulation seemed to be like a daily habit, akin to going to the supermarket to buy groceries.

When a manager at Lloyds Bank was told by a trader about a request made to another trader at the bank regarding a low LIBOR, he was told that 'every little helps … It's like Tesco's.' 'Absolutely,' the manager replied, 'every little helps.'[10]

Large LIBOR panels would require at least a handful of banks to come to some kind of arrangement over the phone or on an electronic platform to have any chance of skewing the fixing. Even so, the impact might be minuscule. Realistically, you would need half the panel on your side to guarantee a favourable outcome. This might be very complicated. There are many different LIBORs. You might want a high six-month LIBOR and a low three-month LIBOR. A high one-month US dollar LIBOR and a low three-month yen TIBOR. And the next day would be different. Your mates could be your friends one day, but your foes the next.

In such cases, interdealer brokers might be used to help out. This is why, on 25 September 2013, the interdealer broker firm ICAP was fined £55 million for its involvement in the LIBOR scandal. On 15 May 2014, Martin Brokers was fined £630,000.

To illustrate how this could take place, consider this exchange between 'Trader A' and 'Broker F':[11]

Trader A: HIGH 6M SUPERMAN … BE A HERO TODAY.

Broker F: I'll try mate … as always.

From this quote, it is clear that the derivatives trader in question would prefer a high six-month LIBOR on that day, and is encouraging the broker to help him achieve that goal.

Brokers do not trade themselves but act as intermediaries between traders at different banks by matching buyers and sellers. For every trade, they receive a commission, and the size of the commission depends on the size of the trade. In other words, brokers have an incentive to get many (and preferably big) deals done.

The first time I heard a broker shouting down the box (the squawk box, the dealer board, the speakerbus, or whatever else we called the telecommunication system used to communicate with each other), I thought it sounded comical. I had never been to a horse race and could not comprehend how someone could pepper the air with so many numbers in such a short time. It almost sounded like a machine gun, '80–83, 80–83, 80–83, 80–83', until the broker said 'Given!', 'Taken!', 'Off!' or changed the ammunition to '80–82, 80–82, 80–82, 80–82'.

'The old image is of East End barrow boys paid to give prices and be entertaining,' a former ICAP broker said during a LIBOR trial.[12] The stereotypical broker came from the East End of London or Essex, leaving school at 16 to work in the City of London. Several of my brokers ticked every single box in that respect, whereas others had joined the broking business after having had a go at trading in one of the large banks. Either way, brokers who survived the cutthroat business of competing against each other to win business from traders were generally good at two things. First, they might not have been mathematicians, but they tended to have a natural flair with numbers. Second, they often had extraordinarily good social skills. No matter how little respect they were shown by traders, who could be angry, ruthless, arrogant or short-sighted, they always managed to make the traders feel on top of the world. Like superheroes.

Brokers communicate with traders all the time via speaker boxes, phones, texts, emails, Bloomberg and other elec-tronic systems. Given the amount of interaction, the personal chemistry between a trader and a broker is therefore tremendously important. Nonetheless, brokers compete with other brokers on price and price information, and, as a trader, you would naturally rather go to a broker showing the best price rather than the second-best price. Likewise, if you were uncertain about where the market was trading at a particular moment in time, you would generally ask brokers. As the brokers speak to other banks as well, they will invariably be able to provide either a firm and tradeable price, or a very good *indication* of where such a price ought to be. If they are unable find an indication, they can make it up. Like the best London black cab drivers, they tend to be good at working out where the grid might be congested and the route commuters are likely to take. Brokers, therefore, are a great source of information.

In a volatile or illiquid market, traders constantly ask brokers for prices or price indications, and brokers ask traders for prices or price indications in return. If you are not particularly active in a specific market, or have simply left the trading desk for five minutes to get a coffee, brokers are the first point of contact when trying to take the pulse of the market – without having the obligation to trade. Active and experienced traders know the important role brokers play in broadcasting prices and price indications to the market. In that respect, the broker can act as a key 'signalling device'. This could be seen as a good thing, as price transparency is supposed to make markets more efficient. If, however, the signalling device is used to broadcast half-truths or outright lies, it is potentially a vehicle for market manipulation.

A common way for brokers to broadcast prices was to send out 'run-throughs'. These were simply series of two-way prices for, say, yen interest rate swaps or euro/dollar FX swaps. Sometimes, these did not consist of firm and tradeable prices, but instead were the broker's best guess at that moment in time. The best guess, or price indication, ought to have been a blend of other banks' prices or price indications given to the broker – coupled with the broker's own judgement.

I used to be given run-throughs over the speaker box many times a day, in different instruments, in different currencies and by different brokers. Increasingly, these were also sent out as emails or messages via terminals provided by Bloomberg, the news and market data provider. In addition, because I was active in the Japanese market, I was also sent run-throughs via text messages. The run-throughs increasingly tended to contain indications of where the brokers thought US dollar and Japanese yen LIBORs would fix during the day. Brokers knew the increased attention LIBOR numbers were receiving, and LIBOR *indications* became part of the overall package of price information and market 'colour'. It was irritating to be woken up at 1.30 a.m. by a string of prices indicating where the Tokyo market had opened, but it became part of the daily routine. I always tended to scroll through the run-throughs on my mobile phone while I was waiting for the espresso machine to do its job first thing in the morning. If I wanted to get into work early, or simply needed a moment to reflect, I would call for a minicab to take me to the City. To get myself in the right mood, I had got into the habit of listening to The Smashing Pumpkins while analysing the prices and indications the brokers had sent me. They became ingredients in the trading strategies I formed in my head on the way to the dealing room.

Should such run-throughs be taken seriously – and I certainly took them very seriously at the time – while containing deceptive indications from a trader at the other end, the broker would in effect be spreading false information. Brokers might do so consciously or unconsciously, but the information would nonetheless influence traders at other banks (like myself) and also LIBOR submitters who were keen to get an idea of where the money market was trading (or at least ought to be trading). In other words, a trader might achieve a manipulated LIBOR quote by colluding not only with other banks, but also with a broker who was trusted by others.

The question is: how could you get brokers to spread false information? As they do not trade derivatives, LIBOR is of no direct relevance to their profit or loss. Why would they play along? This might sound cynical, but they could be threatened to help influence it. A trader could simply cease – or threaten to cease – doing business with a broker and go to a competitor instead, should the broker not comply with their demands. Traders regularly penalised brokers by switching to a competitor, even if it were just for a day or two. This could also take place at a higher level, should the trader be very senior. During my career, I was 'banned' numerous times from speaking to my preferred brokers, simply because they happened to be working for the same firm where another broker had disappointed one of the senior traders in my bank. It was a kind of collective punishment.

The impact of losing a major client can be devastating for a broker. Brokers compete with each other to get the main players on board (these players are often just a handful of individuals) and to retain them. A threat would pose the broker with a dilemma, as their revenue – and that of the company – also depends on their long-term reputation for being fair and seemingly objective. Although brokers tend to have one, two or three key accounts, they cannot be seen to favour these ahead of their other clients. If so, the less active traders providing bread-and-butter business might switch to another broker who provides a fairer service.

On 17 December 2015, a broker said in court that he would never have taken the risk of favouring one bank over another. If the news got out 'it'd spread through like wildfire around the market,' he said. 'You'd go from hero to zero in no time.'[13]

I think his statement is partially correct, but not completely. It would definitively spread like wildfire around the market. Everyone would know that he was favouring that particular bank or that particular trader. However, I am not so sure that the fall from grace would be that dramatic. Everyone knows that, in the end, the powerful banks and the powerful traders get better service from the brokers than less influential players. I think most traders would have been bitterly disappointed, but they would still have forgiven him for playing the game.

Instead of resorting to blackmailing techniques, a trader could also do the opposite: ensnare a broker into a lucrative financial arrangement. The trader could, in theory, simply pay bribes to a broker for complying with certain demands. Bribes would not have to come in the form of brown envelopes discreetly handed over in a dark alleyway. Instead, a trader could put more business through a particular broker and reward them in that way. More business would mean more commission – which would mean a bigger bonus for the broker. There is, however, one problem. Doing more deals just to keep the broker happy would also mean that a trader would suddenly be taking more risk than they might want to at that particular moment. Therefore, bribes could be elaborately constructed in the form of so-called 'wash trades'. In such a case, a trader would buy, say, $1 billion worth of FRAs from a trader at another bank, and simultaneously agree to sell it back at exactly the same rate. There would be no risk involved, as the trades would offset each other perfectly. Such a trade naturally sounds pointless. Why would a trader buy something and sell it back at the same time at the same price? Well, if a broker acts as an intermediary, the two trades would result in having to pay a commission to the broker. The bigger the amount, the bigger the commission (read: bribe) paid to the broker.

Asked in court why he did not refuse to be rewarded with wash trades worth tens of thousands of pounds in commission from a trader, a broker told the prosecutors:[14]

> You've got to bear in mind who he [the derivatives trader] was at the time, like I said he was paying a million pounds a month brokerage to Tokyo. He was the biggest player out there by a country mile. And if I jeopardize the relationship I'm sacked. I'm gone.

What he was saying was that his employer would not have forgiven him for *not* playing the game.

The tricky element of a wash trade would be to get a trader on the other side to agree to such a pointless trade.

'I will do a humongous trade with you … $50,000 trade. I need you to keep it low … I will pay you $50,000, $100,000, whatever you want. If you can just call in some favours … if you've got a mate who will do a flat switch,' Tom Hayes told a broker in September 2008.[15]

It did not matter how much money a broker was paid. At the end of the day, it was necessary to have a bank on the other side that was willing to do a pointless trade. A flat switch meant that the other bank agreed to do such a trade, but at least it did not have to pay commission for it.

As it turned out, JPMorgan Chase agreed to do a switch for ¥50 billion, and RBS did a ¥150 billion wash trade. The broker netted trade commissions worth £32,012 from UBS and £10,244 from RBS. I have no idea why RBS agreed to pay ten grand for something they could have done for free. However, they did get a lunch delivery to the whole trading desk in return, according to the transcripts.

It seemed almost everyone could be a winner in this game. The UBS trader could influence LIBOR, which would generate a profit both for the bank and for himself. The broker, likewise, netted a profit for the firm and himself. Traders at RBS got a nice but expensive lunch (paid for by RBS shareholders, though). JPMorgan Chase did not make any money out of it, unless they also wanted to skew LIBOR in the same direction.

A trader at Merrill Lynch was also asked to help, but according to the transcripts published by a newspaper in 2015 he turned down the request. Although I was not mentioned by name, I had a strong feeling that the trader was in fact me, and this realisation caused me to cry for the first time in years. It was the only occasion since I had left my life as a trader that it had been mentioned in the public domain in a non-negative way. Even though it was just a tiny fraction, a few minutes extracted from 15 full years, it portrayed me neutrally – maybe even positively, considering that it was a criminal case. Insignificant as this might sound, I felt as if I was being seen for who I was.

During the autumn, I was contacted by a couple of journalists who confirmed that the Merrill Lynch trader was indeed me. I asked one of them if he could email me the full transcript he had obtained during the Tom Hayes trial. Here is a conversation between a trader, a broker and myself, taking place on 19 September 2008:

> Trader: Any chance you could wash a trade through with rpms [RP Martin Brokers] for me pls?
>
> Me: [No response.]
>
> *Later:*
>
> Broker: It's UBS both sides basically, you'll be like – you'll take two sides off him and give it back ... at the same level. Don't pay any bro, you've got no risk, no counterparty risk because it's UBS the same, both sides of the deal ...
>
> Me: Oh you mean. I see what you mean. I don't know if I can do that.
>
> Broker: Yeah, if it's a bit dodgy that's fair enough, but I mean ...
>
> Me: Yeah it is actually ... yeah. In these tough times for bankers ... let me think about it.

Later:

Me: I just don't want to do the same thing in and out …

I cannot remember this dialogue. But it obviously took place and those were the exact words I used. One of the problems with extracts from conversations over the phone, via email or in electronic chatrooms is that they don't always give the whole picture. I don't recall thinking that they were involved in something 'dodgy' related to LIBOR at the time, because I remember how much I respected the trader and liked the broker. My main problem with the deal, which was later defined as a 'wash trade' in court, had more to do with the fact that I had come to regard more and more aspects of trading and banking as 'wrong'.

Ironically, the original idea of a switch was rather noble. Flat switches had been common ever since I started as a trader and they probably existed long before that. Because of the sheer volume traded in the market, credit lines were often filled up temporarily. During a crisis, however, and depending on the perceived creditworthiness of the bank on the other side, it could take much longer for the credit department to come back and give a green light. Therefore, if two market makers were unable to trade with each other, a third market maker might step in as a go-between – ultimately to help the suffering bank access the financial markets as in normal times. Again, it was part of the game, an unwritten footnote in one of the many gentlemen's agreements that existed. When a bank was struggling to find banks to trade with, or when its perceived creditworthiness fell dramatically, you would not just stand on the sidelines and watch the bank disappear from the market or face a slow and painful death. No, you would at least consider throwing a lifejacket to enable the trader at the other bank to catch their breath. You would offer to do a flat switch out of pure generosity – because you never knew when you might end up in the same situation, desperately trying to trade at prices in the market only to find that you were unable to grab onto those prices because banks were refusing to trade with you. This was a thing with trading. No matter how ruthless the environment might seem from the outside, there was also a warmth to be found for those on the inside and a great deal of forgiveness.

Nevertheless, some traders would refuse to do a flat switch, and demanded something in return to compensate for the fact that credit lines were being used up. From the outside, this might seem like sound risk management being applied. However, this 'fee' always ended up on the trader's book (and part of it, therefore, in the trader's own pocket), not with the credit officers who were trying to work out the risks involved and how much exposure the bank was willing to have towards another bank. This was another thing about trading. Traders and sales people were 'profit centres', meaning that profits (or losses) on new trades were booked against their names. Credit officers, compliance managers, back office staff, risk managers, financial controllers and others, however, were treated as 'cost centres'. It was very difficult for them to quantify the extent to which their work had paid off.

I remember once being invited home to dinner with a credit officer who was responsible for deciding the bank's credit lines to other banks and large corporations in a whole country.

'Since I joined the bank ten years ago, the credit losses in our department have been zero,' he proudly proclaimed while guiding me through his enormous art collection.

'Hmm, that is not the view we hold of you on the trading floor,' I thought. To us, he was impossible to deal with as he refused to show any kind of flexibility. He was more concerned about his loyalty to the bank than his reputation on the trading floor.

When I told the broker that bankers were having a 'tough time', it wasn't as if I was looking for sympathy. It was my way of expressing the fact that, in the aftermath of the Lehman Brothers collapse, I felt a stronger loyalty towards the credit department of Merrill Lynch than towards a trader at another bank. Technically, I could have accepted to do a wash trade of a few trillion yen. I would not have broken any limits. But it did not feel right.

* * *

There was, however, another serious problem and it had to do with how the LIBOR fixing mechanism was linked to the barometer of fear. According to the rule book, *individually* submitted LIBOR quotes were supposed to reflect 'where the bank can fund itself in the interbank market'. The LIBOR quotes from each individual bank became visible to the whole market at the same time as the LIBOR fixing was published. By comparing the different quotes, you could see which banks had to pay higher interest rates in order to be able to borrow (i.e. which banks were in trouble) and which banks had easy access to money. This signal to the market showing where each and every bank was able to borrow money was important, as the funding cost of the bank and its capital and reputation are closely linked. Downgrades by Moody's or Standard

& Poor's were rare events. Likewise, earnings reports and other financial statements were not published frequently. The individual LIBOR quotes, by contrast, were announced daily and therefore served as snapshots of the perceived creditworthiness of the banks.

A unique thing with banks is that they inherently always have a desire to *appear* 'good and sound'. If depositors lose confidence in the ability of the bank to meet its obligations, there could be a bank run around the corner and the bank could face the risk of being wiped out altogether. Even the slightest of suspicions could cause a sharp decline in the stock price. The problem with the LIBOR fixing mechanism resulted from the individual LIBOR rates being public knowledge (i.e. fully transparent) at the same time as the *actual* funding rate was private knowledge (i.e. secret). LIBOR banks did not have to prove that the rates they were submitting were, in fact, rates at which they were able to borrow. This lack of transparency, coupled with the desire of banks to look 'good and sound', therefore worked as an incentive to conceal potential funding problems publicly through the LIBOR signalling process. An individual quote *above* the average of the others might be interpreted as a signal that the bank had funding issues. An individual quote *below* the others would indicate that the bank was in relatively decent shape. Consequently, there was a stigma attached to signalling a relatively high funding cost via the LIBOR mechanism, similar to the stigma of having to rely on emergency funding from the central bank. Everyone trading in the money markets knew that there was a severe financial crisis, but no bank wanted to look desperate for cash. That would have meant the end. The LIBOR fixing mechanism turned into a vast game of poker, where most of the players were holding terrible cards.

Rumours about which banks needed life support were flying around like confetti. Some of the gossip also leaked out of the dealing rooms. On 3 September 2007, only three weeks after I had put down the axe and returned from the woodshed in Sweden, Bloomberg came out with the following headline: 'Barclays takes a money market beating.' The journalist pointed out that Barclays had submitted the highest quotes among the panel banks for the three-month LIBOR in British pounds, euros and US dollars. They asked: 'What the hell is happening at Barclays and its Barclays Capital securities unit that is prompting its peers to charge it premium interest rates in the money market?'

It was a good question. It was also very bad publicity for Barclays, and senior management at high levels became worried. According to the FSA, managers slightly lower in the hierarchy reacted by asking the LIBOR submitters in the bank to reduce their quotes to avoid bad publicity. The instructions were followed, and the following day Barclays submitted LIBOR rates below those at which they were able to fund themselves in the market. The demand for US dollars was particularly severe. However, all major currencies, to some degree, were affected by the crisis. A few weeks later, an email was sent out stating that Barclays should 'try to get our JPY [Japanese yen] libors a little more in line with the rest of the contributors, or else the rumours will start flying about Barclays needing money because its libors are so high'.[16] This issue was raised in the *Wall Street Journal* in May 2008.[17] The journalists Carrick Mollenkamp and Mark Whitehouse argued that some LIBOR panel banks had deliberately quoted rates that were too low to be justified by their credit standing as reflected in the credit default swap (CDS) market. Although the article did not claim outright manipulation, it argued that banks 'may have been low-balling their borrowing rates to avoid looking desperate for cash'. The contents of the article supported anecdotal evidence from some active market participants (myself included) who had become suspicious of LIBOR manipulation. Already in August 2007, when the LIBOR–OIS spread began to widen, I did not think that LIBOR rose *enough*. It was difficult to work out by how much it should have risen. But given that some large banks were practically shut off from the interbank market, I thought that the 'actual' LIBOR often should have been considerably higher.

* * *

In 2011, I decided it was time to go back to Tokyo. I had not been back in ten years and missed the city. Moreover, the Japanese TIBOR–LIBOR spread was central to the PhD I was writing and Tokyo-based banks now seemed to be under scrutiny from financial regulators. I wanted to broaden my outlook on LIBOR. By now, I had become convinced that banks had misled the public through LIBOR manipulation. However, something else that had bothered me was the fact that not only did the final LIBOR fixing seem to be too low, but also that the individually submitted LIBOR quotes by each bank seemed too *similar*. Most LIBOR panels had many contributing banks, and I found it strange how well they managed to harmonise their misleading quotes. I did not find it plausible that *all* the banks had been talking to each other.

Unfortunately, a meeting I was supposed to have with the Japanese financial regulator was cancelled at the very last minute. Even though I was now an academic, my rogue trader background apparently led them to change their mind about the propriety of me talking to them. I am not totally sure what swayed me to do it, but my instinct told me that it would be good to meet up instead with former traders and brokers in a market where I had been very active. As of February 2009, I had disappeared from that market and was eager to check in again. Not as a trader, of course, but not as a PhD student either. I just wanted to meet people who had been part of my life for years and whom I genuinely liked.

I was expecting to be met with a mixture of suspicion and distance, given that I had left a while ago under somewhat spectacular circumstances. I took it for granted that everybody had read about what had happened, and I was therefore nervous about what the reaction would be. To my surprise, I was welcomed with open arms. Invitations to lunches, drinks and dinners rolled in. The generosity was endless, as if I were still a 'player' in the market. My perspective, however, was now very different. I had returned to see what had gone wrong with the market, or perhaps what ultimately had led me to do something wrong. I was not there to claim any lost territory. But behind the façade, I could also sense a fundamental change in the people I met. Although this was still a group of people with immense confidence and optimism, there was a newly injected concern that I had not seen before. It was as if some traders and brokers were beginning to feel that they had been part of a game all along, but could not really work out its rules.

One evening, I went to a superhero-themed Christmas party organised by Meitan Tradition, one of the large Japanese interdealer brokers that acted as an intermediary between banks in the TIBOR and LIBOR derivatives markets. Traders from different banks came dressed up as Superman, Super Mario or the Terminator. Also invited were competitors from the other brokerage firms ICAP, Totan and Tulletts. Only in the Tokyo market, I thought, did competing banks and brokers still trust each other enough to contemplate writing them a Christmas card, let alone inviting them to a lavish Christmas party. The combination of having been labelled a rogue trader and the fact that everyone knew I understood their market led to some long and deep conversations. Curious as people were about what had really happened to me, they seemed to want to get their own worries off their chests just as much. Whether I met traders and brokers in The Oak Door in Roppongi Hills, in Two Rooms off Omotesando, or in some karaoke bar I would never have been able to find again, the comments I got were now familiar: 'The LIBOR thing was going too far' or 'I was being used.' I thought about the meeting I had had with my ex-broker in Borough Market six months earlier, when he had asked me whether I thought he had done anything wrong by being part of 'it'.

Only a couple of days after the Christmas party, on 16 December 2011, the Japanese Financial Services Agency announced that it would take action against Citi and UBS for having tried to influence TIBOR and LIBOR. Both banks would have to clarify the responsibility of top management regarding the violation, as well as improve controls and compliance. UBS and Citi would also have to suspend derivatives trading relating to TIBOR and LIBOR for one week and two weeks respectively, unless the transactions were deemed 'necessary'.[18]

This was only the beginning, I thought. The manipulation, the low-balling, everything was related to the same behaviour of second-guessing that I had always seen in the markets. Hanging out with the traders and brokers in Tokyo had reminded me of how the system worked. Rather than pinpointing one particular trader, one particular broker or one particular bank, the whole process reminded me of a typical Keynesian beauty contest.[19]

* * *

In 1936, the Cambridge economist John Maynard Keynes published a fabulous book called *The General Theory of Employment, Interest and Money*. He had also been an active trader in the markets, and in Chapter 12 he compared stock market trading to a newspaper competition that was popular in the early 1900s. The rules of the game were as follows. Competitors would have to pick the six most beautiful women from a hundred photographs. However, they would not pick their personal favourites, but instead those six that they thought would receive the most votes. In other words, it was not a game about stating your opinion, but rather about what you *expected* the average opinion to be, what the average option expected the average opinion to be, and so on ...[20]

A typical illustration of such a game (and a classroom experiment I have conducted many times since) goes like this. Students are given a piece of paper and have to write down a number between 0 and 100. They are not allowed to talk to each other, and they have to guess the 'winning number'. The student who picks the number closest to two-thirds of the average wins a prize (which is generally just the honour of feeling smarter than the others). Now, if they were to guess the average, most students would go for 50, because in a large classroom we could assume that the guesses are fairly equally distributed between 0 and 100; 50 would be the logical choice. However, because they have to get close to *two-thirds* of the average, the winning number would be 33 and therefore the rational guess would be 33, rather than 50. But if they predict that the others will do the same, they would have to guess two-thirds of 33, which is 22 … and so on. The outcome is that you might as well pick the number 0 immediately, if you believe that the others believe that the others believe … and so on.[21] As it turns out, when the game is played many times, the winning number drifts towards 0. However, this does not happen immediately. There could be several reasons for this. Firstly, it takes time for players to become 'experts' in this game. Most experiments (including my own) show that the first round tends to generate a number fairly close to 33, the second round close to 22, and the third round close to 15. Thereafter, quite a few 0s tend to be written down. Secondly, even if a student had played the game before and understood what the final outcome might be, they would still have to predict what the others who hadn't previously played the game might guess. Therefore, they know that 0 is rarely the winning number in the first round. Thirdly, some students go for the number 100 in every round. Perhaps they do not care about ridiculous games, or perhaps they genuinely want to stand out from the crowd. If, however, some kind of 'reputational fine' is introduced to the rules of the game, this behaviour changes immediately. Assume I tell students, for instance, that they have to stay after class if their guess deviates by more than a certain distance from the winning guess.[22] Suddenly, the game is taken seriously, and the players avoid extreme numbers. They are incentivised to be 'part of the pack'.

Keynesian beauty contest games can be used to illustrate herd behaviour in stock markets, or why some financial bubbles are created and sustained. For instance, many people argue that the London housing market is crazy. Still, however, there is talk of how important it is to get on the housing ladder (before it is too late), and how 'others' are pushing up house prices in the capital. The same was true during the dot-com bubble. Few people truly believed that even a fraction of the internet start-ups would eventually make any money. Still, money could be made by buying an overpriced stock and then selling it on to someone who paid an even higher price later on. In essence, in dealing with market participants, we are not always concerned about the consensus view of the 'fundamental' value of an asset; rather, we often take a more short-term view to incorporate what we *believe* others will do – and in turn what we think *they* believe others will do, and so on. Whether a fundamental value exists in practice is, of course, another question. When it comes to LIBOR, we know that it is *supposed* to be an objective and unbiased reflection of the interbank money market rate. More specifically, it should be the average of the funding costs subjectively reported by a group of banks. In reality, though, the LIBOR mechanism more closely resembles a Keynesian beauty contest game played once every day, year in year out, by players guided by such higher-order beliefs. Large LIBOR-indexed derivatives portfolios induce banks to submit high, low or average quotes depending on what suits them. Depending on the positions, the LIBOR quotes can be high one day and low the next, but one thing is clear: they do not have to correspond to the actual funding cost of the bank. Sometimes the extreme quotes are trimmed away, and sometimes not. If players are allowed to talk to each other (i.e. collude with each other or with a broker), they are more likely to be able to influence the LIBOR fixing.

However, as LIBOR submitters know that *the others* might manipulate the rates as well in order to reap rewards from the fixing, deceptive behaviour can become the norm rather than the exception. The stigma attached to being perceived as a bank with funding problems gives *all* LIBOR banks an incentive to submit relatively low quotes to distance themselves from the others. For instance, when the US investment bank Bear Stearns was heading for a collapse in March 2008 (and was ultimately bought by JPMorgan Chase), the money markets were exceptionally choppy and illiquid. Looking back, it was probably the closest warning we got of what would happen if a bank the size of Lehman Brothers went under. Bear Stearns was more than just a tremor. It was an earthquake. LIBORs should have gone to the moon. But which banks were prepared to wave a white flag and honestly admit that they were having difficulties getting hold of cash? Very few, I think.

According to FSA transcripts,[23] on Monday 17 March 2008, a LIBOR submitter at Barclays asked a manager: 'I presume that you want me now to set LIBORs … exactly where the market is setting them?' The manager confirmed that he did.

Two days later, a submitter was instructed to lower Barclays' submissions: 'Just set it where everyone else sets it, we do not want to be standing out.'

A couple of weeks after the collapse of Lehman Brothers, on 8 October 2008, a submitter was asked about LIBOR in a phone conversation. The submitter responded that '[Manager E]'s asked me to put it lower than it was yesterday … to send the message that we're not in the shit.'

The banks wanted to look good and sound relative to the others, but at the same time imitate the crowd to be 'part of the pack'. This behaviour resulted in the LIBOR quotes by the different banks becoming too similar (to be justifiable when looking at other financial indicators). Moreover, the fact that nobody wanted to deviate too much from the others at any point in time resulted in a tendency for LIBOR to observe a kind of 'stickiness'. This gave the false impression that the money market was stable, and that the LIBOR banks had fairly similar funding costs. All in all, it was clear that the privilege of being able to influence LIBOR rested with the LIBOR panel banks. This exclusive right certainly gave them the ability to defraud the public. However, another logical, but disturbing, outcome of the LIBOR game was that some players got caught up in the process without necessarily thinking about it. The perception that *others* would act in such a manner meant that *not* submitting a deceptive quote would be punished through the reputational damage of being an outlier, or even because the bank would 'unjustifiably' be regarded as relatively risky. Thus, manipulative behaviour might have evolved into a kind of job routine. And in a market with so many unwritten rules and conventions, it was not totally clear where such routines originated – or how they spread. Moreover, how could they spread without other people knowing about it? To begin to understand why, I believe it is necessary to go back quite far in history – way before 'Trader A', 'Trader B' or 'Broker D' performed their first ever LIBOR trades.

CHAPTER 4

THE LIBOR ILLUSION

Since the credit crunch began, it has become clearer to all of us that LIBOR, not the Bank of England base rate, is what really governs saving and borrowing rates in the high street. It has always been relied on by the market as a reliable benchmark which is also the most transparent. It is appropriate in this global downturn to ensure the continued robustness of this pillar of our financial architecture.[1]

These were the words of the British Bankers' Association (BBA) Chief Executive Angela Knight in a speech given on 18 December 2008. I remember reading the paragraph online and thinking how absurd it was. How could a number, which was not determined by the market, was susceptible to manipulation, and was based on a market that no longer existed, be any of the following: important, transparent or reliable?

In frustration, I wrote down two sentences in a notebook at home: 'Complaints in 2008 from clients and smaller banks that the LIBORs were manipulated went to the BBA, which is run by large banks. Naturally, no change was deemed necessary and no punishment either.' I think I opted for the word 'punishment' because I thought the BBA, the bank lobby that oversaw the LIBOR process, had failed in its responsibility to investigate this properly. It should, at least, have punished a couple of banks by forcing them to temporarily leave the LIBOR panel. At the time, I had no idea that the whole thing would in fact lead to more severe punishments in the form of large fines and even prison sentences. That had never happened before in relation to LIBOR or anything even remotely similar to it.

Looking back, it is remarkable that LIBOR manipulation was seen as unthinkable by almost everyone from its inception in the mid-1980s up until the scandal broke. It is evident that central bankers and governments acted *as if* LIBOR were a perfect proxy for the money market rate. Academics and journalists (with very few exceptions) also treated LIBORs and money market rates *as if* they were synonyms. So did the wider public. Corporations, pension funds and households entered into LIBOR-indexed financial contracts *as if* the money market rate were the underlying benchmark.[2] None of this was correct. I think the only way to fully understand how the foundations were laid for what would become one of the greatest banking scandals in history is to look closer at the origins of LIBOR and specifically at the actors that have benefited from LIBOR: the banks. By doing so, it is possible to reveal not only how and why LIBOR became so important in the first place, but also how and why it came to be perceived as an objective number that was impossible to manipulate. In short, how LIBOR became an illusion.[3]

* * *

A financial crisis tends to be associated with fears of a bank run. If customers desperately begin to withdraw their deposits from a bank, it can quickly turn into a self-fulfilling prophecy. Because if you think that *others* will become afraid that the bank will run out of cash, it might be rational to empty your own savings account first. The typical illustration of a bank run is a picture of a very long queue outside a bank branch or an ATM. The images look similar, whether they are black and white and taken in New York or Berlin during the 1930s, outside Northern Rock in Newcastle in 2007, or somewhere in Greece during the summer of 2015. Before the fear spreads to the public, however, the atmosphere in the dealing rooms has already changed. Trading has turned into a situation in which the hot potato is passed around from trader to trader, from bank to bank. Lending money is a risky business and nobody wants the borrower to default. As a precaution, banks desperately try to borrow money from the others before they stop lending. Nobody wants to be caught off guard when they are the ones left holding the potato.

The financial crisis of 2007–08 led to a freeze in the international money markets where banks lend to, and borrow from, each other. During the height of the crisis, the ECB sent out one of its regular questionnaires to traders at around a hundred different banks across Europe.[4] One of the questions was phrased as follows: 'Has the market liquidity in the unsecured [money] market changed with respect to last year?' Of the respondents, 93 per cent said that it 'had worsened'. Another question to take the pulse of the market was whether traders thought that the money market was efficient. In 2005, over 80 per cent had answered either 'significantly efficient' or 'extremely efficient'. Three years into the Eurozone crisis, in 2013, this figure had dropped below 1 per cent. The situation had been similar for all major currencies. The unsecured interbank money market, where banks lent to each other without requiring any collateral to protect them against a collapse of the *other* bank, died in August 2007. Banks no longer lent to each other the way they used to. And if they didn't lend to each other, why would they lend to companies and households?

The money market freeze should have posed an immediate threat to the use of LIBOR. After all, the benchmark was supposed to reflect where trading in this unsecured interbank money market took place. If there was little trading going on in the market (and sometimes none whatsoever), how could a price be put on it? How could LIBOR still be relevant?

Take the music industry. If players in the music industry want to use a barometer to get an idea of people's taste in music, they might check out iTunes, Spotify, YouTube or the sale of CDs. Cassette tapes, however, no longer provide a reliable indicator for such information, even though they can store music. People rarely buy them anymore, and extremely few artists would contemplate releasing an album on cassette tape. During the last two decades, other ways to store music have become more popular. That is not to say that cassette tapes are useless – just that, effectively, their liquidity dried up and never truly returned. A friend sent me a brand new cassette tape for my birthday a couple of years ago, as a nostalgic reminder. It was still wrapped in plastic and had not been sold at a discount. The artist was Accept (a German heavy metal band) and the album was *Breaker* (their third, released in 1981). I was a huge fan of them in the early 1980s, and every textbook I had at school was inscribed with the iconic Accept logo. My friend conducted some research and found out that precisely eight new cassette tapes had been sold in Finland that year. Although it would be interesting to know what the other seven tapes were, I can say with some certainty that Accept did not represent 12.5 per cent of the Finnish music industry that year. In other words, if analysts in the music industry had based their analysis of the Finnish music taste only upon cassette tape sales that year, they would have falsely come to the conclusion that German heavy metal from the early 1980s was still hugely popular in the country.

Bizarrely, when it came to LIBOR, the opposite happened. Trading in LIBOR derivatives did not stop despite the market on which it was based (i.e. interbank lending) having quite clearly disappeared. Instead, turnover *increased*. Moreover, rather than forcing the benchmark into obscurity, the financial crisis catapulted LIBOR from something boring into an important instrument for the financial system as a whole.

Philips launched a prototype of the cassette tape in August 1963 at the Berlin Radio Show. However, like most inventions, the prototype was based on several earlier prototypes. The same goes with LIBOR. LIBOR was invented in the 1980s. However, banks had constructed a prototype for it a long time before that in the form of the 'Eurodollar' market. The birth of the Eurodollar market occurred in 1957, when banks created a market in Europe where US dollar deposits were re-lent to European institutions instead of being reinvested in the United States. Eurodollars thereby came to be defined as deposits denominated in US dollars in banks *outside* the US. These kinds of deposits were later denominated in other currencies, and these 'Eurocurrencies' in general (Eurodeutschmarks, Euroyen, Eurosterling and so on) came to represent borrowing and lending outside the jurisdiction of the central bank issuing the currency in question.

The Eurocurrency market grew very rapidly, from around $14 billion in 1964 to over $2,500 billion in 1988.[5] This largely mirrored the increase in international trade and investment that took place at the time, although it grew at a much faster rate; world merchandise exports, for instance, grew from $176 billion to $2,869 billion during the same period.[6] In particular, US multinational corporations in Europe sought cheaper, alternative ways to fund their foreign expansion. There was a demand for new and innovative ways to borrow money, and compared with the US domestic interest rate markets, Eurodollars had a number of advantages. Banks and large corporations with relatively high credit ratings were the main players, meaning that they were perceived as less risky. The deals were often large, resulting in lower administrative costs. Because they circumvented some strict US regulations at the time, Eurodollars could be offered at lower, more competitive rates. This, coupled with the sheer size of the market, resulted in tighter bid–offer spreads. Should you, for whatever reason, decide to offset a trade you had previously done in the Eurodollar market, the cost of doing so was smaller than in the old-fashioned domestic money market.

The new market was also boosted by a range of structural economic factors, such as a growing pool of US dollars abroad as central banks had begun to accumulate large currency reserves. Overall, however, the Eurodollar market proved to be a special financial invention. It became systematic. It had a clear purpose. After some initial resistance, it was also approved by authorities. Ultimately, the Eurodollar market resulted in what today we simply refer to as the 'international money market'.

The first ever Eurodollar *trade*, however, seems to have been triggered by fears of sovereign and political risk, rather than by the economic and regulatory factors mentioned above. The international political climate that existed during the Cold War began to intensify towards the late 1950s. The mounting supply of dollars on 'the other side' of the Iron Curtain needed to be invested, but preferably not in the US. The first to exploit this opportunity was, perhaps paradoxically, the Soviet Union, when it transferred deposits to its bank in Paris, the Banque pour l'Europe du Nord (more commonly known by the telex address 'Eurobank'). US dollars deposited at Eurobank became known as Eurodollars.[7] Investors in the Middle East also began to place US dollars in Europe, quite possibly influenced by the resulting instability after the outbreak of the Suez War in 1956, when the US reacted by freezing some US assets held by foreigners. Later, with the oil shocks of 1973 and 1979, OPEC countries began accumulating large US dollar surpluses that they preferred to invest in European countries with large funding requirements.

However, the key driver of the Eurodollar market was *financial regulation* – or, more specifically, the banks' determination to avoid it. Money markets were heavily regulated at the time, particularly in the US, making a strong case for setting up a US dollar money market outside the jurisdiction and scrutiny of the Federal Reserve and other US authorities.[8] This also coincided with the end of the foreign exchange controls that had existed in Western Europe. With the Eurocurrency market, a free, competitive and global money market was beginning to take shape for the first time.

A platform for engaging in regulatory arbitrage was formed, and European banks jumped at the opportunity to exploit loopholes in different jurisdictions. As policy makers began to realise that this market was impossible to curb (there was no global regulator, no global central bank nor any global state), they began to embrace and even encourage it. As such, this marked the beginning of a process of competitive deregulation on both sides of the Atlantic. Seen from a different perspective, if the Eurocurrency market was the banks' response to regulation, the subsequent deregulation phase was individual states' response to the regulation of other states.

The deregulation process did not, however, happen overnight or completely without friction. Opponents raised concerns surrounding the possible inflationary effects caused by excessive lending by banks, the weakening role of the central bank in controlling the monetary system,[9] the difficulties for smaller banks of competing with the new 'universal' banks, and the Eurocurrency market's destabilising impact on exchange rates. Some argued that the market had created a set of semi-independent international interest rates over which no single country or institution had control.[10] Questions were also asked about the vulnerability of domestic banks as a result of the opaqueness of the new financial innovations and whether and how they should be regulated.

In fact, the arguments used back then were surprisingly similar to some of those used during and after the financial crisis of 2007–08. Banks were seen as having lent recklessly. Banks had created financial instruments that hardly anybody understood. The deregulation process had gone too far. Many banks had become too big to fail. Central banks had to resort to extraordinary measures to save the global financial system from collapse. And so on …

* * *

On 12 December 2012, the United States of America charged two of my former trading counterparties, Tom Hayes and Roger Darin, with conspiracy, wire fraud and price fixing in relation to LIBOR.[11] In a bid to dismiss the charges (which he lost), Roger and his lawyer argued that the US authorities had no jurisdiction over his actions. Not only was he a *foreign* citizen but he had also been charged with 'conspiring to manipulate a *foreign* financial benchmark, for a *foreign* currency, while working for a *foreign* bank, in a *foreign* country'. Considering that the Eurodollar market was invented in 1957 to avoid US authorities, it is striking how LIBOR (which is based upon the Eurodollar market) returned to the issue of jurisdiction more than half a century later.

* * *

It is possible to explain the birth and rapid growth of the Eurodollar market by relying on a range of macroeconomic and political factors. However, these factors cannot explain why the Eurodollar market continued to grow so fast even after the international political climate had stabilised. Demand by multinational corporations definitely played a crucial role in justifying the market, but obvious causality becomes difficult to establish as the growth rate of the Eurodollar market overtook that of international trade and investment.

The rapid deregulation of the financial markets around the globe during the 1980s was also crucial. The City of London changed remarkably after Margaret Thatcher launched the 'Big Bang' in 1986, and similar fireworks took place in a number of financial centres around the same time. In fact, since then, the Eurodollar market has often been downplayed as a historic 'event'. Rather, focus is placed on the processes of liberalisation, globalisation, privatisation and financialisation that appear to have started in conjunction with the financial deregulation that took place in the 1980s. Whereas this might be logical, the approach can also be misleading.

Financial deregulation did not prompt Eurodollar trading. It was the other way round: Eurodollar trading was pivotal in prompting financial deregulation. If we see it this way, as a key innovation that led to change, we need to look closer at the 'innovators' – the banks.

* * *

In the summer of 2009, I had lunch with a former competitor at Roka, a Japanese restaurant on Charlotte Street in London. He clearly felt sympathy for what I had been through, following my turbulent exit from the market. But it was also as if he wanted to justify why he was still there, doing the same job he had always done. What was his actual contribution? What had *our* contribution been?

'We *make* the interest rate,' he proudly proclaimed, suggesting that market making was a craft that came with a great degree of responsibility and importance.

It reminded me of an evening back in the 1990s. It had been a volatile day in the financial markets and the whole FX trading desk at HSBC needed a drink or two. When we strolled past the Swedish central bank, which was located just around the corner from our new office, the chief dealer suddenly burst out: 'The Governor has never made a two-way price in his life!'

Everybody laughed.

The joke referred to the fact that not even the Swedish central bank governor Urban Bäckström knew what it felt like being a market maker. He was an economist and ex-politician, not a trader, and now he was the most influential person in the Swedish foreign exchange market. He was not 'one of us' and therefore could not hope to understand how difficult it was to quote a bid price and an offer price at exactly the same time in a volatile market.

Both of the remarks above might sound out of touch, perhaps even arrogant. However, they highlight an important aspect of the financial markets that is often overlooked or simply mis-understood. Markets do not evolve automatically. Markets are *made*.[12] The cassette tape did not evolve into a CD and then into an MP3 file. Each format drew lessons and inspiration from the former, but ultimately they were made separately. The same goes for the Eurodollar market. It did not emerge automatically and autonomously within an already existing money market. The Eurodollar market was *made* by the banks.

And just as the banks made the Eurodollar market, so they went on to *make* LIBOR. The interest rate at which Eurodollars were trading became known as the Eurodollar rate. These Eurodollar rates were not 'official' in any way. They were simply prices at which trading had taken place. Although LIBOR soon came to be associated with the derivatives market, it was the syndicated loan market that had begun to develop during the 1980s that created a need for it. This referred to large loans to corporates and institutions that were put together by a group of banks to spread the risk, rather than being arranged by one single bank. Thus, an appropriate interest rate for these loans had to be agreed upon. Initially, an average interest rate was taken from three reference banks at 11 a.m. two days before a loan was due to roll over. Sometimes, the bank syndicates tried to retain the right to name substitute banks if the majority of syndicate members felt that the original reference bank had lower borrowing costs than would be representative for the syndicate as a whole.[13] With time, however, members of large loan syndicates became insistent that the reference banks used should be representative of the various bank syndicate members. In 1984, UK banks asked the BBA to develop a calculation method (or fixing mechanism) that could be used as an impartial basis for calculating the interest rate on syndicated loans. This led to the creation in 1985 of BBAIRS, the BBA Interest Rate Settlement, which in 1986 became LIBOR.

Originally designed using the tradeable Eurodollar market as a template, LIBOR came to bear – and still bears – a close *resemblance* to a market. In effect, the LIBOR panel banks are the largest banks in the world, which are competing fiercely against each other. However, LIBOR was never an outcome of a market-determined process. As mentioned previously, the submitted quotes are not binding, tradeable prices. Instead, LIBOR (and its equivalents elsewhere) can be seen as a benchmark for where the selected panel banks *argue* that the money market is.

The Eurodollar market prompted regulatory arbitrage between different jurisdictions, which resulted in a competitive deregulation process among states. Likewise, LIBOR (with its roots in the Eurodollar market) managed to escape the confines of particular regulatory jurisdictions. The benchmark remained unregulated up until 2013.[14] The definition, the fixing mechanism and the panel bank compositions of the LIBOR benchmarks managed to remain remarkably unchanged, despite far-reaching changes in financial markets more generally from the 1980s onwards.

Leaving the susceptibility to manipulation aside, a fundamental issue is the discrepancy between what LIBOR *is* and what it has been *perceived to be*. It is a benchmark, but it has been perceived to be the Eurodollar market, the international money market, the short-term interbank money market or an objective reflection of all these. Financial derivatives offer an insight into why LIBOR *cannot* be synonymous with the underlying interbank money market. Whereas syndicated loans justified the need for some kind of objective reflection of the Eurodollar market, the derivatives market *required* a benchmark.

A derivative can broadly be seen as an instrument whose value depends on the value of an underlying asset, index or measurement. Prior to the 1980s, the best known and most traded derivatives markets were the agricultural commodities markets of North America: derivatives on wheat, corn, soya beans, coffee and so on. Academic textbooks often look back to these as typical, perhaps because they help to illustrate the 'need' for derivatives. The theoretical approach has its roots in neoclassical economics,[15] and goes something like this: we do not know what the future will look like, and some people do not like uncertainty. Derivatives enable people to transact in the future. Being able to transact in the future *right now* reduces uncertainty. Therefore, because some people do not like uncertainty, derivatives increase overall economic well-being in society.

A classic textbook illustration of how this works in practice would involve a farmer. Imagine a wheat farmer. Nobody knows what the price of wheat will be next year. The price could fall, for instance because of oversupply in the market for wheat. Or perhaps consumers switch from eating Weetabix to cornflakes for breakfast. In both cases, the wheat farmer will be paid less for his harvest. To protect against a fall in the price of wheat, the farmer could enter into a derivative whose value depends on the price of wheat, such as a wheat futures contract.

Assume that John Wheatley has a farm outside St. Louis, Missouri. He knows he will have 5,000 bushels of wheat to sell in September next year. The current price of wheat is $3 per bushel and the September futures price is $4. By selling one September wheat futures contract (which is based on 5,000 bushels) at $4 now, he can 'lock in' that price. He can make sure that a potential loss from the price of wheat will be offset by a gain from the position in the wheat futures contract. Should the wheat price end up being $2 next September, the futures price will also settle at $2. In comparison to today's price, he will lose $1 per bushel on the crop (the price having fallen from $3 to $2), but will make $2 per bushel on the futures contract (the price having fallen from $4 to $2). Likewise, should the wheat price end up being $5 next September, the futures price will also settle at $5. In comparison to today's price, he will make $2 per bushel on the crop (the price having risen from $3 to $5), but he will lose $1 per bushel on the futures contract (the price having risen from $4 to $5). By entering into the derivatives market, he can rest assured that $4 is what he will be paid for his efforts come September.

The theory is almost beautiful in its simplicity. However, there are two problems with it. First, my father-in-law is a wheat farmer. He is also a civil engineer and a retired maths teacher. He would not have any trouble in understanding the pricing and valuation of rather complex derivatives instruments, including wheat futures contracts. But he has never traded wheat derivatives. In fact, I have met numerous farmers in my life and all of them, it seems, have yet to set up derivatives trading accounts. Academics do not seem to pay attention to the fact that farmers rarely trade derivatives. Instead, it appears that they are mostly occupied doing something else, such as farming. The main users of derivatives are banks. And banks, as we know, do not belong to the agricultural sector. Second, the theory does not explain the phenomenal growth in derivatives in recent decades. Why is the market so phenomenally large, and why do speculators, rather than hedgers (such as farmers), seem to drive the market forward?

One of the main issues lies in how derivatives are taught and explained. This can lead to confusion, misunderstanding or even fear of derivatives as 'weapons of mass financial destruction'. Some of the confusion can be cleared up by dividing derivatives into two groups: an old-fashioned, concrete type and a modern, abstract version. The concrete type is the one that normally appears in textbooks or in basic explanations of derivatives as useful tools to make markets more efficient and societies better off. The concrete type is like the cassette tape: visible, physical, easy to grasp, but increasingly rare. The abstract type is the opposite: almost invisible, virtual, difficult to understand – but hugely popular.

Before the 1980s, derivatives were always settled physically (100 per cent were of the concrete type). When the wheat futures contract expired, the farmer had to deliver the wheat in return for cash. Whoever was on the other side of the contract did the opposite. Since the expansion of derivatives trading in the 1980s, however, the vast majority of derivatives are no longer settled physically. Instead, they are settled purely in cash. Cash-settled derivatives function *as if* an underlying commodity-like exchange occurs. But the exchange of whatever the underlying 'thing' is – be it coffee, gold, the FTSE 100 stock market index or LIBOR – never actually takes place.

The revolutionary aspect of cash-settled derivatives is that the only thing that is delivered is cash – not an asset, commodity, security or anything else that could be seen as tangible. When you buy a bottle of water, cash is exchanged for a bottle of water. We could also imagine a bottle of water being exchanged for cash at some point in the future (some kind of physically settled derivative). In a cash-settled derivative, however, the amount of cash that needs to change hands in the future would depend on where people *argued* the price for a bottle of water was. This would then require some kind of bottle-of-water benchmark, so that the buyer and the seller would be in complete agreement with regard to how much one party owed the other in cash.

The benchmark itself cannot be bought or sold, nor can it be delivered in exchange for cash. A benchmark can, however, determine the amount of cash due in other financial instruments. This has two important consequences. First, it makes derivatives less useful for those who want to exchange the underlying *asset*, but perfect for those who want to capture price changes in the underlying *benchmark* through buying and selling. Banks, of course, have no real interest in storing wheat. Second, it enables a vast expansion of the quantities that can be traded by removing the need to source and deliver the underlying asset. It can be complicated or expensive to source, store and deliver gold, oil, equities, bonds and so on. Money, however, is incredibly easy to exchange. This is clearest in the most 'developed' forms of derivatives, such as volatility, inflation or weather derivatives, for which delivery of an underlying asset is simply impossible. You cannot source and deliver a unit of market turbulence, an item of inflation or a specific type of weather. Consequently, it is not possible to create physically settled derivatives that are indexed to, say, the inflation rate or the temperature. Cash-settled derivatives, however, are possible as long as you can agree upon a benchmark. The benchmark could be the UK Consumer Price Index (CPI) as reported by the Office for National Statistics, or the outside temperature in Fahrenheit or Celsius measured by the Met Office.

You cannot protect yourself against Mother Nature through derivatives. However, by trading derivatives on Mother Nature, you can protect yourself against (and speculate on) movements in the *benchmark* used to measure the force of Mother Nature. The temperature, measured at specific times and in specific locations in London, Amsterdam, Cincinnati or Kansas City, is of interest not only to farmers and residents in and around these cities, but also to futures and options traders around the world who are active on the Chicago Mercantile Exchange (CME), where weather derivatives contracts can be traded. Using a weather benchmark, a derivative could also, for instance, be constructed that would pay out if global warming intensified. Weather derivatives are an extreme example, because there is obviously no market for temperature. You cannot buy or sell Fahrenheit or Celsius. However, it serves as a good illustration as to why, once a benchmark has been agreed upon, derivatives on Fahrenheit or Celsius can be constructed, traded and then have a life of their own. It enables the cash-settled derivatives market to expand beyond the limits of the underlying market, whether or not such a market exists in reality. The point is that the outstanding amount of weather derivatives does not need to be directly related to the number of sunny days in a year, nor does the amount of LIBOR derivatives need to be directly related to the size of the global banking system, for example, or to how much banks lend to each other. Retrospectively, it is easy to come up with reasons why there is a need for each new derivative instrument that is made. A snow derivative, whose value would depend on, say, the number of millimetres of snow falling in a Swiss city over a certain period of time, might make sense. If you operate a ski lift, work as a snowboard instructor or sell hot chocolate up on a mountain, your future revenue would depend on the existence of snow during the winter season. How could you 'protect' yourself against disappointing weather? A snow derivative could be a solution, if constructed so that it would pay out in cases when the slopes remained green. Even a winter without any snow whatsoever might involve the buying and selling of snow derivatives, as you never know when the clouds might roll in and a few snowflakes begin to fall.

In September 2009, Adair Turner, the chairman of the FSA at the time, delivered a speech in London that went on to be cited frequently in the British media.[16] He was critical towards the City and the role banks had played in the run-up to the financial crisis.

'Not all financial innovation is valuable, not all trading plays a useful role, and a bigger financial system is not necessarily a better one,' he said.

'There are good reasons for believing that the financial industry, more than any other sector of the economy, has an ability to generate unnecessary demand for its own services – that more trading and more financial innovation can under some circumstances create harmful volatility against which customers have to hedge, creating more demand for trading liquidity and innovative products.'

Banks had been at the forefront in creating all these new derivatives, and no matter how useful they might seem, he questioned whether they brought any benefits to society as a whole. In reality, farmers or snowboard instructors did not trade derivatives. The main players were banks, which traded them to make money.

* * *

Banks *made* the Eurodollar market and subsequently *made* LIBOR. It is no surprise then that banks also *made* LIBOR derivatives. As I said, it is impossible to actually trade LIBOR. It is only possible to trade derivatives based on LIBOR. However, the derivatives market increased the *importance* of LIBOR. At the same time, it reduced the attention paid to the 'real' underlying market: namely the interbank money market that was supposed to form the basis for LIBOR. This process can be seen as having taken place in four different phases – each overlapping, each strengthening the appearance that LIBOR was a 'market', even though it never was such a thing.

The first phase started with the invention of the world's first cash-settled futures contract, the Eurodollar future, which was launched by the CME in 1981. It quickly became the world's most actively traded short-term interest rate contract.[17] In a Eurodollar futures contract, the underlying 'asset' is a three-month deposit of precisely $1 million. This means that the underlying benchmark is an interest rate corresponding to such a deposit. The counterparties involved exchange the equivalent of the change in the interest rate on a three-month deposit of $1 million. Although no actual deposit is made or required, for each contract they exchange *as if* they had borrowed or lent $1 million. To ensure that the market is liquid, the maturity dates of Eurodollar contracts are standardised according to the IMM convention, using four quarterly dates per year; these dates are the third Wednesday of March, June, September and December. If, for instance, I sold 1,000 June Eurodollar futures contracts, it meant that I was putting on a trade that *replicated* a deal whereby I borrowed $1 billion for three months starting in June. If interest rates went up by June, I would hypothetically be able to lend those $1 billion to someone else at a higher rate and therefore make a profit. In reality, though, I never borrowed or lent any money. I only entered into contracts that would pay out the same amount *as if* I had done so.

Up until 1996, the CME used a benchmark based on a survey of which randomly selected banks had been willing to lend to 'prime banks'.[18] In January 1997, however, the contract began to be fixed and settled against LIBOR, although it still bore the name 'Eurodollar futures' (reminding us of its link to the Eurodollar market). Between 1981 and 2006, more than 2.7 trillion CME Eurodollar futures contracts had been traded, and in 2011 the value of Eurodollar futures contracts traded on the exchange reached $564 trillion. To put this into some kind of perspective, the total market value of *all* goods and services produced in the world in 2015 was 'only' $73 trillion. The corresponding figure for the EURIBOR futures contracts traded on the London International Financial Futures and Options Exchange (LIFFE) was not far off: €241 trillion. For short sterling (the equivalent future on British pounds) LIBOR futures, the turnover was £58 trillion.[19]

The success of Eurodollar futures also prompted competing exchanges, such as the LIFFE, the Singapore International Monetary Exchange (SIMEX) and the Tokyo International Financial Futures Exchange (TIFFE), to offer similar instruments. Euroswiss, Euromarks and Euroyen all became more closely associated with their respective LIBOR than the Eurocurrencies themselves. The name of the benchmark also ended up being copied in a range of other international financial centres: FIBOR in Frankfurt, PIBOR in Paris, TIBOR in Tokyo, STIBOR, NIBOR and so on. A whole new landscape opened up for derivatives exchanges, futures brokers and banks. I remember when SIMEX tried to launch its new Euroyen LIBOR futures contract. It must have been around 1999, in the aftermath of the Japanese banking crisis and the subsequent swings in the TIBOR–LIBOR spread. SIMEX already had control over the Euroyen TIBOR futures market and presumably wanted to capitalise on the fact that the yen market had two frequently used benchmarks. A futures broker from Credit Suisse First Boston, trustworthy and sharp as a sushi knife, asked if he could come into the dealing room and explain all the benefits of this new product. I still have the pamphlet from the marketing campaign, which opens with a quote by Rudyard Kipling: 'Oh, East is East, and West is West, and never the twain shall meet.' Then, above a British and Japanese tea set, it says: 'At SIMEX, we beg to differ.' The derivatives exchange in Singapore proudly proclaimed that it did not subscribe to the view held by the writer from the British colonial period. By being able to offer financial instruments indexed to both TIBOR *and* LIBOR, they could bring Asia and Europe together.

Marking the twenty-fifth birthday of the Eurodollar futures contract, CME Executive Chairman Terry Duffy said:[20]

> Perhaps no other contract exemplifies our spirit of innovation better than the CME Eurodollar contract. As the world's first cash-settled contract, CME Eurodollar futures transformed financial markets and paved the way for future contracts, such as stock indexes and weather, which cannot be physically delivered.

As Duffy stated, this was truly a remarkable innovation – just like the Eurodollar market had been during the 1950s. The conviction that this innovation had brought, and would continue to bring, benefits to society as a whole was echoed by comments made by CME's Chief Executive Officer Craig Donohue:

> The ability to hedge interest rate risk has had a tremendous impact on the global economy, as it has allowed banks and other financial institutions around the world to manage their interest rate risk in ways that otherwise would not be possible.

He continued: 'In addition to lowering the risk of lending, the ability to hedge interest rates lowers the cost of lending, which ultimately benefits both corporate and consumer borrowers.' The logic is exactly the same as in the example of the farmer. A farmer benefits from being able to trade wheat derivatives, because it makes farming less risky. This lowers the cost of wheat, much to Weetabix Limited's delight. The company can lower the price of its breakfast cereal, which is made of 95 per cent wholegrain wheat. Consumers who like Weetabix gain. The lower price of Weetabix might even push down the price of cornflakes, as Kellogg's might want to remain competitive in the cereal business. So consumers gain even more. The same logic applies to LIBOR-indexed Eurodollar futures. A bank benefits from being able to trade Eurodollar futures, because it makes lending less risky. This lowers the cost of lending, much to the delight of the bank. The bank can lower the interest rate it charges on its loans, which is linked to LIBOR. Households with mortgages gain. Companies can borrow at lower interest rates, invest more and create more jobs. And so on.

Despite the success story of the exchange-traded LIBOR-based derivatives, such as Eurodollar futures, it was the OTC derivatives market that truly changed the market place. This was the largely unregulated market for interest rate and foreign exchange derivatives that always involved two counterparties: a bank and a client, or, more frequently, a bank and another bank. OTC derivatives, such as IRSs, CRSs, FRAs, caps and floors differed from exchange-traded derivatives in the sense that they were much less standardised and could be tailor-made to suit the needs and wants of those involved in the transaction. They offered much greater flexibility in terms of amounts, maturities, currencies and benchmarks, and they stimulated further financial innovation. A US dollar forward rate agreement (FRA) is, for instance, very similar to a Eurodollar future. However, rather than always being $1 million, it can be any amount. Any business day in the future can be chosen as the start date. Rather than having to resort to three months, any

LIBOR maturity could be chosen. If I bought a $1 billion three-month FRA starting in June, the idea would be the same as selling those futures contracts in the example above. I would be putting on a trade that replicated a deal in which I borrowed $1 billion for three months starting in June. The contract would pay out *as if* I had borrowed the money for real. An interest rate swap (IRS) could be explained non-technically in several ways. The easiest way is to think about it as a string of many FRAs in a row. If I bought a $1 billion two-year IRS starting in June, it would be as if I had bought eight consecutive three-month $1 billion FRAs: the first starting in June, the second in September, the third in December, and so on. Again, I do not borrow or lend any money; I only enter into a contract that pays out the same amount *as if* I actually did.

The Bank for International Settlements (BIS) estimates that the IRS market grew from just $3 billion in 1982 to around $100 billion to $150 billion in 1985. Since then, growth has been phenomenal, with *daily* turnover in 2013 reaching $1,415 billion.[21] In June 2014, the notional amount of outstanding OTC interest rate derivatives contracts amounted to $691 trillion.[22] Of these, it is estimated that between 60 per cent and 90 per cent are linked to LIBOR, EURIBOR or TIBOR. LIBOR and its equivalents are by far the most frequently used benchmarks for IRSs, FRAs and OTC interest rate options.

* * *

When I was working for Citibank in London during the late 1990s, I became involved in *making* a derivatives market for IRSs indexed to the one-month Norwegian interest rate benchmark, NIBOR. Back then, IRSs had been around for 15 years, and they also existed in Norway. However, no derivatives market existed using the one-month NIBOR as a benchmark. The relatively short maturity of the benchmark made the price of the swap more sensitive to swings in the interest rates at which banks funded themselves in the very short term, and also to potential central bank rate changes in the near future. As with any derivative, the 'usefulness' of it could be explained by what kind of benefits it offered to the potential buyer and the potential seller: the buyer would profit from central bank rate hikes and/or funding squeezes in the Norwegian banking system. The seller would profit from the opposite scenarios.

A market does not exist unless it has at least one buyer and one seller. To begin with, the market had this bare minimum requirement: a trader at Chase Manhattan and myself. As in any derivative market, traders often disagree upon whether the current market price is justifiable or correct given all the information that exists out there in the universe. Consequently, prices went up and down and the actual trading activity was a bit like a snowball fight. I threw first, and sold him around 250 million Norwegian kroner worth of swaps (I cannot recall the precise amounts). He threw one back the next day, selling 250 million back to me. Then he threw another, and sold me 100 million, and perhaps 50 million more. I went on the defence, and was hit by another 100 million, then attacked and sold 250 million. At some point, a few other banks also began to play. Interdealer brokers got involved to match trades at better prices than we could have achieved by simply calling each other directly. I was rather excited by this development, and happy that others had come on board. Looking back, I don't think I ever reflected on the fact that the market, as a result, got bigger and bigger. I had already become immune to large numbers, and being so involved in the process of constructing the market only served to make me less aware of what it might look like from the outside.

It was often cheaper to enter into price negotiations through brokers and pay them a commission, rather than having to trade directly on the relatively wide bid–offer spreads we quoted each other at the time. The audience grew, and after a while more onlookers were keen to have a go at the new game in town. More interdealer brokers entered the market. Soon, at least half a dozen banks could proudly claim that they were market makers in one-month NIBOR IRSs. The sales people on the trading floors loved it. They now had a new product they could sell to clients. It offered something slightly different that other products could not. If you wanted to protect yourself against higher (or lower) Norwegian interest rates in the near future, the one-month NIBOR IRS market was the right place for you. If you wanted to speculate on a surprise rate hike (or cut) by the Norwegian central bank, the one-month NIBOR IRS market was the right place for you. By being able to offer a solution to a potential future problem, or an opportunity to profit from such a problem, the banks could portray themselves as smart, sophisticated and customer-oriented, all in one go. Something that might be of genuine interest from the trading desk gave sales people a reason to pick up the phone and talk to clients. It might not necessarily result in an actual trade, but the customer might, while on the line, express an interest in something completely different – perhaps a different derivative in a different currency. Years later, it got to the stage that you *had to* be a market maker in one-month swaps if you wanted to be taken seriously in the Norwegian krone market.

So, the cash-settled derivatives market did not simply 'evolve' from the 1980s onwards. Banks and traders made derivatives and derivatives markets, in the same way as Apple made the iPhone. The iPad did not evolve from the iPhone or from the typewriter. Apple *made* the iPad.

* * *

The second phase began during the 1980s, when the global economic situation and accompanying financial market regulatory changes transformed the character of the financial markets. Despite the fact that the Eurodollar market was still growing, these changes led to a reduction in its *relative* importance as a funding source or investment outlet for the banks. Instead, Eurodollars gradually turned into the prime tool with which to speculate on short-term interest rates in an increasing range of currencies. This was an area where banks had a superior competitive, informational and economic advantage. Further, the abolishment of capital controls made it possible for any bank to become involved in the Eurodollar market by constructing 'synthetic' Eurodollars. According to the so-called 'covered interest parity', an FX swap could theoretically be seen as the difference in interest rates in two currencies. By entering into an FX swap, you effectively borrowed in one currency and lent in another. Therefore, if you believed that the interest rate would increase (or decrease) more in one currency than in another, the FX swap market presented itself as a perfect outlet for such speculation. Moreover, because you actually borrowed from and lent to the same counterparty at the same time (in different currencies, though), there was considerably less credit risk involved. If the counterparty defaulted halfway through and therefore was unable to pay back what you, in effect, had lent them in one currency, you, on the other hand, were sitting with the other side of the trade: the money they had lent to you in the other currency. The lower credit risk boosted the FX swap market, which ultimately made it much more liquid than the deposit market in the underlying Eurocurrencies.

Eurocurrencies as a proportion of total credit creation had already begun to slow down and diminish in the 1980s.[23] However, LIBOR derivatives, as a proportion of banks' total *exposure* to LIBOR, increased and began to all but completely replace the Eurocurrency market as a vehicle for hedging and speculating. Derivatives enabled banks to expose themselves to LIBOR in very large notional terms with little real or physical exposure to the underlying money market. It did not matter if you believed in higher or lower interest rates, trading derivatives *as if* you borrowed or lent money was much cheaper, safer and easier than *actually* borrowing or lending money. An important reason why the outstanding amount of derivatives grew so fast was that they were traded *as if* they could be bought or sold again and again – although in reality they could not. Because, like loans, they were contracts between two counterparties, and until the trades matured (which could take a day, a month or 30 years), OTC derivatives were kept on the banks' books. Although they often netted each other out, new trades were put on faster than the old ones expired. As a result, the outstanding notional amount of the derivatives market ballooned.

* * *

In 2002, when I was working for the French bank Crédit Agricole Indosuez, I found myself at an award ceremony in a hotel near Sloane Square in Chelsea. Traders, sales people, brokers and clients were regularly sent surveys and questionnaires to determine which banks and traders were perceived to be the 'best' in various categories. Surveys were conducted by industry journals such as *Euromoney* or *Risk*. Ranking lists were then published, and prizes were handed out to the winners. This particular evening it was time to find out who had won the awards in derivatives ranging from synthetic CDOs and FTSE 100 equity index options to South African FRAs and Polish zloty interest rate options. *Risk*, which conducted the survey and organised the event, had put on a lavish do in the banqueting hall. Around ten traders and managers sat around each table – this was not a night when you sat down next to your competitor or your friend from Deutsche Bank, Goldman Sachs or Credit Suisse. Traders wore dark suits and *ties*, even though the formal dress code in the dealing rooms had long since been consigned to the history books. During the height of the dot-com bubble, banks had decided it was time to catch up with the times and began to introduce a Friday dress policy. Dark suits and ties gave a boring image of investment banking and discouraged talented graduates with IT skills from applying. Deemed a success, 'business casual' quickly became the accepted norm among traders and sales people Monday to Friday, as long as clients did not get a glimpse of you. From then on, coming to work wearing a tie always prompted one of these two questions: 'Which client are you meeting?' or 'Which bank are you interviewing with?'

With the ties loosened, and a more relaxed atmosphere enabled by generous amounts of champagne, wine and cognac, it was time for the results. When our bank was announced as the winner in the one-month NIBOR IRS category, I could not help feeling both flattered and proud. However, this feeling turned out to be short-lived. Before I had the chance to put down my cutlery, my manager, ignoring me, stepped up to the podium and accepted the prize on behalf of the bank. He nodded gracefully to the audience, half of which applauded politely and half of which was now more interested in ordering another round of drinks. For a while, I expected my manager would hand the trophy over to me. As the evening progressed, however, I began to realise that this was not going to happen. I never found out where my engraved glass trophy ended up. Looking back, however, perhaps some achievements are better forgotten. Was there ever a *need* to make that market?

The last big trade I remember doing in the one-month NIBOR IRS market was for exactly 80 billion Norwegian kroner (around $10 billion). To put this into perspective, Norwegian exports of military equipment amounted to 2.4 billion in 2015.[24] But then Norway is not exactly famous for its military exports. How about culture? According to the Norwegian Ministry of Culture, the total expenditure on culture by the government, county authorities and local authorities amounted to 23.6 billion kroner in 2014.[25] Still only a fraction of that single derivatives trade. Of course, nobody would, in all seriousness, call a bank manager to ask whether it would be possible to borrow $10 billion. To enter into a derivatives contract *as if* you were borrowing $10 billion is, however, something completely different.

* * *

The third phase that made LIBOR appear market-determined involved a gradual reduction – and at some points even the disappearance – of the underlying Eurodollar market. Just as the

FX swap market had outgrown the actual market for borrowing and lending money, so too did the LIBOR derivatives market. Paradoxically perhaps, new regulatory requirements promoted the use of financial derivatives.

An important development in banking during the 1990s, and particularly towards the end of the decade, was the increased attention to credit risk. New regulations were being implemented and banks had to follow the new rules. According to the 1988 Basel Accord, different kinds of bank assets were to be classified according to pre-set brackets. The brackets ranged from 0 per cent (no risk) to 100 per cent (everything at risk), and banks were required to hold capital equal to 8 per cent of the risk-weighted assets. If you lent $1 million to another bank or to a corporation for one year, there was always a risk that they might default before it was time for them to pay back the loan. In a worst-case scenario, nothing would be paid back. This was an example of an asset that would attract a high risk percentage. If you did a one-year FX swap in $1 million, however, the risk was much smaller as the other side of the trade (in another currency) would offer protection. The exchange rate might swing – say, 10 or 20 per cent during the course of the year – but you would not lose everything. FX swaps therefore received a lower risk percentage. Interest rate derivatives were even better because you never physically *lent* any money. The only thing that was exchanged was the profit or loss *as if* you had done so.

Although the Basel rules put new constraints on banks, they simultaneously opened doors. Excessive 'on-balance-sheet' asset usage (Eurodollars belonged to the risky type) was 'penalised', while 'off-balance-sheet' product trading – which was perceived as low risk (LIBOR derivatives, for instance) – was, relatively speaking, 'rewarded'. From a traders' perspective, this meant two things. Firstly, excessive usage of the bank's balance sheet was seen as a bad thing. Old-fashioned borrowing and lending was to be avoided whenever an alternative could be found. I remember watching a PowerPoint presentation where the word 'assets' had been crossed out and a symbol of two syringes and a skull inserted. Assets were seen as deadly. Secondly, according to the new rules, off-balance-sheet trading was to be rewarded. In other words: 'Trade derivatives, because they were off balance sheet!' Although the Basel rules were designed as a deterrent to excess risk taking (lending is a risky activity because the borrower might default), they also came to have a perverse effect by acting as an incentive for increased derivatives trading by banks. The fear of risky assets, combined with the generous treatment of derivatives by regulators, led to a kind of 'regulatory arbitrage'. Financial derivatives increasingly became part of the daily trading and funding routines. And as the banks' risk appetite grew, their speculative activity increasingly took place via derivatives that replicated the *idea* of borrowing and lending. Instruments were created that looked like old-fashioned borrowing and lending but were not treated as such – because that was not what they were. At the centre of this transformation were LIBOR derivatives. They acted as a natural bridge between what banks used to be and what they would become. The derivatives market grew, with trade amounts now often in billions, not millions, of dollars. And along with it, the importance of LIBOR itself also increased.

This did not happen overnight but was introduced gradually into the psyche of traders. Credit officers would increasingly complain when traders traded 'real' cash, whereas derivative traders were left to their own devices. Bid–offer spreads narrowed in the derivatives market but were left largely unchanged in the 'real' market. This gradual change was also reflected in the various pricing spreadsheets and systems used by traders and banks. Like all traders, I also used spreadsheets to help with the pricing of the financial instruments I traded. As the spreadsheets were fed with live market data, they were key tools in spotting new trading opportunities. During the hour or so before I left the dealing room to go home, or when the market was quiet, I would spend time fine-tuning my spreadsheets, adding new mathematical formulae to make them more sophisticated, removing parts to make them faster, or simply changing some colours if I got bored. Over the years, more and more live feeds from the cash markets were removed because there was little or no trading going on in them. The indicative bid–offer spreads were too wide or too sticky to provide much meaningful information about what was going on in the markets 'here and now'. Increasingly, such feeds were replaced by derivatives prices that seemed to provide a more accurate picture of the market.

Traders in the derivatives market also seemed to be rewarded with bigger bonuses than those in the real market, and they came to be seen as more glamorous. During the trial of five former Barclays employees accused of conspiring to rig the US dollar LIBOR, the prosecutor claimed that the IRS desk was where the 'glamour boys' and 'big dogs' worked.[26] On 17 May 2016, he said that one of the defendants, Jonathan Mathew, a LIBOR submitter on the money market desk, had attempted to boost his career by giving derivatives traders certain favours.

Mathew denied the allegations, but also testified that the IRS desk was 'the desk that people wanted to get onto. All the graduates wanted to become swaps traders, they didn't want to be on the money markets desk.'[27]

The STIRT desk, where I used to work, tended to rank somewhere in the middle on the glamour scale. We traded FX and money market instruments, which were rather old-fashioned. On the other hand, we also traded short-term IRSs and other derivatives, giving the desk a more exotic feel. There was no doubt, however, that the long-end IRS desk (trading derivatives maturing far beyond the two- or three-year horizon we were focused on) was perceived to be more sophisticated and attractive.

Half a year after joining Merrill Lynch I was approached by Goldman Sachs, who asked whether I would be interested in a position on their long-end IRS desk. I felt honoured, of course, given not only the status of the investment bank but also the prestige of the role that potentially was on offer. However, having agreed to meet them in a quiet café near Blackfriars Bridge, I was unable to show much passion for the opportunity and, instead, ended up recommending one or two of my competitors for the job. It didn't feel right to leave Merrill Lynch after just six months. That would have been rude. More than this, though, the idea of turning my back on the STIRT desk made me very uncomfortable. Over the years, it had almost started to feel like a second home, and I knew how much I would miss it.

* * *

The budgets for traders in the derivatives markets also increased. To meet those targets, there was a need (but also a desire) to take more risk. The trade tickets got bigger – much bigger. Standard and conventional amounts, be they $10 million or £25 million, came to be regarded as peanuts. Market conventions still dictated what should be considered a 'reasonable' or 'standard' market amount when one market maker called another for a two-way price. Gradually, larger amounts became the accepted norm, rather than rare exceptions.

Gentlemen's agreements regarding the amounts market makers were supposed to quote each other did not apply in cases where a trade was done through a broker. And since brokers often acted as intermediaries between two banks, even larger trade tickets could be printed. The negotiations regarding not only the price but also the *size* of the derivatives trade could turn into a game of arm wrestling, much to the delight of the interdealer broker standing in the middle of it all. If one bank indicated an amount of, say, ¥100 billion, the trader at the other bank might reply 'Can do more!' 'Can do more!' meant precisely that: the other trader was willing to do more, say ¥200 billion at that price, perhaps even up to ¥500 billion. Depending on your conviction about the direction of the market and your assessment of the other trader's (and, of course, your own) ability and skill to predict the future, you might counter with 'What's your full amount?' If it got to the stage where the full amount was disclosed, this generally ended with a mutual understanding that one trader would clear their total amount – ¥450 billion, say – with the trader at the other bank at that price and at that moment in time. The selling trader would not return a few minutes later, spraying the market with another hundred billion Japanese yen. That would have been seen as unethical, and strictly against the prevailing gentlemen's agreement. 'Full amount!' was therefore synonymous with a firm handshake, where one trader got rid of everything they needed or wanted to get rid of, and the other trader swallowed the whole lot, even though it might have been somewhat more than their normal risk appetite would allow. The accepted norm was that the deal price was favourable to the trader who accepted to carry and gradually offload the heavy luggage. It might take some time to do so, and the process could be extremely nerve-racking if the market was volatile, but if the other trader behaved fairly, such trades were generally quite lucrative.

But not always. I remember when a large hedge fund contacted me wondering if I would be willing to quote a two-way price on a gigantic interest rate swap in their 'full amount'. The owner of the fund had almost celebrity status and the traders always featured prominently on the lists of the highest-paid hedge fund managers in the world. I had never dealt with them before, and was surprised by their approach. Normally, sales people would make the first introduction to a new client.

Quoting a price would have had huge PR value for the bank, for my boss, for me. I should have been alarmed by the fact that the amount was 40 times the normal market size, but at the time I was extremely confident in my risk-taking abilities. It turned out that the banks the hedge fund normally dealt with had declined to quote a price, and that they had contacted me because of my reputation. Incredibly flattered by hearing this, it made me even more amenable to accommodating their polite, but sizeable, request.

The market was very thin, however, and soon my competitors figured out that I was holding bad cards. Whenever I called a bank requesting a price quote, in a fraction of the amount needed to reduce my risk, they had already read my intentions and adjusted their quotes accordingly. The position took weeks to get out of. Drained of energy, it was like slowly being run over by a bulldozer. I lost a fortune on the trade.

As the market grew even larger, the meaning of a 'Full amount!' began to change somewhat. It signalled that there might be a client trade that had triggered the desire or need to trade in an amount that, no matter how large, was *limited*. On the other hand, everyone knew that such client trades had become minuscule in relation to the speculative activity expertly undertaken by traders at banks and hedge funds. 'Full amount!' began to signal a kind of weakness, because it involved a limitation in the trader's conviction or ability to take risk. Being a flow trader, whose only job was to execute trades on behalf of clients, was more glamorous than being a broker, but not by much. This led to a new phrase gaining popularity: 'Your amount!' 'Your amount!' was a double-edged sword. One the one hand, it meant a trader generously offered to accommodate whatever amount another trader required at an agreed price at that particular moment in time. However, it also planted a seed of doubt in the brain of the other trader. What does the trader know that I don't? How can the trader be so convinced about selling that they are willing to buy *any* amount at that price? Have I missed something? This could happen after an important macroeconomic data release or, more frequently, a central bank monetary policy committee meeting – something that might cause traders to suddenly change their view about where interest rates would be at some point in the future, and where certain derivatives should therefore be priced. The psychological warfare was now in full swing. Once a trader had said 'Your amount!', there was no way out. The trader had to accept ¥900 billion or ¥2 trillion if that was the amount you suggested. A gentlemen's agreement stipulated that. It goes without saying that some of these poker games, sometimes cleverly orchestrated by brokers to boost their commissions (and the egos of everybody involved), would become legendary in the financial markets. Whereas 'Can do more!' was a statement by a rather self-confident trader, 'Your amount!' was the joker in the pack that bordered on hubris. Admittedly, it was one of my favourite cards.

The FX swap market was much more liquid than the money market. It was cheaper to put bets on interest rates via the FX swap market than the money market, and cheaper to take the bets off. The FX swap market also involved considerably less credit risk, which meant that more trading could be done with other banks (and also with clients) before the credit department became worried. Larger bets could be put on. The LIBOR derivatives market became, in most currencies, even more liquid than the FX swap market. What is more, it worried credit departments even less. This development, coupled with innovative sources of funding (often through so-called securitisation), made the old-fashioned international money market all but unnecessary. After all, borrowing and lending was expensive, risky and ultimately detrimental to the share price. It was an activity that should be avoided rather than embraced, and it was therefore transformed into a platform for rather boring and routine bank operations. Maturities became much shorter, as trading in and out was a highly capital-intensive activity. LIBOR, as a reflection of the term money market, therefore became *even less* linked to a market that was actually trading. For instance, according to the ECB, 99 per cent of turnover in the unsecured euro money market in 2015 involved transactions with up to one-month maturities. Hardly any trading took place in three-month or six-month maturities, to which most EURIBOR derivatives were indexed.[28] A similar pattern could be seen in other money markets around the world. And, contrary to what many people seem to believe, the market had shown signs of disappearing long before the outbreak of the 2007–08 financial crisis.

However, trading in very short-term maturities (such as overnight or for one week) had little to do with interest rate expectations and credit provision and more to do with daily funding and liquidity requirements to square up bank balances before going home for the day. There was no derivative that could replace this daily bank routine, which is why it was predominantly done in the FX swap market. Invariably, these tasks were left to the treasury desk, to junior traders, or to the FX swap traders themselves who were most active in the respective currency pairs. I remember often hating doing that job, day in and day out. I would try to square up the accounts using the help of brokers before the 'proper' market opened at 8 o'clock, but if the balance was large this was not possible. I could occasionally be stuck for hours trading 'tomnext' (contracts with a start date tomorrow and an end date the day after tomorrow) – losing focus on what I believed was a more important market. But I have to confess that I would not have liked giving it up either. The activity reminded me of how things used to be when I was a junior trader. For brokers, it was a way of getting my attention, and I found the morning habit quite pleasant. Naturally, it also gave me an insight into which banks regularly borrowed and which banks regularly lent US dollars, for example, via the FX swap market. There was generally a logical reason behind such patterns in their trading behaviour, and often it could provide useful clues as to how the other banks were positioned – or how they wanted to be positioned. It was the true barometer of fear.

* * *

The fourth, and perhaps most abstract, phase took place when the benchmark needed to become anchored to something else. However, if the original market had all but disappeared, what could be the next-best thing? It turned out to be its *own derivative*, rather than the underlying market it was supposed to reflect. The liquidity of LIBOR derivatives increased as they became more suitable for trading 'needs' than the underlying Eurocurrencies were. Importantly, superior liquidity as reflected in bid–offer spreads gave them an advantage over the underlying asset (the money market) in the price determination process. Money market traders began to look more towards the LIBOR derivatives markets rather than the money market itself, both in terms of risk taking and for indications of the future direction of LIBOR. It was many times cheaper to put bets on three-month Eurodollar futures, for instance, than to *actually* borrow or lend US dollars for a period of three months. If you wanted to know where the market thought LIBOR would be in a few weeks' time, you could simply look at the Eurodollar futures contract expiring next month. There was even a FRA market for tomorrow's LIBOR, which gave an even better indication of where LIBOR should be today. If one bank was prepared to bet that LIBOR would be higher than 3.00 per cent tomorrow, and another bank was prepared to bet that it would be lower than 3.01 per cent tomorrow, surely today's LIBOR could not be vastly different from a 3.00 to 3.01 per cent range – unless a special event was supposed to happen sometime during the next 24 hours.

The LIBOR rate for longer maturities, such as six months, became less driven by actual money market trading in those maturities and instead reflected interest rates implied by the prices of a range of LIBOR derivatives. There was hardly any activity in interbank borrowing and lending for such maturities. However, plenty of derivatives made it possible to imagine and mathematically calculate the interest rate at which borrowing and lending ought to have been taking place – if such a market had existed in reality. LIBOR, as a 'thing', became more and more imaginary. Imagine a referee uncertain as to how many yellow cards 'reasonably' to hand out during a football match. Way too many, and players, coaches, fans and commentators will blame the referee for interrupting the play too much. Too few, and players, coaches, fans and commentators will blame the referee for losing control of the game. A way to avoid being blamed for poor judgement would be to glance at the football betting market, which provides a reasonable assessment of how many yellow cards *others* expect during the 90 minutes of play. This, in effect, is what happened to LIBOR. It became dependent on the betting market, which was betting on it, in a continuous feedback loop.

Given that the money market dried up during the financial crisis, it would be logical to think that LIBOR derivatives also all but disappeared in 2009. However, LIBOR continued to be used not only when the interbank money market ceased to exist; it continued to be used even though everyone *knew* that the interbank money market no longer functioned. In fact, the absence of an underlying market did nothing to halt the growth of the derivatives market relating to it. The daily global turnover of the LIBOR-indexed FRA market, which is a kind of bespoke OTC Eurodollar futures market, gradually grew from $74 billion in 1998, to $129 billion in 2001, to $233 billion in 2004, and to $258 billion in 2007. Rather than eliminating it because of the lack of an underlying market, the financial crisis injected the market with steroids. By 2010, the turnover had more than doubled to $601 billion.[29]

This statistic highlights how illogical the cash-settled derivatives market can seem to be. However, it is something that is very fundamental to it. Just as the weather derivatives market is built on imaginary 'prices' in temperature, raindrops or snowfall, the LIBOR derivatives market was built on imaginary prices in the money market. As long as we can treat the temperature or LIBOR as 'prices', and as long as it is possible to trade and profit from changes in these imaginary prices, the derivatives market can grow. Although the underlying LIBOR was never a market per se, its relative significance gradually increased. The astonishingly large turnover of derivatives referencing LIBOR sustained the illusion that the underlying index reflected a large, liquid and efficient money market. More specifically, it served as 'evidence' that LIBOR was indeed an outcome of a market-determined and objective process. Perhaps no better illustration of the faith in LIBOR-equivalent benchmarks can be found than in the fact that EURIBOR was first published on 30 December 1998, two days *prior* to the euro becoming an accounting currency on 1 January 1999. This enabled a EURIBOR derivatives market to emerge before physical transactions could possibly be made, as the currency did not yet exist.

* * *

We can see how these four phases led to a perception that LIBOR was a market-determined benchmark, even though the mechanism was no such thing. We can also see how, propelled by the extremely large volume of derivatives trading, LIBOR gradually took on an objectivity that enabled the derivatives market to eclipse the Eurodollar market. This, in turn, enabled LIBOR to replace the money market as an objective 'fact'. This did not happen only in dealing rooms. Because LIBOR had turned into something so important, it came to be used – or misused – in other areas as well.

For instance, given its importance in finance and economics, LIBOR became frequently quoted (and misquoted) in scholarly and professional literature. Before the LIBOR scandal erupted, benchmarks in financial markets were rarely mentioned as more than footnotes in the academic literature – or by the financial press or regulators, for that matter. In many ways, this is not surprising, as benchmarks are used like yardsticks. They are simply standardised indicators measuring and analysing performance and predictions for the future of *something else*. Take inflation, for example. Inflation refers to an increase in the general price level of a country. However, a benchmark such as the CPI is used to measure it. Very few people know (or are interested in) precisely which products count towards the basket that makes up the index. The same goes for stock market indices such as the FTSE 100 or the S&P 500. Many people know that they are useful benchmarks for measuring the performance of the UK and US stock markets, but few would be able to recite the names of the 100 or 500 companies whose share prices make up the benchmarks. Most people simply trust that the benchmarks are correct in measuring whatever they are supposed to measure.

A Eurodollar future or interest rate swap cannot be properly explained without mentioning the underlying benchmark. Take the following from the classic academic textbook *Introduction to Futures and Options Markets* by John Hull (the 1991 edition):[30] 'The variable underlying contract … is the 90-day Eurodollar interest rate. A Eurodollar is a dollar deposited in a U.S. or foreign bank outside the United States.' Whereas the definition is correct, the following quote (from the same book) highlights how the underlying benchmark becomes known as the underlying market: 'The Eurodollar interest rate is the inter-bank interest rate earned on Eurodollars and is also known as the 3-month London Interbank Offer [sic] Rate (LIBOR).' Finally, trading in the Eurocurrency market is described as almost synonymous with trading LIBOR itself – which, of course, is impossible: 'LIBOR … is a floating reference rate of interest. LIBOR is determined by the trading of deposits between banks on the Eurocurrency market.' This widely translated classic textbook by Hull is not only to be found in all prominent dealing rooms around the world; it also belongs to the core derivatives literature at business schools and universities. The use of the derivatives benchmark, rather than the underlying market, in academic textbooks, journal articles and the financial press further cements the facticity that had been developed through banks' trading practices. 'Facts' in important textbooks should not be underestimated. Even when I am writing this today, on 21 April 2016, LIBOR is described with the heading 'Interest rates: market' in *The Financial Times*, to distinguish it from central bank interest rates, which are coined 'Interest rates: official'. LIBOR is not, and cannot be, a market interest rate. Like Celsius or Fahrenheit, it is a measurement, and therefore it cannot be bought or sold.

Another example, and arguably the most powerful justification for the use of LIBOR, occurred when it became accepted and adopted by the *state*. As mentioned previously, the interbank money market rate is important in central banking as it acts as the first step of the monetary transmission mechanism, measuring how policy rate changes ultimately affect lending and borrowing in the real economy. Central banks around the world need a measurement for this interbank money market rate, and this turns out to be LIBOR. It is easily observable on Bloomberg and Reuters screens or in the daily press.

The importance of this is considerable. For instance, when the 'barometers of fear' surged in virtually all developed countries during the height of the financial crisis, central banks introduced a wide range of extraordinary measures to alleviate the stress in their banking systems. The common measure for this was the LIBOR–OIS spread, which was widely perceived as being based on actual market transactions. In other words, LIBOR had become a key variable that was used in assessing the effectiveness of central bank policy in dealing with the financial crisis.[31] If LIBOR reacted promptly to what central banks did, the policy measure was deemed successful. If it didn't, the measure was seen as misplaced or insufficient.

Some central banks went even further, making LIBOR a strategic policy tool in itself. Since January 2000, the monetary policy strategy of the Swiss National Bank has consisted of three elements: 'a definition of price stability, a medium-term inflation forecast and – at operational level – a target range for a reference interest rate, the three-month Swiss franc LIBOR'.[32] Norges Bank, the central bank of Norway, publicly announces its projected monetary policy rate and also the future three-month Norwegian krone risk premiums, based on the three-month NIBOR.[33] All of this might seem like a paradox, considering that the Eurodollar market was created in order to *avoid* the jurisdiction of the central banks. If central banks, as part of the state, accept LIBOR as a fact, surely it can be trusted?

LIBOR was, however, of importance not only to derivatives traders, academics and central bankers. Cemented as 'the world's most important number', banks could put LIBOR into use in other areas of the economy as well. LIBOR became not only the benchmark of choice for a variety of derivatives contracts, but the underlying benchmark for seemingly unrelated agreements such as residential mortgages, credit card debt and student loans. The Eurodollar market was never intended to be an investment outlet or a place to raise funds for households, university students or pensioners. However, as a vast number of people and organisations became directly exposed to the movement of the LIBOR rate through these agreements, it became a focal point that was easily followed in the daily press, which opted to publish the LIBOR rate as it would any other important number, such as the local weather or the closing level of the stock market index. Companies and households entered into LIBOR-indexed financial contacts falsely believing that the money market was the underlying benchmark.[34]

The LIBOR scandal turned this upside down. On 30 April 2012, a lawsuit[35] was filed in New York (and many others followed) alleging that a group of defendants had conspired to manipulate LIBOR. The list of defendants read like a Who's Who of global banking: Credit Suisse, Bank of America, JPMorgan Chase, HSBC, Barclays, Lloyds, WestLB, UBS, RBS, Deutsche Bank, Citi, Rabobank, Norinchukin Bank, Bank of Tokyo-Mitsubishi, Royal Bank of Canada. The plaintiffs who initiated the lawsuit were two ordinary citizens, Ellen Gelboim and Linda Zacher, who had exposure to LIBOR. Gelboim, from New York, had a retirement account that owned a debt security that was issued by General Electric. Linda Zacher, from a small town in Pennsylvania, was the sole beneficiary of her late husband's retirement account that owned a debt security that was issued by the State of Israel. Both of these financial instruments were indexed to the US dollar LIBOR. The plaintiffs alleged that the banks 'collusively and systematically suppressed LIBOR' so that the interest rates paid were lower than they otherwise should have been.

They also argued that they 'did not know, nor could they reasonably have known, about defendants' unlawful conduct until at least March 2011'. Indeed, the exclusive privilege to determine LIBOR was always in the hands of a few banks. This naturally benefited the banks as long as the illusion was maintained that LIBOR was not susceptible to manipulation and represented a tradeable market.

In February 2009, during my final days at Merrill Lynch, a UBS trader asked a broker at RP Martins to help manipulate LIBOR because he had 'heard [he] knew magic'.

'Yes I've got my wizard's hat on today,' the broker replied, having agreed to assist.[36]

LIBOR, however, was always much more than just an extremely elaborate magic trick.

CHAPTER 5

THE VALUE OF SECRETS

'What does the industry do to people working in it? Do you recognise yourself in characters that feature in *Wall Street*, *American Psycho* or *Cosmopolis*?'

I have never stopped thinking about the question I got from a journalist in 2012. It would be logical to think that the financial 'industry' has a tendency to change individuals. Money often has a strong influence on people, and the activities taking place in dealing rooms are closely connected to money. Therefore, a person who has spent 15 years in a dealing room ought to have gone through a fundamental life transformation. Moreover, because of my past and my turbulent exit from this industry, it was automatically assumed I would identify myself with characters in books and films set in or around such dealing rooms.

I will come back to my response in a later chapter, but in many ways I think the question is much more interesting than the answer. To me, it captures two of the most widespread and important perceptions – or perhaps misperceptions – about the 'industry'. From different perspectives, both of them illustrate how powerful banks are, and how much of this power is linked to various forms of secrecy.

The use of the word 'industry' in the question by the journalist highlights the fact that the distinction between the 'market' and the firms operating in these markets (mainly banks) can be blurry. As a trader, however, you are never employed by the 'market' – the system or the place where the financial instruments are bought and sold. You are not hired by the 'industry' either – 'industry' referring to the collective of all the institutions and organisations providing services that relate to these financial instruments. I have been employed by Dresdner Bank, HSBC, Citi, Crédit Agricole Indosuez and Merrill Lynch, but never by the industry or by the market. It is an important difference, because when elaborating on what is going on in this industry and how it affects you, you must, in effect, reveal what is going on inside the *bank*.

Problematically, it is extremely difficult to talk about what the bank looks like from the inside without almost immediately breaking a string of rules. When you enter a dealing room as an employee for the first time, you have already signed an agreement to keep secrets. And these secrets are supposed to last forever. One of the first agreements regarding secrecy and confidentiality I signed read like this:

> Stenfors may not without authorization disclose what he, during his activity at the Bank, has gotten to know about others' business or personal relationships. This duty remains even after the termination of your employment.

This sounds fair enough. It would not be pleasant if you had a colleague who kept on gossiping about your private life.

Another deal with my signature on it was somewhat more detailed when it came to protecting clients (and the bank, of course):

You will keep secret all trade secrets or other confidential, technical or commercial information which you may use, see or obtain regarding the affairs of the Bank or its clients. This includes, in particular, intellectual property, software packages, specialist know-how, names of clients and customers and any information concerning its or their dealings or affairs.

How about scribbling some interesting stories or revelations in a diary kept in the dealing room, so you have some anecdotes to share in the future? This, too, is impossible without breaking secrecy rules. I have signed this agreement as well:

You may not make, other than as necessary for your duties, any notes or memoranda relating to any matter concerning the dealings or affairs of the Bank. Nor shall you during your employment or at any time after you have left the employment of the Bank, use or permit the use of any such notes or memoranda.

However, of all the secrecy clauses I have signed, this paragraph remains my favourite:

You agree to keep confidential and not divulge to others, during the course of your employment, secret and confidential information and data regarding the business of the Bank, its customers, products and services, methods, systems, business plans or marketing methods and strategies, costs or other confidential, secret or proprietary information. Further, you agree to keep confidential the secret and proprietary information of the Bank's customers, clients and vendors. In the event that your employment with the Bank terminates, you agree not to divulge or use such confidential information, and to return promptly to the bank all documents and other materials owned by the Bank.

When you take away colleagues, customers, vendors, data, products, services, methods, systems, business plans, marketing methods, strategies, costs and other confidential, secret and proprietary information, what is there really left to talk about? If banking were an industry producing bicycles and the trading floor the factory floor where the assemblage and production took place, you would never be able to tell anyone what was going on *inside*. You could describe the colour of the walls and the air-conditioning system, and you could elaborate on the selection of drinks in the vending machines, but that would be it. You could never explain how the bicycles were made, how many, for whom and how working on the factory floor affected you and others around you. You could only speak about the bicycle industry. But nobody is employed by the 'bicycle industry'.

Secrets can be very valuable, or, as Professor George Simmel wrote in the *American Journal of Sociology* in 1906, 'what is withheld from the many appears to have a special value'.[1] Secrets are almost like commodities. Let us say that Max tells Rupert in the playground 'I know something that you don't.' This immediately elevates Max's status, whereas Rupert is demoted. Regardless of whether there is any truth in the secret or not (maybe Max is just pretending that he knows something), jealousy and admiration kick in almost inevitably.

On the other hand, unless there is value (or perceived value) in secrets, there is no point in collecting secrets like stamps.

In the old days, pricing and valuation spreadsheets and various risk management systems could be saved onto floppy disks and then slipped into a suit pocket. These days, banks are more sophisticated in protecting trade secrets. Downloading something to a USB flash drive or emailing a large attachment is rather difficult from a dealing room computer. However, information is still smuggled out because the human brain is like an enormous memory stick. Client contact lists, for instance, easily emerge in the dealing rooms of competitors.

I did not pay much attention to the small print about secrecy when I signed these contracts. I doubt many other traders did. However, in August 2009 I contacted 20 or so ex-colleagues and ex-competitors to ask whether they would be willing to act as character references should the FSA want a few unbiased opinions about me. I only got in touch with people I trusted and who knew me well enough as a trader working *inside* the bank. Whereas a few were kind enough to show support, the majority found my request highly problematic. One potential reference initially confirmed that their whole company was 'happy to be associated with me', only later to stop responding to emails, phone calls or text messages. Two supported me wholeheartedly and wished me good luck, but wanted nothing to do with me in writing. In fact, they did everything they could to distance themselves from me formally, and even openly told me how they were seeking reassurances from their own banks that their previous connection with me would not become a hindrance to their future careers. A couple who had left the industry altogether were afraid that commenting on former colleagues might jeopardise their right to exercise their stock options. Writing a statement about me (which I would then be able to show to the financial regulator) meant that their pensions might end up being in danger. And so on. The task was much harder than I had ever imagined, as everyone, of course, had signed similar agreements to me. Everyone had sworn secrecy to the banks. Breaking the agreement to keep secrets came at a price that was measurable in money. And the price was very high.

* * *

In some respects, confidentiality agreements are broken almost by default. This is particularly true when it comes to the hiring process of traders and sales people. Players in the market are not like football players, where everyone is able to assess who is talented and who is not simply by watching a game. Because dealing room expertise (often defined in terms of the ability to make money) is difficult to verify, sales people might exaggerate how closely connected they are to important clients and how instrumental they were in generating those enormous trading profits for the bank. Traders, likewise, often brag about their know-how, how much money they make and how powerful they are in the market. Therefore, with so much money and prestige at stake, the kind of jealously, admiration and Schadenfreude that exists in a children's playground is probably even more common on a trading floor.

'My last game tomorrow at Parc des Princes. I came like a king, left like a legend,' the Swedish football player Zlatan Ibrahimović posted on Twitter before moving from Paris Saint-Germain to Manchester United. I was nicknamed both 'The King' and 'Legend' by some traders, but, equally, I know I was called 'Stealth' and a range of other much less flattering things by others. Legends are born, heroes fall, and myths are created all the time in the financial markets – and secrecy plays an important role in this.

When Citi agreed to pay $425 million to the US authorities in May 2015 for its involvement in benchmark manipulation, the transcripts revealed that a senior derivatives trader was described by managers thus: 'This guy has forty percent of the market, and he knows where all the fixes are, he knows everybody on the street, he's a real fucking animal, this guy owns it.'[2] As a trader, it is difficult to get a more ringing endorsement than that. If such a reputation slips out, competitors soon take notice and the headhunters begin to call. Even though I usually ignored headhunters, they were instrumental when I joined both Citi and Merrill Lynch. In the former case, London and the reputation of the bank persuaded me. In the latter, I was attracted by the bank's investment bank status and attitude to risk. After all, banks hiring senior traders and sales people are 'buying' a specialist skill and expertise that those individuals have acquired at another bank. As there is no free trial period or returns policy, banks have to rely on promises, hearsay and open secrets. Bonuses, in particular, are the sort of open secrets that induce respect and jealousy in equal measure. Whereas well-paid traders, sales people and managers are happy to let others know how much they are worth (their 'market value'), this information is by no means supposed to reach the wider market – especially not the customers of the bank or the general public.

* * *

On 15 September 2008, the day when Lehman Brothers filed for bankruptcy, financial markets panicked and became paralysed at the same time. Share prices in banks and other financial institutions collapsed, whereas the money markets froze completely. For many banks around the world, the day of the largest corporate collapse in history will probably remain their worst for years to come. Having put very large bets on a worsening financial crisis, the day will also go down in history as the best day ever in my trading career. Trading-wise, I had managed to remain calm throughout a marathon poker game that had lasted since August 2007. When it was time to reveal our hands, I was the one with the royal flush. But now the game was over, and rather than being a day of celebration, this was the day on which I began to have very serious doubts about the industry, Merrill Lynch and myself.

Without outside help, Merrill Lynch would also have gone under on 15 September 2008. Like a number of other banks, my employer had kept on writing down the value of its sub-prime mortgage-related assets throughout the crisis. With Lehman Brothers gone, the word on the street (and on the trading floor) was that we would be next in line. The newsflash that Bank of America had agreed to buy Merrill Lynch was met with a feeling of relief and resignation. We did not want to be escorted from our high-tech office next to St Paul's Cathedral carrying brown cardboard boxes containing the very few personal and non-secret belongings we kept in the dealing room (toothbrushes, family photos, business cards, crime novels, etc.). However, Bank of America was a dinosaur. Merrill Lynch was, as the famous company logo illustrated, a charging bull. We were strong and aggressive. It did not matter that managers tried to convince us how lucky we had been to be thrown a lifeline just before drowning. The attempts at improving the mood were half-hearted at best. You could almost smell the humiliation.

But it could, of course, have been much worse. Many of us had friends who worked at Lehman Brothers or had traded with them – if not daily, then at least frequently enough to get a sense of how they must have been feeling. It was like a close cousin had died.

But the mourning process was very short. The cousin had no widow or children to look after the estate (yet), so within a couple of days Lehman Brothers was surrounded by vultures looking to eat whatever pieces were left of them. Trades had to be unwound and all ties had to be cut to a 150-year-old investment bank with which, it seemed, every trader and every bank had managed to enter into deals. It was one of the ugliest scenes I remember having seen in the market.

When Merrill Lynch announced its results in mid-January 2009, it turned out that the fourth quarter had been terrible. Losses ultimately exceeded $15 billion during the period, more than twice as much as Bank of America shareholders were led to believe when they approved the merger on 5 December 2008.[3] Despite such huge losses, the bank had still managed to pay bonuses amounting to $3.6 billion to an army of traders, investment bankers and managers. Rather than having a traditional bonus day during the early spring, after the results had been announced, a more convenient date had been chosen: 31 December 2008, which just happened to be the day before Bank of America formally took over Merrill Lynch. At that point, I had no idea how bad the situation was for the bank as a whole, but it did not feel right. I remember beginning to feel sick when I was quietly told which day had been picked as the bonus day.

The announced losses were so huge that the Federal Reserve had to step in and outline an emergency package to Bank of America. A large majority of the toxic assets the bank now had on its books came, as the press release stated, 'as a result of its acquisition of Merrill Lynch'.[4] If the public was not already furious with bankers by then, the Merrill Lynch bonus saga truly came to symbolise what the financial crisis looked like from the outside. Andy Stern, the President of the Service Employees International Union in the US at the time, neatly summarised it as follows: 'Bank of America took taxpayers' money and allowed Merrill Lynch to hand out bonuses at the same time as it was preparing pink slips for 35,000 employees.'[5]

On 5 March 2009, the *New York Times* published an article with the headline 'Undisclosed Losses at Merrill Lynch Lead to a Trading Inquiry'.[6] It was about me. However, most of the story related to the takeover by Bank of America, the huge fourth quarter losses reported by Merrill Lynch, and those bonus payments. The timing of the article was extremely unfortunate, as, although it did not state so specifically, a reader would automatically draw the conclusion that the two stories were connected. For me, the situation turned Kafkaesque. Merrill Lynch had suspended me, pending the outcome of an internal investigation. Depending on the outcome, I would then most likely be contacted by the FSA, the UK financial regulator. During this stage of the process, any discussions surrounding me would be held between Merrill Lynch and the FSA without my involvement. The fact that I was 'co-operating' with Merrill Lynch meant I was assisting them as much as I could during the investigation. It also meant I was still employed by Merrill Lynch and had to adhere to the contract of employment I had signed. In addition, I was requested not to come into the office, not to speak to the press, and not to speak to any colleagues at Merrill Lynch or in the market. I wasn't even allowed to reply to emails or text messages.

When, the next day, the New York Attorney General sent a letter commanding me (and presumably others) to 'testify in connection with an investigation concerning executive compensation', my situation became precarious. The US government wanted answers about what was really going on inside Merrill Lynch. Bank of America shareholders wanted answers about what was really going on inside Merrill Lynch. US taxpayers wanted answers about what was really going on inside Merrill Lynch. Lawyers for Merrill Lynch and Bank of America, however, argued that the names of those traders, investment bankers and managers should remain secret. Bonuses were discretionary and a private matter between employer and employee. Revealing them to the public could also affect their security (some people were *that* angry). Moreover, it was claimed that bonuses could be seen as 'trade secrets'. Somehow, competition for talented staff would be harmed if everyone knew the compensation structure at Merrill Lynch. This would be unfair. Neither John Thain (the ex-CEO of Merrill Lynch) nor Ken Lewis (the CEO of Bank of America) wanted to speak out. On the other hand, they were unable to pinpoint an exact policy stating that compensation was supposed to be kept secret at all costs. In fact, when asked if he 'had an understanding of whether Merrill's employees routinely disclosed compensation information during the recruitment process', Thain answered 'Yes'. Ken Lewis testified as follows:[7]

Q: Have you ever given anyone instruction to keep their compensation confidential?

A: No.

Q: In the 40 years that you have been at Bank of America?

A: Not that I recall.

In my naivety, I was rather keen to speak openly about what I knew and what I didn't know. It was 'a misunderstanding'. My instinct was similar to what it had been a few weeks earlier, when suggesting to my lawyer that it might be better to talk to the FSA directly, rather than leaving everything up to Merrill Lynch. As I had never met a financial regulator in person, I had not given much thought to how the process worked in reality. Now I knew that although I had a form of trading licence issued by the FSA (which quickly switched from 'active' to 'inactive' on their website), it was the banks, not the regulator, that ultimately regulated the traders. Traders were not supposed to talk to regulators.

By speaking up, I would obviously be breaking an unwritten rule. Having committed to being co-operative just a few weeks earlier, suddenly going rogue (again) would be unwise. And perhaps I did not know anything that was of interest? But who knew what I knew or what I didn't know? The end result was that I continued to pay the lawyers who were working on my behalf in relation to having going rogue in the first place, whereas the bank paid for an extra team of lawyers that were working on my behalf to prevent me from going rogue again, but in a rather different manner.

* * *

In a democratic society, transparency and public awareness are normally seen as good things. Every citizen should be informed about facts and relationships that matter to them. Although financial markets are in no way democratic, a somewhat similar logic is often applied. Without transparency, markets become less efficient – and efficiency is seen as something good. In financial markets, therefore, transparency is also seen as a good thing.

Central banks illustrate how important transparency has become in financial markets. Until only a few decades ago, central banks tended to be highly secretive. Acting on behalf of the state, they often took the markets by surprise and did so deliberately. Since the 1990s, however, the opposite strategy has been adopted. Economic theory gave support to the idea that surprises generally resulted in a welfare loss for society, whereas certainty and openness were beneficial. The new ideas made sense and led to a range of changes in the way central bankers communicated with banks, and ultimately with traders who were betting on what their next actions would be. Whereas monetary policy committee meetings used to be held on an ad-hoc basis, central bankers began to announce their exact meeting schedule, often a year or two in advance. The discussions in these meetings used to be secret. Now, central bankers began to disclose the minutes on their websites. The same happened to their interest rate forecasts. Before, a trader needed to scrutinise every single word they said in order to get clues about the direction in which interest rates were heading, how fast, and by how much. Recently, several central banks have gone so far as to publicly announce their own projections or interest rate 'paths', and some even their own LIBOR forecasts. All in all, this transparency has resulted in the increased predictability of central bank policy. This fits well with the idea that societies aim for greater transparency. However, as the LIBOR scandal has shown, not only was this openness one way (from central banks to banks), but communication remained secretive and deceptive the other way round (from banks to central banks). Therefore, unless central banks were consistently aware of the problem (which I don't think they were) and were able to quantify that problem (which they could not), policy decisions that were supposed to work towards a 'social good' would inevitably be distorted. Manipulated quotes would result in a deceptive market signal, which in turn would then have been picked up by the central bank. In other words, a decision would be made based on a lie. A rate cut, for instance, might have been delayed, or the 'wrong' kind of liquidity might have been injected into the banking system.

Individual rights to privacy should, of course, be protected. This also applies to secrets that belong to corporations. Trade secrets have an economic value precisely because they are secret. If, through industrial espionage, they are revealed to a competitor or to the wider public, the value of the secret to the firm is diluted. The corporation suffers. Societies therefore try to find the right balance between transparency and secrecy. The LIBOR scandal is a perfect example of where this balance was wrong.

Although I had not been involved in industrial espionage, my mismarking episode in 2009 had publicly exposed some of the bank's failures with regard to supervision, financial control, and risk management. However, these failures were described in just 65 words in the bank's settlement with the Irish Financial Regulator. Despite the fact that the bank was praised for having been 'open and transparent throughout the examination',[8] the 65 words did little to reveal what these failures actually were. This is not surprising. As I mentioned previously, banks have an inherent desire to *appear* good and sound. No bank wants failures. Therefore, if failures *do* materialise, no bank would want the details of them to be revealed to the wider public.

After I became labelled as a rogue trader, I met people who took a surprisingly positive view of my situation. There were those who argued that the City and Wall Street represented the worst sides of capitalism, and that the whole system ought to be brought to its knees. My actions could therefore be seen as an 'attack from the inside', making me into a kind of anti-hero. The fact that I was doing a PhD at SOAS, a university famed for its radical outlook, undoubtedly seemed to confirm that, despite having spent 15 years as a trader, I was 'one of them'.

On the other hand, I also encountered those who were fighting tooth and nail to protect capitalism against 'people like me'. If I agreed to work for *them*, I would be able to turn my unusual experience into something productive – in poacher-turned-gamekeeper fashion – and thereby pay back my debt to society. After a widely publicised rogue trading scandal at UBS in 2011, I was contacted by one of the Big Four accountancy firms (the Big Four audit 99 per cent of the FTSE 100 companies and are Deloitte, Ernst & Young, KPMG and PwC). The prosecutor had called the rogue trader an 'accomplished liar' who 'played God' with UBS's money. The money lost was bad news for UBS, but so was the reputational damage caused by the event. Managers – not only at UBS but also at other banks – had their work cut out in order to convince people (and themselves) that their trading systems and controls were bulletproof. The accountancy firm saw a business opportunity and was wondering whether I would be interested in a job related to trading systems and controls in an American bank. The idea was that I, having exposed defects and weaknesses in one bank, could try to do the same in another, or perhaps even in several other banks by becoming a 'white hat'. I had to Google the expression, learning that it was another term for a 'legal hacker'. I found the pitch exciting and absurd in equal measure. If governments could hire skilful hackers, why not banks? Maybe this was the logical next step for traders who had been on the edge (and beyond) of what was considered reasonable and ethical. Employing an ex-hacker or an ex-rogue trader might make perfect sense. However, I had three reservations. First, why would a bank take the risk? The reputational risks seemed way too large should it get out that the bank was so worried about its procedures it was willing to employ a former rogue trader such as myself. The arrangement was too sensitive publicity-wise and would be difficult to keep secret. Second, why would I take the risk? What if something went wrong and I was blamed? With my credibility, who would want to protect me? Third, although it was portrayed to me as 'a way to pay back my debt to society', I was not sure how helping another bank would benefit society, and at the same time clear my conscience. I regretted my actions deeply, but this project had nothing to do with the guilt I felt. In the end, these questions did not matter, because the project never got the green light anyway (at least not with me on board). Instead of employing ex-rogue traders as ethical hackers, the accountancy firm told me that the bank in question had instead decided to involve 'management knowledgeable of the trading environment but not engaged directly in trading'. I should have trusted my initial instinct that the whole idea was absurd. A bank would never *voluntarily* expose itself to the risk of revealing secrets that related to trading.

* * *

Secrets are well protected because they are valuable to the bank. Or, put differently, secrets that are exposed can cause harm. Because of the nature of the relationship or contract with the bank, it is therefore complicated for a trader to divulge 'what the industry does to people working in it', unless they talk in very broad terms about the industry. The second part of the journalist's question ('Do you recognise yourself in characters that feature in *Wall Street, American Psycho* or *Cosmopolis*?') touches upon this indirectly. Wall Street is not only a small section of lower Manhattan or a film directed by Oliver Stone. It is also a metaphor for the speculative activities that take place in dealing rooms on Wall Street, in the City of London, and in other financial centres around the world. The tremendous amount of money that flows through these dealing rooms makes them showrooms for capitalism. Visitors and TV crews might be allowed to catch a glimpse of the action that takes place: seas of flickering computer screens, shouting, celebration, despair, and a few hand gestures by traders indicating that they want to buy or sell something. For an outsider, a dealing room can look a bit like a casino, where dice are rolled and fortunes made and lost every day. Surely, something could be said about this environment and these markets without revealing valuable secrets? The answer is yes. However, this automatically leads to *another* layer of power and secrecy that is fundamental to how the FX, money and derivatives markets operate. The fact that the international, and often self-regulated, financial markets have become more 'powerful' is hardly a controversial statement. We only need to look at the seemingly large, liquid, competitive and efficient markets described in this book (the FX, interest rate and derivatives markets) to find evidence of the phenomenal transformation that has taken place over the last decades. In this context, governments around the world could be seen as having given up power, willingly or unwillingly, to the speculative activity of the players in this global 'casino'. In simple terms, power has shifted from states to markets, from Main Street to Wall Street, from the 99 per cent to the 1 per cent, and so on. When political economist Susan Strange coined the term 'casino capitalism' in 1986,[9] she could hardly have foreseen how important and powerful the international financial markets would become.

Because of this development, it is quite logical that the 'market' has come to be regarded as a kind of courtroom in itself, where policy decisions by governments or central banks receive an instant verdict. An ambiguous outcome in an election or a referendum often acts as a strong 'sell' signal in the market. Stock markets fall, bond prices tumble and currencies get slaughtered. Such an assessment by the market is not democratic by any means, and the industry shows no compassion or mercy. For instance, following the result of the EU referendum in the UK on 23 June 2016, the pound fell sharply. Although most experts and analysts had warned that Brexit would mean a weaker currency, the victory of the Leave campaign came as a surprise. On the other hand, when a result has been well predicted (most US presidential elections before Trump, for instance), the impact has often been negligible.

However, the markets have increasingly tended to be seen as objective and fair, precisely because they are perceived to be so immensely competitive. 'The market is always right,' many observers claim. 'The market hates uncertainty,' others say. But *who* is this market that is always right? And *who* is this market that hates uncertainty? This is where the focal point tends to become blurry. The search for answers stops, and instead the conclusion is reached that 'this is what the market wants' or 'this is what the industry prefers'. But when it comes to a real casino in Las Vegas or Monte Carlo, it is also claimed that the house always wins. If we use the casino as an analogy for the market, we should be equally precise. We should look more closely at the house involved in writing the rules and keeping control of the markers, those who decide when the casino opens and shuts, and who is allowed to spin the roulette wheel. In the markets, the house consists of the banks.

The global markets in foreign exchange and money markets (for both cash and derivatives) are phenomenally large. We know this. But *who* are these markets? According to *Euromoney*'s FX and rates surveys,[10] 87 per cent of the global FX market belongs to the top 15 banks. Thirteen LIBOR panel banks accounted for 96 per cent of this portion. A similar pattern can be seen in the interest rate markets, where the top 15 banks had a total market share of 94 per cent (for both cash and derivatives) in 2012. Eleven LIBOR panel banks accounted for 81 per cent of this portion. When we discuss these markets, or the industry behind these markets, it is impossible not to talk about a very small group of very large banks. In fact, it is impossible not to mention the LIBOR panel banks, which are completely dominant within this small group of banks.

Banks are corporations, but the banking system is also different from other industries. For instance, information asymmetries where one party (the borrower) knows more than the other (the lender) are natural in banking. Banking assets can also be difficult to value, as it is impossible to assess the likelihood of default for every counterparty at every moment in time. Moreover, banks provide transaction and accounting systems. All of these aspects help make the banking sector 'special' and allow it to be supervised and regulated differently from other industries. According to Charles Goodhart,[11] an economist and former member of the Bank of England Monetary Policy Committee, the central bank automatically emerges as a kind of 'manager of the club of banks'. The kind of relationship that exists between the central bank and the banks is unique. No other industry is protected by the state to the same degree (through the taxpayers and via the central bank). As banks form the spine of the financial system, it is in the interests of a country's citizens to know if something is not quite right inside a bank. It would therefore be logical that even though the public might not have the right to gain access to relevant information, the central bank should.

When I spoke to central bankers during the financial crisis, I got the impression that they did not suspect anything was 'wrong' with LIBOR. In the aftermath of the LIBOR scandal, however, the tone had changed. 'Through all of my experience, what I never contemplated was that there were bankers who would purposely misrepresent facts to banking authorities,' Alan Greenspan said. 'You were honour bound to report accurately, and it never entered my mind that, aside from a fringe element, it would be otherwise. I was wrong.'[12] Greenspan, who had often been referred to as the world's most powerful banker, or even one of the most powerful people in the world, was a man you listened to as a trader. The Federal Reserve had a tremendous amount of power, and Greenspan had been the captain of the ship for almost two decades.

Being what they are, central banks have an interest in participating – at least as an observer – in important matters relating to financial markets and benchmarks they are active in or influenced by. For instance, they are founding members of the Association Cambiste Internationale (ACI), more commonly known as Forex – the leading trade organisation for dealers in foreign exchange and money markets. Central banks also participate in the International Capital Market Association (ICMA), which represents a broad range of capital market interests and is the forum for market conventions and standards within such markets. The International Swaps and Derivatives Association (ISDA) is also an important organisation, more specifically in the derivatives market. Here, central banks tend to be so-called 'subscriber members', whereas the market-making banks are 'primary members'. Sometimes, central banks are required to take a more active role. Through incentives, or various 'carrots and sticks', they are able to get the banks to act in a certain way. For instance, central banks have the power to grant bank licences, thereby giving certain financial institutions privileges that are attached to simply being a bank – such as accepting deposits. However, these privileges naturally depend on certain restrictions and conditions, ranging from capital and reserve requirements to rules on governance and reporting. The central bank also decides which banks are allowed to enter into repurchase agreements ('repos') with them, which is where banks put up collateral in return for cash, or vice versa. For central banks, repos are a crucial element in order to conduct monetary policy. Doing repos with the central bank can be lucrative for the banks, and the central banks know this.

A similar logic applies to the power of the central bank, the treasury or debt office to grant 'primary dealerships' in the local T-bill, government bond or FX markets. Primary dealers are, in effect, 'official' market makers that commit to follow certain rules and regulations that are somewhat stricter than those followed by normal market makers. They might, for instance, be required to provide central banks with some valuable information about the state of the market or to follow stricter rules when it comes to providing liquidity. In return, primary dealers are given certain privileges. A central bank might choose to intervene in the FX markets only through its primary dealers. As an intervention, by definition, is intended to move or support the market price, getting the information first-hand means a slight, but important, informational advantage over other competing banks. One second can mean a lot in the FX markets.

Once, I was invited to a Christmas party organised by the Bank of Japan for all the primary dealers in the Tokyo FX market. Compared with the lavish parties organised by brokers, such as ICAP, Tullett Prebon or Meitan Tradition, it was a rather dull event, consisting of a huge conference room dotted with small round tables where you could stand and mingle, while being offered wine and canapés. The *gaijin* gravitated towards one part of the hall, and the locals to the other. Speeches, when serious gentlemen gave serious talks about the Japanese economy and the financial market, were held at a podium. These generally finished with the conclusion that it had been an interesting year, and that next year would be even more interesting. Applause. The party was over in two hours exactly, and, when leaving the building (and, I admit, desperately looking for people who wanted to continue somewhere else), I asked one of my Japanese colleagues why *everyone* from the market had turned up at the party. 'Ah,' he said. 'In a speech a few years ago, the Governor told the room that if he was in their shoes, he would not go home "long yen". Since then, nobody dares to miss the party, or forgets to bring a mobile phone.' My colleague explained that Bank of Japan had effectively given the traders a 'tip', by saying that unless they immediately sold the positions they had in yen and bought other currencies instead, the central bank would step in and intervene in the currency markets the following day. It worked. Traders, as soon as they could, scrambled for their mobile phones to call the junior traders who were still back at the office, and told them to sell Japanese yen before everybody else did. I can never be sure whether the central bank had actually given the traders in the room this non-public information. Maybe it was just an urban myth, or maybe 'if I were in your shoes' simply meant that the Governor thought the Japanese yen was fundamentally overvalued at the time, and this view corresponded with their economic outlook at the time. It is difficult to say.

Some years later, and back in London, my manager at the time got a phone call from the Federal Reserve. The caller wanted his opinion on what he thought the market reaction would be if they decided to cut the central bank interest rate at the next meeting by a remarkable 50 basis points, rather than the widely expected 25. After hanging up, my manager explained what had happened and, without hesitation, bought LIBOR-indexed Eurodollar futures contracts that would soar in value should the Federal Reserve decide to take the market by surprise. In this case, the central banker had provided no clues whatsoever about what they were up to. He had, however, revealed something that hardly anyone in the financial market had considered – that they were contemplating 50. The unimaginable turned into a probability. A secret thought or discussion was, perhaps unconsciously, transmitted to traders who immediately tried to profit from it.

Close relationships with central bankers, whether in foreign exchange or interest rate markets, can give an informational edge. The same goes for primary dealerships in government bonds and T-bills. The ability to participate in auctions or to be a vehicle through which interventions take place is often profitable, but sometimes also loss making. The information, however, is useful. If you cannot profit from it directly, it is still perceived to be valuable, as others not belonging to the club might think you know something they don't. This enhances your reputation tremendously in the market place. When I was working for HSBC in Stockholm, we were desperate to become primary dealers in government bonds. Being part of the T-bill club was not enough. Some of our sales people even complained that their customers refused to trade with us unless we also joined the bond club. The information they got from the primary dealers was superior to what we had to offer. When we gave them some market colour, it was already old news. So we hired a team of bond traders, applied for primary dealership and got the membership card. It was seen as an investment.

While being a club member was in itself seen as prestigious, it goes without saying that once you got to sit at the table with the big boys, you wanted the best seat possible. In the Swedish FX market, one route was to do well in the annual primary dealer survey, an assessment by the competing club members on behalf of the central bank. In the questionnaire, you had to assess how professional you thought the others in the club were on a scale of 1 ('Poor') to 5 ('Excellent'). Then, you subjectively ranked each bank from 1 to 10 (there were 11 primary dealers and you could not vote for yourself) according to their expected performance in the forthcoming years. In 2004, I ticked Den Danske Bank for the top spot. They were brilliant. The survey, of course, was supposed to be confidential, but JPMorgan Chase 'accidentally' managed to copy in a few interdealer brokers when emailing the reply to the central bank. According to them, we should be last. I had already rated *them* last, so there was no point in thinking about possible revenge. Even though it felt personal and seemed like a public insult, we managed to win the category for FX swaps that year. That meant being invited to sit next to the Deputy Governor at an exclusive lunch organised for the foreign exchange dealers. Apart from the incident with JPMorgan Chase, however, I genuinely believe that most traders took such surveys seriously and refrained from strategically marking each other down. In any case, central bank surveys were always constructed *as if* traders were honest and forthcoming people. And *as if* they were playing a fair game.

Other clubs were perhaps less elitist or formal. Nonetheless, membership in, say, Bank of England's London Foreign

Exchange Joint Standing Committee, or in the Canadian Foreign Exchange Committee, was highly exclusive. Minutes from the meetings (those that are in the public domain) read like a Who's Who in the FX markets. The chief dealers at the major banks are there, and so are the central bankers. But the 'market' is notably absent, unless, of course, the market is purely defined as the dozen or so global banks that buy and sell the majority of those $5.1 trillion worth of currencies on a daily basis.

In contrast to stock markets, therefore, activities in foreign exchange and interest rate markets are often managed through certain 'clubs'. And it almost seems natural that the central bank becomes the logical manager of the club of banks.

* * *

LIBOR, however, was different. Although the LIBOR clubs look strikingly similar to, say, primary dealerships in that a group of banks control a money-related instrument or price, the central banks lack authority. LIBOR has never been under the jurisdiction of a central bank, and until 2013 it had always lacked regulatory oversight. Due to its roots in the Eurodollar market, it could be argued that it was intended never to be under any government scrutiny *at all*. However, LIBOR was not self-regulated by the 'markets' either. However, this did not this imply that LIBOR lacked rules. What set LIBOR apart was that the LIBOR banks themselves, not the market, had authority. The group of LIBOR clubs had steering committees deciding upon the rules and structure of the benchmark. These committees consisted of, and were appointed by, the LIBOR fixing panel banks themselves. Although the LIBOR panel compositions changed over time (mainly as a result of bank mergers), the LIBOR clubs always included the large universal banks that were also the most active market makers in the money, FX and derivatives markets. Likewise, despite the differences in size (ranging from just five members in the STIBOR club to 43 in the EURIBOR club), they also tended to increasingly include international banks that were not under the direct jurisdiction of the central bank issuing the underlying currency for that particular benchmark. In other words, they were either typical so-called too-big-to-fail banks within a country, or international banks of gigantic proportions. For instance, 14 of the 18 members of the US dollar LIBOR club were classified as 'global systematically important banks'.[13]

The clubs, in turn, appointed an organisation to govern and supervise both themselves and the process. This was not the 'market' or any kind of financial regulator, such as the Securities and Exchange Commission (SEC) or the FSA. Instead, it was usually the prevailing banking lobby organisation in the country. The main objectives and tasks of the lobby organisations are, of course, to promote the interests of their members. For instance, the BBA (which governed LIBOR) aims to influence decision makers by 'promoting a legislative and regulatory system for banking and financial services ... which takes account of our members' needs and concerns and provides an effective and competitive market place in which their businesses can prosper'. The banking lobby also 'promote[s] and defends the [banking] industry' by engaging 'with government, devolved administrations and Europe as well as the media and other key stakeholders to ensure the industry's voice is heard and to highlight the strength and importance of UK banking'.[14] Among the guiding principles of the European Banking Federation (which governed EURIBOR in conjunction with the ACI) is 'to promote the principles of self-regulation and better regulation within the EU, so as to alleviate the burden on banks'. The lobby also aims to 'ensure that the experience and the views of banks are taken into consideration in the shaping of relevant policies'.[15] The point is that the banking lobby is not working for the market, but for the banking industry. That the banks selected a lobby as the governing body for the most important financial benchmark in the world is logical, but also quite remarkable. As with many things in banking, the idea would be unthinkable in other industries. It would be the equivalent of the National Rifle Association being responsible for the supervision and governance of the US firearms industry.

The BBA even managed to register the BBA-LIBOR as a trademark in the same way as Coca-Cola did with its famous contour bottle about 100 years ago. Just as the Coca-Cola recipe still remains a protected trade secret, the true ingredients of LIBOR were also fiercely guarded by the banks and the bank lobby. Following queries into the integrity of the LIBOR process in 2008, the BBA said: 'It is not possible to receive the details of individual dealt rates as the confidentiality agreements between brokers and their clients preclude these from being disclosed.'[16] After a more thorough review of the whole process, the following statement was released by the BBA:

In conclusion, all contributing banks are confident that their submissions reflect their perception of their true costs of borrowing, at the time at which they submitted their rates. They are therefore prepared to continue with their individual quotes being published with the day's LIBOR rates. As there was no real support for any

of the proposals to limit stigmatisation, the FX & MM
Committee has therefore decided to retain the existing
process.[17]

The integrity of LIBOR (or the lack of it) was protected by the
clubs or by the associations working on their behalf. It should
not come as a surprise that the lobby organisations often
acted as defendants on behalf of the banks with regard to the
integrity of the LIBOR fixing mechanism, despite pressure
from individual non-member banks and end users such as
pension funds, corporations and hedge funds.[18]

The LIBOR rate-setting process was always secretive by
nature. Banks did not have to provide any evidence that their
submissions were accurate. In fact, actual trades between banks
are considered trade secrets. Even so, to prevent unnecessary
suspicion, banks actively tried to conceal what they were up
to. When, on 29 May 2008, the *Wall Street Journal* reported
that banks might have been manipulating LIBOR rates, panel
banks were quick to refute the claims.

'We continue to submit our LIBOR rates at levels that
accurately reflect our perception of the market,' a Citi spokes-
man said.[19]

This was a far cry from what was being discussed within
the bank, though.

'WSJ article on LIBOR getting a lot of attention. So under
pressure to be in middle of pack so will be moving up a couple
today,' a Citi US dollar LIBOR submitter had commented,
according to transcripts obtained by the regulators.[20]

Being in the 'middle of the pack' basically meant submitting
LIBOR rates similar to the average of the others, regardless of
their accuracy.

HBOS, the British bank later acquired by Lloyds Bank, also argued that the contents of the newspaper article were unfounded. The official statement argued that the bank's LIBOR quotes were a 'genuine and realistic' indication of its borrowing costs. The word on the trading floor was somewhat different. Just three weeks before the article was published, an HBOS senior manager sent an email to two other senior managers and other HBOS personnel, including the senior manager of the LIBOR submitters, saying: 'It will be readily apparent that in the current environment no bank can be seen to be an outlier. The submissions of all banks are published and we could not afford to be significantly away from the pack.'[21]

Banks not only mislead customers and the wider public. Deutsche Bank, for instance, went so far as to mislead the lobby and the financial regulator. On 4 February 2011, the Financial Conduct Authority (the FCA, which had replaced the FSA) sent out a request to all LIBOR panel banks asking them to confirm that they had proper systems and controls in place for the submission process. Two months previously, the BBA had asked all banks to confirm that an audit had been carried out; this was signed by a compliance officer at Deutsche Bank. That, however, was incorrect. There had been no audit of LIBOR. Instead, the compliance officer had said in an email that the BBA confirmation was 'an arse-covering exercise [by the BBA]'.

Deutsche Bank sent a signed document to the regulator on 18 March 2011, claiming that it had 'conducted spot checks on a random sample of LIBOR submissions across a number [of] currencies' and that the bank 'monitor[ed] all email and instant messaging communications of all front office staff'.

In sum, it was concluded that the bank had 'adequate systems and controls in place for the determination and submission of Deutsche Bank's LIBOR fixings'. This was also incorrect. The bank had not conducted any spot checks on LIBOR submissions. The bank did not have adequate systems and controls in place. The bank did not include any LIBOR-specific terms in the monitoring of communications of front office staff. Moreover, the FCA also found that Deutsche Bank had failed to give accurate information regarding audio recordings, and even shredded important documents that were required to be stored, according to the regulator.[22]

* * *

Although I was very active in trading various LIBOR derivatives, I was either working for a bank that did not belong to any LIBOR clubs (Merrill Lynch in London), working for a bank that belonged to LIBOR clubs in other countries (HSBC in Stockholm), working for a bank that belonged to LIBOR clubs in other currencies (Crédit Agricole in London) or working for a bank that belonged to various LIBOR clubs but I was located on a different trading floor or within another trading entity (Citibank London and Tokyo).

If a non-member wanted change, they could of course try to become a member of one of the clubs. This would have given the new member not only a VIP card to be part of the process in determining LIBOR, but would also have provided them with a voice in the meetings where decisions regarding the whole structure were made. However, a membership card was incredibly difficult to obtain.[23] First, it was not enough that you had exposure to LIBOR or could claim to be a financial institution. You had to be a bank, and a bank with a good credit standing. Second, you needed to be a very large bank. You had to show that your trading activity was 'sizeable', which meant that small and medium-sized banks would be disqualified even before the application process started. A third hurdle was 'market-making ability'. To act as a market maker in a specific currency, you had to be either a very large domestic bank or one of the few universal banks that had extensive local expertise everywhere in the world. Some clubs also required branch presence in a particular country.

Once, a trader at RBS called me to tell me he was keen to take the initiative in getting his bank to join one of the LIBOR clubs. RBS was a big bank. RBS had a sizeable trading activity. RBS was a market maker. When he called back a while later, I patiently listened to him as he furiously told me that they had been rejected because of a lack of branch presence. I did not really know what to say. At various points during my career, I had started inquiries into whether it might be possible to join a few of the clubs. Every time I was rejected even before seeing a proper application form.

The clubs and their governing bodies were almost like secret societies. Outsiders knew they had influence and power. But the rituals and formal tests you had to pass in order to become a member, or just to attend as a guest, were too difficult. In the unlikely event you passed, you were still met by an informal resistance among the existing members to broaden or diversify the membership roster. 'Reputation' in the market belonged to more informal criteria. In hindsight, we now know that the reputation requirement had little to do with reputation outside the clubs. Despite numerous fines, lawsuits and criminal investigations since 2013, the club members have remained almost precisely the same and their members continue to submit LIBOR quotes on a daily basis. None of the banks have been disqualified for lack of reputation.

No major overhaul, or rule change, with regards to LIBOR took place from its inception to the aftermath of the scandal. A few groups of banks retained exclusive privilege to influence LIBOR throughout these decades. And the same clubs managed to keep control of the rule book. In that sense, LIBOR was a fundamentally anti-competitive process from the start, which then benefited from deception, secrecy and disguising itself as a competitive and free market. The status quo of maintaining control over the underlying benchmark while keeping its integrity intact probably suited the banks' interests and gave them a kind of 'secret power'. Or, as Steven Lukes, a sociologist, once said: '[T]he most effective and insidious use of power is to prevent such conflict from arising in the first place.'[24]

However, power and secrecy stretched beyond the world of *benchmarks* that were used in derivatives, mortgages, corporate debt, student loans and central bank policy. They also ensnared the largest market in the world: the foreign exchange market.

CHAPTER 6

CONVENTIONS AND CONSPIRACIES

In 1995, I was sent to the HSBC Group Management Training College in Hertfordshire to learn the basics of foreign exchange trading. It was nice to leave dark and icy Stockholm behind for two weeks to join 15 or 20, mainly London-based, soon-to-be traders and sales people in the leafy English countryside. HSBC was very good at FX, probably in the top three in the world at the time, so my expectations of the course were high. We got to play a computer-based trading simulation game, designed to replicate a realistic situation in a dealing room. It was fun, and the teacher was both knowledgeable and engaging. I remember how we were repeatedly told to 'galvanise our HPs', as if our calculators (manufactured by Hewlett-Packard) were like musical instruments needing to be restrung before a concert. We had to practise, practise, practise – to master the most difficult mathematical problems that could arise in FX and money market trading. However, after a day or two I think most of us found the classes rather tiresome. The young orchestra – wanting to *play*, rather than simply learn the chords – became frustrated and began to miss the buzz of the London dealing room, even if at this stage of their careers they probably did little more than tea and sandwich deliveries for the desk. I just felt lucky to be there, but perhaps also a little looked down on by some of the others who, I thought, saw me as an unsophisticated relative from some distant wilderness. Frustration turned into desperation, and one night, after we had stayed up chatting and bragging, someone had the idea of breaking into the bar inside the training centre; as with everywhere else in England at the time, it had closed at 11 p.m. Two fearless traders-to-be turned the vision into reality by somehow managing to find an entry point. Perhaps the bar had been left unlocked? I cannot remember more than the fact that soon thereafter the drinks were flowing. 'Gold' by Spandau Ballet was playing on the sound system. Even now, whenever I hear Tony Hadley singing about being 'indestructible' I cannot help but wonder what happened to my classmates when they got back to London. I am not just thinking about the two mischievous ringleaders, who seemed both ruthless and smart. Any trading desk would have been delighted to have them on board, and I doubt the incident was ever reported. No, I am thinking about those who cheered them on, who tried to persuade them to stop, or who, like me, neither actively helped nor actively prevented it from happening. Those who just happened to be there.

* * *

In November 2014, six global banks received fines totalling $4.3 billion for manipulative trading conduct in the FX markets.[1] Despite the incredibly large fines, which matched or even trumped those in relation to LIBOR, things were by no means settled. 'This isn't the end of the story,' said Martin Wheatley, then head of the FCA.[2] The six banks were HSBC, RBS, UBS, JPMorgan Chase, Citibank and Bank of America. I had worked for half of them: HSBC, Citigroup and, technically, Bank of America after they bought Merrill Lynch. On reading about the fines, I remembered the HSBC training course I had participated in almost 20 years earlier. Not that it had anything directly to do with the FX scandal the whole world was now reading about in the newspapers. Instead, I thought about how black and white everything looked from the outside. Before this day, LIBOR seemed to have been the problem, and the FX market had not. Some banks had paid large fines for manipulating the FX markets whereas other banks had paid nothing. Some FX traders were mentioned in the transcripts (again, without revealing their true identities) whereas others were not. You were either innocent or guilty.

To me, LIBOR derivatives and FX had always been extremely closely connected. Traders in the two markets always fed off each other, sat close to each other, or, like me, were equally involved in both. Camaraderie was mixed with enmity in a peculiar way, and once you were 'inside', the world was fluid rather than solid, grey rather than black and white. The rules were different from those followed in the rest of society and evolved differently. The problem was that these rules, having become almost conventional for those who abided by them, looked from the outside like a crystal-clear case of conspiracy.

Earlier, just a few months after the LIBOR scandal broke in 2012, I met a former colleague who was now a managing director in foreign exchange sales at one of those six banks. We had both been 'inside', and our discussion quickly gravitated away from LIBOR and towards FX.

'Just imagine all the shit they would find if they began digging into FX,' he said.

He was not referring specifically to the manipulative practices that have been made public by regulators and law-makers since then, but more generally to the perception of the

FX desks as the Wild West of the various dealing rooms across the City, in Canary Wharf and elsewhere around the world. FX trading was like nothing else, yet it had hitherto managed to escape the attention of the media. Strange, but it was only a matter of time before it was in the firing line, we both thought. The FX market did not have a particularly bad reputation. It was just that it had a different 'culture', something that the more well-behaved stockbrokers and equity analysts on the trading floor would often comment upon. If they, with their knowledge and experience, found the culture sometimes questionable, surely the person on the street who was not familiar with dealing room practices would be interested in knowing what *really* went on.

Throughout my career in trading, I was proud of belonging to the LIBOR derivatives community, but even more so to the FX community. At the same time, traders or sales people in FX had to learn to live with certain stereotypical perceptions. For instance, FX traders tended to be noisier than others in the dealing room, and usually cared less about what others thought about them. Because of the extremely fast market, FX traders often had shorter attention spans – they tolerated less bullshit. In addition, FX traders were more street-smart (less educated, others would say) and, supposedly, lived by different rules.

It should come as no surprise then that the most hilarious (or shocking) stories of traders misbehaving related to FX traders rather than to LIBOR derivatives traders, let alone strategists, analysts, stockbrokers or others in the dealing room. For instance, I recall an FX options trader being dismissed after urinating on an important client; he had probably lost money on a trade and thought that the client had behaved unprofessionally. Although the FX desks tolerated quite a lot of irrational and sometimes indefensible behaviour, this clearly crossed a line. Reputation was important. However, most 'incidents' tended to be hushed up without repercussions, as long as the trader made money for the bank. After all, it was quite common for senior managers to have a trading background, which meant they often felt sympathetic towards how difficult life could be as a trader. FX was not for the faint-hearted and it was deemed natural that traders should be allowed to let off some steam every now and then. During my 15 years in trading I was called into the HR department only once to discuss anything remotely related to improper conduct. An FX spot trader had lost his temper, with a senior interest rate options trader the target of his fury. As I happened to be seated back-to-back with the options trader and facing the FX trader, I became a key witness to the physical fight that ensued between the two. I had not seen anything like it since I was 11 years old. Behind the closed doors of the HR department, I tried to convey an unbiased view of what I had seen, expecting that, as usual, everything would be settled with a man hug or a firm handshake. However, when I came into work one morning soon after, the interest rate options trader was gone. I was told that he had left to take up a new opportunity. The incident and the background to it had already been erased from history, leaving behind many more questions than answers. But it added to the trading room folklore.

However, it was not the extracurricular activities of certain traders that made me doubt that LIBOR was going to be a one-off scandal. It was activities within the working culture itself. Six months after the first batch of FX fines, Bank of America,

Barclays, Citigroup, JPMorgan Chase, RBS and UBS were fined $5.6 billion for engaging in collusive practices in the same markets. According to the FBI, the activity involved criminality 'on a massive scale'.[3] Very few have since stepped forward to try to defend the behaviour leading up to the fines, which, when revealed to a wider public not familiar with FX trading 'activities', gave banks and traders even more of a headache.

To understand what went wrong, and perhaps in order to improve how trading and banking are conducted in future, we need to look closer at the rules and conventions that allowed these activities to happen. Before doing so, however, it is important to keep in mind that up until the LIBOR scandal broke two years earlier, the global FX market was still widely perceived to be completely free from manipulation or collusive practices. This is not surprising. Whereas LIBOR was a benchmark and not a market per se, the FX market was (and still is) by far the largest market on the planet. It is difficult, perhaps even unthinkable, to imagine being able to manipulate traded currencies in a market with a daily turnover of $5.1 trillion,[4] either single-handedly or in collaboration with a few other traders. The global equity market is huge when all the stock exchanges in the world are put together. The turnover in the FX market, however, is more than ten times larger still. The FX market also appears to be way too competitive for such things to happen. From the moment Wellington wakes up on Monday morning until San Francisco switches off the lights on Friday night, traders quote and deal on immensely tight bid–offer spreads. Even during times of extreme uncertainty and crisis, when some stock markets are forced to temporarily shut down, the FX market continues to work. The FX market simply seems too large, too competitive, too efficient – too 'perfect' even – to possibly be rigged.

But, as with LIBOR, perceptions can be deceptive. Despite being astonishingly large, the global FX market is concentrated within a relatively small group of very large banks. Roughly half of the market belongs to Citi, Deutsche Bank, Barclays and UBS. Add a few more key players, such as HSBC, JPMorgan Chase, Bank of America Merrill Lynch, Credit Suisse, BNP, Morgan Stanley and Goldman Sachs, and this number surpasses 80 per cent.[5] The banks are few, but they are also very large. Deutsche Bank has around 100,000 employees, Citi and JPMorgan Chase more than twice as many each. The FX market is not only getting larger but also more concentrated. In Japan, for instance, 19 banks represented 75 per cent of turnover in 1988. In 2010, just eight banks accounted for the same proportion.[6] In sum: the pie has become bigger, while being sliced into fewer and fewer pieces.

Furthermore, the number of FX *traders* is surprisingly small. You could comfortably fit 80 per cent of the market in any currency pair into a sizeable hotel conference room. Even though I never worked on an FX spot desk, to which the FBI comment related, I still knew or had heard of around half of the traders mentioned in the transcripts. It's a small world. Three-quarters of those working in the FX swap market for US dollars against, say, Norwegian krone could feasibly do lunch together. It is a tiny market. But everything is relative, and what does it mean if a market with a daily turnover of $43 billion is considered tiny by those in the industry? Until relatively recently, you could literally fit the whole FX market into your pocket. Hambros Bank (a British bank later bought by the French bank Société Générale) used to publish a book listing almost every bank, every dealing room and the Reuters Dealing 2000-2 code for every trader and sales person in the global FX and money markets. Before the internet, 'Hambros', as the little red book was called, was indispensable.

The major FX trading banks operate in many countries and in diverse cultures. The FX market, after all, is by definition an *international* activity. One might think that this automatically means that there are as many FX cultures as there are countries or languages. On the contrary, the language, customs and norms of the FX market are highly standardised. Even though every global financial centre has its own linguistic features, the lingua franca in the FX market is a curious mix of English, Cockney (a working-class London dialect) and electronic abbreviations – peppered with rhyme, history and a great deal of humour. 'Cable' and 'Loonie', the standard terms for the currency pairs of US dollars against British pounds and Canadian dollars respectively, are derived from the old Atlantic communication cable between Britain and the US and the bird depicted on the Canadian one-dollar coin. 'Spaniard' (referring to the number one, which sounds like the Spanish name Juan), 'Bully' (50 points on a dartboard and hence number 50) or 'Yard' (rhyming with the French word *milliard*, i.e. 1 billion) are other examples. Abbreviations (similar to text message shortcuts) such as BIFN ('Bye for now') and CUL ('See you later') have been around for ages in order to save precious seconds in hectic markets, and add to a trading lingo that is inclusive for those who speak it but is incomprehensible to those who don't. A foreign trader who might struggle with dinner party conversation in London can often 'click' within seconds with a hitherto unknown trader at a different bank in another country. Regardless of whether deals or conversations take place on the phone, via Bloomberg, on Reuters Dealing or through interdealer brokers across the world, misunderstandings are rare. Planet FX might be gigantic, but the population density is remarkably low and the inhabitants speak the same language.

From the outside, the FX market could also be seen as an extremely 'efficient' market, where traders behave rationally at all times. Following good news, traders immediately try to buy. Following bad news, traders immediately try to sell. The outcome of such an environment is that exchange rates always incorporate all relevant and available information (whether it is good news or bad news) immediately. If traders do not behave rationally, other traders immediately spot this and exploit the opportunity provided by a mispricing in the market. Furthermore, the irrational traders lose more and more money, so they either stop trading or are sacked. The market is left with the rational, emotionless traders who ensure that the FX market remains hyper-efficient.

This is the logic of the so-called efficient market hypothesis, developed by professor and Nobel laureate Eugene Fama. For decades, it has been part of the core curriculum at business schools and in economics faculties around the world. It is one of the theories in finance that truly has had a major impact – from students learning the basics of how financial markets work to policy makers and regulators assessing how markets can be made more efficient. Efficiency is, of course, seen as a good thing, as the opposite implies waste. From the outside, the FX market certainly *looks* efficient, a place where there should be little room for emotion – or, indeed, a special 'culture'.

However, in my experience, the FX market is far from hyper-efficient. Traders are not more rational than other people, and many are positively irrational.

From the Citibank Tokyo dealing room, we could see Mount Fuji when the weather was good. The image of the snow-capped mountain, the line of trees and the water has been reproduced on postcards endless times, and also features on the back of the ¥1,000 banknote. A trader I worked with claimed that whenever he was able to see the famous scene from his desk, he traded well and made money. When he could not, the opposite happened.

'Nowadays, I force myself not to trade when I cannot see Mount Fuji,' he told me.

I remember being perplexed by his explanation. Although I understood how important religious and cultural rituals were (even to traders), I had never come across someone admitting to something so irrelevant being of relevance to their trading strategy.

Professors in behavioural finance have long argued that the efficient market hypothesis makes unrealistic assumptions about human behaviour. In short, they argue that there is no room to account for psychology in the most influential theory on how traders should behave. In the real world, people are not always rational. Moreover, people tend to be irrational over and over again, and in similar ways. For instance, people often exaggerate how predictable things are. Sports betting companies know this all too well. Millions of people *think* they can predict the outcome of a particular football, hockey or baseball game, yet the bookmaker is always the long-term winner. Sometimes, people see patterns or are able to find predictability even when it is highly unlikely that they exist. The Tokyo trader happened to be a money-making machine, but I doubt if it had anything to do with the weather.

People also tend to be overconfident in their ability to estimate things precisely, and their level of overconfidence tends to increase in line with the difficulty of the problem in hand. Imagine having to guess whether the next person appearing around the street corner is a man or a woman; there are around 101 females to every 100 males in the world, which makes it a slightly uneven bet. The likely distribution might differ depending on the location and the time of day. However, unless you had thoroughly researched the area, guessing the right answer would be like flipping a coin. When I did my internship at Dresdner Bank, I was sent to a training camp in the German countryside to learn about FX and interest rate derivatives. This time around, the traders and sales people were much more senior and no plans to break into a bar were discussed. The boredom and frustration grew steadily, though, and after a few days the PIBOR futures trader decided that he had had enough and made his escape in his Porsche. I declined his kind offer of a lift back to Frankfurt. Not only was I working in the back office, I was a temporary member of staff and actually found the intensive course very interesting. On the nights not spent in my room, listening to Sonic Youth or Theatre of Hate on my Walkman, I tried to hang out with the traders and listen to their stories. One FX spot trader told me how they used to play the male/female guessing game when he used work in the New York office. The standard wager was $1,000. The game was not like roulette, which, of course, is completely random. Instead, it was *almost* random, which made it incredibly difficult to play with any degree of success. However, the game seemed to appeal to certain traders, particularly overconfident male traders like him. I cannot remember whether he had been a skilful player at this game, but given that he happily ordered and paid for round after round of drinks, I have a feeling that he must at least have felt like a winner.

In fact, overconfidence appears to be more common among men than women,[7] and also in professions where blame can easily be shifted to others if things go wrong. Given the limitless number of unforeseen circumstances in the financial markets, this shifting of blame comes almost instinctively to traders in the male-dominated dealing rooms. Blame is constantly apportioned to central banks, politicians, competitors, brokers, customers, sales people, back office staff, risk managers or interns. It is much more convenient to interpret information in a way that is beneficial to yourself, even when trying to be objective and unbiased. If you have bought a new car, information that contradicts how smart your purchase was is uncomfortable. Reading a car magazine praising your chosen model, on the other hand, feels great. The same applies to trading. If the market goes your way, it is like music to your ears. If the market goes against you, however, it is tempting to pick up the phone to someone who you know is on the same sinking ship so you can convince each other that you are right and the market is wrong.

I remember being reminded of this in the late 1990s, after gradually having increased my position in a specific type of interest rate swap. Confident that I was doing the right thing, and that everybody else in the market was blind to the magnificent trading idea I had formed in my mind, I kept on adding to my position. The fact that market prices then moved in my favour convinced me that I was right, and gave me further justification for adding a bit more to what was already a very large bet. One day, when the market suddenly stopped going my way, one of my managers came over to me. 'Your position is massive,' he said, red-faced, almost as if he had been waiting for this moment to arrive. 'You know which bank is on the other side of your trades. They are *professionals*. Have you thought about why they keep being on the opposite side?' I had, perhaps unconsciously, suppressed the thought that I was betting against very experienced traders who knew what they were doing. I might have scored a few goals in the first half of the match, but they had begun to detect a fragility in my defence. They could see my overconfidence had taken over, and had started to bet on the fact that the market (and my luck) would turn. I felt like a schoolboy being told by a teacher to stop doing dangerous tricks high up on a climbing frame. It was humiliating, but he was right. I reduced my positions and escaped with some minor scratches. I could recite countless more examples where I have traded irrationally as a result of exuberance, hope, regret or fear – or have witnessed colleagues or competitors doing so.

* * *

I saw a psychotherapist on a weekly basis from March 2009. Then, after two years, I stopped. I no longer felt a need to explore my inner thoughts by going to the sessions. Instead of sitting in the comfortable armchair and talking non-stop for 60 minutes, I had begun to ask more and more questions about psychology in general. I guess I had begun to learn some of the tools, or knew what the toolbox consisted of, should I ever need psychoanalytic theory again to solve personal problems.

I knew more about myself than she did. She, however, knew more about psychology, having spent years studying the subject and listening to people in the comfortable armchair.

Academics and experts in behavioural finance emphasise that investors and traders should be aware of their own – and others' – psychological biases and take them into account when trading. This makes perfect sense. The financial markets consist of human beings (or, increasingly, computer algorithms programmed by human beings), and human beings do not always behave rationally. However, even though this contradicts the efficient market hypothesis, proponents of the two different schools have one thing in common. Both tend to assume that traders act as market *takers* (approaching a market, which somehow already exists) rather than as market *makers* (creating that market). In other words, traders are seen as patients who either are rational or can learn to become more rational by visiting a therapist. Traders are not, themselves, the therapists.

Prices such as exchange rates are therefore seen as being generated by the interactions of a large number of day traders, investors, retirement planners and other customers approaching a market place that is somehow 'already there'. The profession of market *makers* tends to be ignored. I find this strange, because although few traders I know have received any formal training in psychology, if there is one thing market makers share, it is the ability – even the necessity – to 'read' the market. Market makers don't just sit in the comfortable armchair. They constantly switch roles between asking for prices and quoting prices, between knowing when to buy or sell and knowing when others want to buy from, or sell to, *them*.

Therefore, I have generally found that the strongest critics of the efficient market hypothesis are neither behavioural finance academics nor economists critical of conventional finance. Rather, they tend to be market makers quoting prices all day long, all the while not knowing in advance whether the other person is a buyer or a seller. They have spotted the theoretical flaws in a different way: by witnessing others (and themselves) losing money as a result of irrational behaviour. Constantly exposed to the psychology of the market, market makers develop skills that help them recognise predictable psychological flaws in others. Having the ability to read the market, or see behavioural patterns faster and more clearly, has obvious advantages. If you can detect fear, exuberance or hubris in others, you can incorporate it into your own quoting behaviour. Traders know this, and traders also know that *other* traders sometimes might be better informed about the likely direction of the market. If the other person trades on a two-way price you just quoted and bought from you, your price is quite likely to have been too low. It is unlikely that you would be able to buy it back from someone else without making a loss or hoping that the market would turn the other way. If the other person just sold to you, the price was probably too high. Once, a mortgage bond trader I was sitting close to was so delighted at having quoted a price that was left alone that he leapt up and raised his arms with joy. Having to quote a tight bid–offer price in a large amount to a fierce competitor in a volatile market could be nerve-racking, especially if your gut feeling told you that the other trader knew in what direction the market was heading. It was like trying to save a penalty kick by Cristiano Ronaldo. He must have felt like the best goalkeeper in the world at that moment.

Market making is not only about quoting prices to others, it also involves asking others for prices. Thus, market makers are both goalkeepers and strikers at the same time. As in sports, it is easier to win a contest if your opponent is weak. By the same token, if you are weak, or perceived to be weak, you opponent is more likely to launch an attack. Market makers are therefore good at spotting each other's weaknesses, and will sometimes use (or abuse) those weaknesses if and when the opportunity arises. In other words, just as market makers can learn how to detect and avoid their own habitual mistakes, they can learn to exploit the psychological flaws of others.

Market making does not come without its drawbacks, one of which is visibility. Other players *know* that market makers are able to suck up information and sentiment from the market by quoting prices throughout the day. This is one of the reasons why, when I was a trader, clients and sales people often tended to ask market makers for 'market colour' – a string of intangible factors that gave a feeling for the direction of the market. Sometimes this feeling was underpinned by real or potential trading activity. Sometimes it was just a gut instinct. Whatever its basis, market colour was a sought-after form of expert judgement that predominantly came from the market makers.

However, the existence of such market colour (regardless of whether it is revealed to others or not) can also lead to unwanted copycat behaviour. The logic goes like this. Because of fear or greed, other players try to imitate the actions of a market maker, who is presumed to have unique information. If the market maker buys, others try to buy. If the market maker sells, others sell. Consequently, executing a large amount can be difficult, as *others* figure out the market maker's intentions and jump the queue before the mission has been completed. What is more, competing market makers who have snapped up some information might warn others of an incoming attack. Brokers might be told that 'the Big German Guy is selling!' or that 'the Oil Tanker is out spraying the market in size!' Even without mentioning real names, market moving information spreads like wildfire in an environment where everyone knows everyone else. The market maker might therefore want to divert unwanted followers. Rather than attempting to execute a very large amount, which is immediately spotted and ultimately proves to be loss making, the market maker can turn copycat behaviour to their advantage. Instead of trying to sell a large amount, the market maker might *buy* a smaller amount via a broker. The broker, unaware of the market maker's true intentions, whispers to his best clients that 'the Big German Guy is out buying!' or just shout 'Taken!' down the speaker boxes to a number of dealing rooms around the world. Now, knowing that other traders have been warned of the opposite, the market maker begins to *sell* frenetically, taking advantage of the fact that other traders have read the market maker the wrong way: as a buyer rather than a seller. Trading techniques have also been refined to exploit the fact that human beings tend to be psychologically affected by real, observable and recent events – such as a fear of flying after a recent and widely reported plane crash. Traders have similar biases. If something special happens *for real* in the financial markets, players often adjust or anchor their perception of reality around that event. If a market maker puts in a ridiculously low bid – let's say '83' – with a broker, nobody takes any notice. A price at which nobody in his right mind would be prepared to sell is of little interest.

However, if another trader (perhaps conspiring with the market maker) suddenly decides to sell at that price, everyone is immediately alerted to the fact that the market has been 'given at 83!' The instinctive knowledge *that* the market has suddenly collapsed often has more impact than the knowledge of *why* this has happened. A similar logic applies to 'spoofing' and 'layering', which involves placing fictitious orders in the market with the purpose of influencing other traders' perception of the prevailing market. These could be seen as either clever trading tactics or outright deceptive behaviour.

When my ex-colleague pondered what might happen should regulators shift their investigations from LIBOR to FX, he was referring to an open secret – that numerous forms of bluffing (or double-bluffing) had been regarded more as 'trading techniques' than as 'deceptive and market abusive practices' in the FX market for as long as both of us could remember. There was no textbook, manual or crash course on the subject. Instead, poker tricks such as these were taught on the job, passed down from one generation of market makers to the next – informally, of course. Put differently, behaviour that would be unacceptable in, say, stock markets had long been cynically regarded as 'part of the game' in the global FX market. Although the culture was not considered criminal, it was not always considered ethical.

* * *

Recently, without thinking too much about it, I sent a LinkedIn request to my psychotherapist – not to book a session, but simply to add her as a 'friend' on social media. She declined, and wrote me a personal email instead. 'I saw your invitation on LinkedIn and just wanted to say thank you, but unfortunately it is leaning towards being unethical.' Having embarrassingly completely forgotten about the obvious patient–therapist relationship issue, I apologised. The boundary was clear – rather more so than has sometimes been the case in banking.

One of the banks' 'criminal activities', to paraphrase the FBI, related to how they had exploited some of their clients. In particular, banks had tried to trigger so-called 'stop-loss orders' to profit from them.

I still remember my first ever stop-loss order. I was a junior trader and my manager asked me to watch his position of 5 million deutschmarks against Swedish kronor during the day, and then to pass it on to another bank overnight. I cannot recall the prevailing exchange rate at the time or whether he was 'long' (betting that the market price would rise) or 'short' (betting that the market price would fall), but for the sake of simplicity let us assume that he was long 5 million deutschmarks and that the market exchange rate was trading at 5.0000. Thus, if the exchange rate appreciated by 1 per cent to 5.0500, he would make 50,000 worth of deutschmarks (250,000 Swedish kronor) and if the exchange rate depreciated by 1 per cent to 4.9500, he would lose the same amount. By leaving me a stop-loss order at, say, 4.9500, he instructed me to 'close the position' (do an opposite trade to eliminate the risk) should the market exchange rate fall to 4.9500. He could be assured that no matter how much the market moved against him, his maximum loss was capped at 250,000 Swedish kronor.

Nothing happened during my watch. It was nerve-racking, though, to stare at the flickering market prices that changed every second, perhaps dropping as low as 4.9580 but nevertheless not quite reaching the predefined level at which the ejector seat was to be activated. I sweated a lot, I couldn't leave the desk for a second, and I almost felt relieved when I could call the trader at the other bank and leave it all up to him. As we were not market makers in the specific currency pair at the time, I was treated more like a client (a patient) than a competitor (another clinic offering therapy sessions). However, nothing happened during New York trading hours either, and the stop-loss order was passed to Hong Kong. In the morning, the trader called me up to say that nothing had happened overnight, and that the order could therefore be cancelled and passed back to me. I started watching again.

Leaving a stop-loss order overnight should have enabled me to relax, as the worst-case scenario was limited. In all honesty, though, I don't think I slept at all that night. I was way too nervous that the stop-loss might be triggered and that I would have to deliver the sad news to my manager that he had lost money. However, the downside was limited. The trader at the other bank had guaranteed that if the market moved to 4.9500 (the predefined level), he would do a trade with me at that price before the market had time to move even further. If so, the hot potato became his problem. If he then believed that the market would drop further – to 4.9200, say – he would sell the 5 million to someone else. If he believed the market would rebound, he would keep it, hoping to make a profit at some later stage.

Banks receive numerous stop-loss orders from clients, but also 'take-profit orders' (assume that my manager wanted to close his position at a *profit* should the exchange rate move to 5.0500). They offer this service free of charge.

Why would a market maker voluntarily absorb the fear and anxiety of customers and other traders for free? An important factor is information. Being able to (almost secretly) read the cards of customers and other traders is a valuable asset: for example, a Swedish car company's position in US dollars against Swedish kronor or a mobile phone manufacturer's position in British pounds against South Korean won. Such orders add up to information about the supply and demand of the market. If nine clients leave stop-loss orders to protect them from lower prices and only one client the opposite, it appears as if the client base (and perhaps the whole market) is 'long': in other words, they are betting that the market will rise. In that case, an unexpected collapse in the price would trigger a string of stop-loss sales, causing the market to plummet. Similarly, if many orders (or large orders) are given within a certain price range – 4.9000 to 5.1000, for instance – they indicate that such price levels are particularly sensitive. If these levels, for whatever reason, are reached, sharp market movements will follow.

Generally, we tend to think about markets being driven by the buying and selling of products. Prices then fluctuate according to the 'real' buying and selling. Stop-loss and take-profit orders are somewhat different, because they are not actual trades until they are executed – and most of them never are. They are, however, very important in revealing what clients want to do *if* something happens in the future: 'If the euro falls below 1.10 against the US dollar, I want to buy €10 million' or 'If the Swiss franc rises to 3.30 against the Brazilian real, I want to sell 15 million francs.'

The problem is that a market maker with a substantial client order book could, technically, ensure that the 'if' happens. This is where the unethical part comes in. Let us return to my own stop-loss order above. If the market had been trading at, say,

4.9520 in Asia (when I was desperately trying to get some sleep in Europe), a bit of selling might have been enough to push it down to 4.9500, at which stage the bank with which I had left my order would automatically have executed my order to sell 5 million to *them*. It would not matter if the market then immediately bounced back to 4.9520. The bank would already have booked a profit by having sold to someone else at 4.9520 and having bought them from me at 4.9500. Triggering a stop-loss is a manipulative technique to ensure that the 'if' happens, even if it is just for a very brief moment in time.

'Love them … free money … we love the orders … always make money on them,' an HSBC trader had told a colleague according to transcripts released by the UK financial regulator, following a string of fines imposed upon a handful of major banks. To traders at other banks, an HSBC trader had said: 'Going to go for broke at this stop … it is either going to end in massive glory or tears' and 'Just about to slam some stops.'[8]

Not all orders in the FX market relate to *if* something happens. Orders can also reveal what clients want to do *when* something happens in the future: for instance, 'When it is 4 o'clock in London, I want to buy £20 million against euros.' In other words, clients not only give take-profit or stop-loss orders to banks, but also specific orders to buy and sell various currencies at a particular moment during the day.

This type of order is widely used in the global FX market. The so-called WM/Reuters 4 p.m. fix is the world's most widely referenced FX benchmark. In contrast to LIBOR, where banks *argue* about the level of a price, the 4 p.m. fix is based on actual FX trading by market participants just before and just after 4 p.m. London time. This foreign exchange benchmark, like LIBOR, has become increasingly important over the years. From having mainly been used for valuation purposes, it is now used not only in a range of derivative instruments and other contracts, but also by clients as a trustworthy and 'official' closing rate for a range of currency pairs. The market continues to trade after the fixing. However, given that around 40 per cent of the global foreign exchange turnover takes place in London, and that the FX market conventionally 'closes' at 4 p.m. (i.e. it then shifts to New York), it appears to be a cleverly chosen snapshot in order to capture the market when it is very liquid. Bundling as much buying and selling as possible into one minute gives clients time to focus on other important matters during the rest of the day.

'Banging the close' is a technique to try to influence a benchmark, such as the 4 p.m. fix. Rather than trying to buy or sell in order to push the exchange rate to a level at which a stop-loss order gets triggered, it involves trying to buy or sell in order to push the exchange rate as far as possible in one direction or the other at a specific time during the day.

This might, or might not, involve collaboration between several market makers. Assume that three fictitious traders, Andy, Bruce and Charlie, despite working for three banks in fierce competition with each other, happen to be good friends. A pension fund has placed an order to *buy* €200 million against US dollars from Andy at 4 p.m. A life insurance company has placed an order to *buy* €20 million from Bruce, also at 4 p.m. And a dishwasher manufacturer has placed an order to *sell* €50 million to Charlie. Looking at the order books, it is clear that Andy would prefer a very high 4 p.m. fix as he will sell €200 million to the client at whatever the closing rate will be. Bruce has the same interest, although he will sell only €20 million. Charlie, however, would prefer a low 4 p.m. fix, as he will buy €50 million from the dishwasher manufacturer. Andy and Bruce, in other words, have the same incentive, whereas Charlie has the opposite incentive. Andy and Bruce will do whatever it takes to achieve a high exchange rate at 4 p.m. Charlie, however, will try to push it lower. But all three are friends, and they don't want to deliberately cause each other losses or missed opportunities in order to make money.

Given Charlie's limited amount of ammunition (€50 million versus Andy and Bruce's combined €220 million), he would be the likely loser. Therefore, he could give a €50 million buy order to Andy that perfectly offsets the one he has received from the dishwasher manufacturer. Andy would then have sell orders worth €150 million, Bruce would still have sell orders worth €20 million, but Charlie would effectively have nothing left. Instead, he can sit back and watch the action from a comfortable armchair.

It could also be that David, a fourth market maker, has the opposite interest. If that is the case, Andy might wish to reduce his exposure further (from €150 million to, say, €90 million) to 'clear the decks' or to 'take out the filth' from the market – in other words, to prevent other market makers from working against him and Bruce.

'Hopefully taking all the filth out for you ... hopefully decks bit cleaner,' a Barclays trader told a UBS trader, having matched €196 million worth of orders to help his friend ahead of a benchmark fixing on 15 February 2012.[9]

Ultimately, the large banks get the vast majority of orders and are therefore able to benefit from superior information.

Moreover, the larger the orders, the greater the potential there is to make more money. Another tactic would therefore be to 'build ammo', where orders are actively increased to create an even stronger desire to make the 'if' or 'when' happen. Bruce, with orders worth €20 million in the example above, might transfer his orders to give Andy even more ammunition ahead of the fixing battle.

* * *

One afternoon, the following scenario was played out on the FX spot desk at HSBC (with spelling mistakes as they were typed in the chatroom forum), according to transcripts released by the FCA.[10]

3.25 p.m.: HSBC has orders to sell £400 million against US dollars, and Bank A has sell orders worth £150 million. 'Let's go,' HSBC tells Bank A. 'Yeah baby.'

3.28 p.m.: 'Hopefulyl a few more get same way and we can team whack it,' Bank A says. HSBC asks Bank C to do some 'digging' to see if anyone else has orders in the same direction.

3.34 p.m.: Bank C has sell orders worth £83 million.

3.36 p.m.: Bank A now has sell orders worth £170 million and Bank B has £40 million in the same direction. Bank D steps into the conversation and exclaims: 'Bash the fck out of it.'

3.42 p.m.: Bank A warns HSBC that Bank E is 'building' in the opposite direction to them and will be buying at the fix.

3.43 p.m.: Bank A tells HSBC, '[I have] taken him [Bank E] out ... so shud have giot rid of main buyer for u ... im stilla seller of 90 [million] ... gives us a chance.'

Between 3.32.00 p.m. and 3.59.00 p.m. that day, HSBC sold £70 million against US dollars, and the exchange rate fell from 1.6044 to 1.6009.

Between 3.59.01 p.m. and 3.59.05 p.m., HSBC sold a further £101 million, and the exchange rate fell to 1.6000.

Between 3.59.06 p.m. and 4.01.00 p.m., HSBC sold £210 million.

The WM/Reuters 4 p.m. fix rate for British pounds against US dollars fixes at 1.6003.

A client naturally hopes – even expects – that their foreign exchange orders will be executed in a competitive market. Given a turnover of $5.1 trillion per day, it would be difficult to think otherwise. However, during the crucial minutes before and after 4 p.m., HSBC accounted for 51 per cent of turnover in the market in the currency pair above. If one bank is able to exercise such power, even if it is just for a few minutes, it gives the bank a significant advantage in influencing the price in a direction that is amenable to the bank rather than the client.

According to the UK financial regulator,[11] HSBC had a financial motive to manipulate the market, the profit from doing so amounting to $162,000. A large sum, but small when considering that this was only one bank and one currency pair on one specific day. The losses obviously did not disappear into thin air. Instead, they ended up elsewhere – with HSBC's clients or others involved in the foreign exchange market. Given the vast number of client orders in the FX market, it would be difficult to determine how much has been transferred from clients and other market participants to the large banks systematically in this way. Like any amount in the global foreign exchange market, it would, however, probably be quite substantial.

Thus, the FX market has never consisted of purely rational traders. Even in the largest market on earth, psychology has always mattered. While this makes the FX market more 'human' than many outsiders might think, it also creates an ethical problem. Unless there are rules and enforcement mechanisms for what kind of behaviour is right and what kind of behaviour is wrong, the market can evolve into a culture in which almost any behaviour is tolerated, perhaps even encouraged.

'We self-detected this matter and reported it to the US Department of Justice and other authorities. Our actions demonstrate our determination to pursue a policy of zero tolerance for misconduct and a desire to promote the right culture in our industry.' This is what UBS Chairman Axel Weber and CEO Sergio Ermotti said in a joint press release after regulators subjected UBS to a large fine for manipulating the FX market. 'The conduct of a small number of employees was unacceptable and we have taken appropriate disciplinary actions.'[12]

The official statement by UBS suggested that it was the bank which had discovered that the FX spot desk had gone rogue. Despite it being one of the most prominent and vocal desks in any dealing room (FX spot dealers can be loud sometimes), up until this point 'the bank' had not overheard any of their conversations and had, so it claimed, been totally unaware that the behaviour of its dealers had transgressed the morals, norms and conventions of the market and of society as a whole.

I have never worked for UBS and therefore cannot comment on the culture of its FX spot desk. However, having done trades worth trillions of US dollars with UBS over the years, and having sat within metres of various FX spot desks for 15 years, the idea that the issue concerned only a few traders seems far-fetched. A scandal of such magnitude rarely evolves in such isolation.

A trading desk is not an island within a bank. The personal space in a dealing room is minuscule, which means that even in a vast dealing room you sit fairly close to everyone else. The FX spot desk tends to be located very close to the FX options and FX swap desks. This is logical, because even though the traders focus on different types of contracts, they all relate to foreign exchange. The FX spot desk focuses on agreements to buy or sell currencies *now* (generally in two business days' time, to be precise). The FX options desk, often located next to the FX spot desk, trades derivatives that give the buyer the right, but not the obligation, to buy or sell currencies at a specific price at some time in the *future*. The FX swap desk deals with agreements to buy or sell currencies in the future (FX forwards), as well as combinations of FX spot and FX forward transactions done simultaneously, but in the opposite direction (FX swaps). The FX swap desk tends to be located close to the money market or interest rate swap desks, or maybe even integrated into a STIRT desk trading LIBOR-indexed derivatives. Bond trading desks might also be nearby, whereas commodities and equities are situated further away. The seating arrangement in a dealing room is as meticulously organised as a wedding party. And as at weddings, people tend to mingle, switch seats, go out to smoke, powder their noses in the washroom, or listen to rumours told elsewhere.

Trading desks are also connected to trading desks at other banks. Traders trade with each other, talk to each other, learn from each other. Traders constantly move: in, up or out. The layout of the dealing rooms in the major banks is very similar, regardless of where they are located. It might take traders some time to familiarise themselves with the IT systems and to get to know new people, but everything else follows a logical pattern. Most dealing rooms have around five clocks on one wall, showing the time in a selection of international financial centres such as Sydney, Hong Kong, Tokyo, London and New York. Most dealing rooms lack vast collections of books, magazines and newspapers containing yesterday's news. Instead, computer screens ensure that the focus is on current and future news. Even though some trading desks can be loud, carpets and a trend towards electronic trading act to reduce the noise levels. Traders are expected to start performing quickly. As in competitive team sports, you are not given a full season to acclimatise to a new bank and a new dealing room; rather, you must find your feet in a matter of weeks. Unless you are a trainee, you are expected to have received your 'training' elsewhere.

There is no official educational background or diploma required to become an FX trader in a bank. Although a degree in finance, economics or another quantitative subject increasingly tends to be desired (and is now often standard), numerous FX traders I used to work with or against had come in via other routes. They had spent their youth studying medieval history or biology or did not go to university at all. Many traders came in from secondary school, the back office, the army or the rugby club. If trading is difficult to learn, it is even more difficult to teach. Diversity is therefore natural.

There is, however, one kind of foreign exchange trading certificate or diploma that *has* been around for years. Since 1975, the International Code of Conduct and Practice for the Financial Markets (or simply the Model Code) has worked as an industry standard for the global FX and money markets. It is published by the ACI (more commonly known as Forex), which, since 1955, has acted as the trade organisation for banks and central bank dealers in the FX and money markets around the world. Forex also issues 'Dealing Certificates' following an exam process. The following question appeared in the Forex Association London Diploma exam in June 1995:

> You have a position, long of USD [*US Dollars*] against GBP [*British pounds*]. The market has moved your way and is being quoted 1.6085–1.6095. A bank calls for a cable [*British pounds against US dollars*] price and you are thinking of closing your position. Which of these prices would you quote?

a) 1.6085–95
b) 1.6080–90
c) 1.6088–98
d) 1.6083–93

The question is directed at a potential FX spot market maker (not a client of the bank). To answer it, you first need to take into account that you are 'long' US dollars, which automatically means that you are 'short' British pounds. If you are thinking about closing your position, you therefore need to sell US dollars and buy British pounds. (You also need to know that the currency pair is quoted in terms of how many dollars can be bought or sold for one pound, rather than how many pounds can be bought or sold for one dollar.) Because you are the market maker, you want to *tempt* the other bank to deal at your price, while quoting a price that is *as beneficial as possible* to you. If you opt for the same quote as the rest of the market, i.e. 1.6085–95, your quote is not tempting enough. If you go with 1.6080–90 or 1.6083–93, you show the other bank that you are keen to sell British pounds for fewer US dollars than the rest of the market. However, you want to show the opposite interest: that you are prepared to pay more dollars for your pounds. The correct answer is therefore 1.6088–98.

Although a real trading scenario would include additional aspects that ought to be taken into account when quoting a price, the question captures one element of market making very well: market makers do not always want to 'win' a trade. Sometimes, the status quo can be good, which is why acting like a chameleon and mimicking the others by quoting 1.6085–95 could be an option for a trader who is *not* thinking about closing their position.

However, the question also contains an oddity. Why not quote, say, 1.6088–96 or 1.6088–99? Why do all four possible answers contain different prices, but *exactly* the same bid–offer spread? The figures 85–95, 80–90, 88–98 and 83–93 all represent ten 'pips'. Why ten pips and not eight, nine or eleven? More importantly, perhaps, does the fourth decimal really matter? Well, currently, the average *daily* turnover in the global FX spot market for British pounds against US dollars stands at around £175 billion.[13] One pip represents $17,500,000 per day. Assuming 252 trading days per year, this figure becomes $4,410,000,000. Expanding the calculation exercise to other currency pairs and types of FX contracts would yield a phenomenally large amount. Even the slightest change in the bid–offer spread matters. On balance, a wider spread is good for market makers (banks) and a narrower spread is good for market takers (everybody else).

The phenomenon that prices, or bid–offer spreads, often tend to cluster around numbers ending with 0 or 5 more frequently than, say, 7 or 8 is referred to as the 'round number effect', whereby human beings put greater emphasis on digits and numbers that are easier to process. Given the numerical system we are used to, ten – or multiples of ten – is much easier to handle than nine or eleven. This observation has also been shown to be prevalent in the FX market.[14] A psychological explanation for this kind of behaviour might lie in the desire to look for approximate 'anchors' when exact precision might be difficult.[15]

Another theory explaining such behaviour is the 'price resolution hypothesis'. Some researchers argue, plausibly, that volatile markets force market makers to form some kind of grid, or price matrix, in their brains.[16] It is simply too complicated and time-consuming to think about which bid–offer spread is appropriate each time you quote a price. The market is too fast and there is too much to think about. Therefore, market makers follow a self-imposed pattern in order to quote and transact faster.

The third option is that there is some kind of *conspiracy*.

* * *

When HSBC was fined by the FCA in the previous example, the regulator pointed out that manipulative practices were not confined to HSBC alone. Confidential information was shared with other banks about the clients and their identities; these clients included central banks, large corporates, pension funds and hedge funds. It was often a team effort, involving traders at banks that ought to be competing with each other.

Judging by some of the traders' comments in the chatroom after 4 o'clock, released by the regulators, the tactics worked well for the banks involved in the conspiracy: 'Nice work gents … I don my hat', 'Hooray nice team work', 'Bravo … cudnt been better', 'Have that my son … v nice mate', 'Dont mess with our ccy [currency]' and 'There you go … go early, move it, hold it, push it'. The HSBC trader also sounded pleased: 'Loved that mate … worked lovely … pity we couldn't get it below the 00 [1.6000]'; 'We need a few more of those for me to get back on track this month.'

Sometimes, secret code words were used instead of real names. In fact, not only did traders use secret code words and nicknames for individual clients and other traders in the market, nicknames such as 'The Bandits Club, 'The 3 Musketeers', '1 Team, 1 Dream', 'A Co-operative', 'The A-team', 'Sterling

Lads' or 'The Mafia' could also be applied to various teams of foreign exchange traders from different banks specialising in a particular currency pair. For instance, a group called 'The Cartel' had members from Barclays, Citi, J. P. Morgan, RBS and UBS. Membership in the electronic chatroom was by invitation only, and required particular expertise in euros against US dollars. Information sharing came with benefits, of course, and when a Barclays trader desperately requested to join the club in 2011, existing members pondered whether he 'would add value'. He received a one-month trial membership, but was told 'mess this up and sleep with one eye open at night'. (The Barclays trader ultimately passed the test.)[17]

In other words, it could also be that banks secretly agreed upon which bid–offer spreads they promise to quote to each other in the FX market – and to their clients. In the stock market, such behaviour would be problematic. For instance, in the US, Section 1 of the Sherman Anti-Trust Act prohibits contracts, combinations and conspiracies in restraint of trade. These can refer to spoken *or* unspoken agreements. A potential conspiracy with regards to bid–offer spreads in financial markets was brought to light during the 1990s. Two academics found that market makers on the NASDAQ stock exchange tended to quote stocks in increments of one-quarter and one-half dollars rather than, say, three-eighths or five-eighths of a dollar.[18] This prompted the question as to whether they tacitly colluded to maintain wide bid–offer spreads. The scandal resulted in a regulatory investigation, significant financial settlements and new rules relating to transparency.[19] Following the reforms, savers and investors who bought and sold stocks on NASDAQ were seen as winners. The archives from that scandal reveal that market makers generally treated the convention as a 'pricing ethic, tradition, or professional norm that other market makers were expected to follow'.[20] Some traders even testified that they had been trained by senior staff to follow this convention. A failure to comply with the 'unwritten rules' sometimes led to harassment or a refusal to trade by other market makers. In the end, the SEC and the Department of Justice decided not to refer to the convention as 'an express agreement reached among all of the market makers in a smoke-filled room'. Instead, the behaviour failings were seen as a convention that 'had anticompetitive consequences and was harmful to the interests of investors'.[21]

In 2014, the European Commission fined a handful of market makers for agreeing:

> to quote to all third parties wider, fixed bid–offer spreads on certain categories of short-term over-the-counter Swiss franc interest rate derivatives, whilst maintaining narrower spreads for trades amongst themselves. The aim of the agreement was to lower the parties' own transaction costs and maintain liquidity between them whilst seeking to impose wider spreads on third parties. Another objective of the collusion was to prevent other market players from competing on the same terms as these four major players in the Swiss franc derivatives market.

In this case, the collective behaviour of RBS, UBS, J. P. Morgan and Crédit Suisse was classified as a cartel. Joaquín Almunia, Commission Vice-President in charge of competition policy, said in the press release that:

unlike in previous cartels we found in the financial sector, this one did not involve any collusion on a benchmark [*such as LIBOR*]. Rather, the four banks agreed on an element of the price of certain financial derivatives. This way, the banks involved could flout the market at their competitors' expense. Cartels in the financial sector, whatever form they take, will not be tolerated.[22]

In competition law, therefore, the bid–offer spread is seen as a 'price component' or 'an element of a price' – the equivalent of a bicycle chain or computer keyboard, for example. It is illegal for a group of computer manufacturers to conspire and fix prices for their PCs, as it is for their keyboards.

Legal scholars, therefore, seem to agree that if companies stand in competition with each other (such as computer manufacturers or banks), they should not collude to agree upon a predefined price component or bid–offer spread. Instead, it should be determined *competitively*. In 2015, the Bank of England, the UK Treasury and the FCA published a joint assessment of the financial markets following the manipulation scandals. In the *Fair and Effective Markets Review*, the message is clear; it states that 'no distinction is made between wholesale and retail markets, or between FICC [fixed income, currencies and commodities] and non-FICC markets' with regards to UK and EU competition law. The report specifically stressed that it 'also applies to financial markets, including FX spot, which may currently fall outside of the direct scope of financial market regulation'.[23]

In fact, a class action has already been filed in the US in which the claimants (a long list of clients in the FX market) allege that the defendants conspired to fix bid–offer spreads for various currency pairs in the FX spot market. Such collusive practices, it is argued, have acted to deprive their clients of active price competition, resulting in higher prices. Moreover, given that FX spot prices are often used as *components* in a range of other FX instruments, clients entering into, for instance, FX forward or FX futures contracts would also have been harmed. The defendants in this lawsuit are familiar names: Bank of America, Bank of Tokyo-Mitsubishi, Barclays, BNP, Citi, Credit Suisse, Deutsche Bank, Goldman Sachs, HSBC, JPMorgan Chase, Morgan Stanley, RBC, RBS, Société Générale, Standard Chartered and UBS.[24]

* * *

At the time traders were sitting the Forex exam in 1995, did traders in the FX spot market for British pounds against US dollars actually quote each other ten pips? I cannot remember, but presumably they did. Whoever wrote the exam paper must either have been a dealer or had checked with a market maker that the question was realistic enough. Bid–offer spreads in the FX and money markets not only tend to cluster around a few digits, but are also remarkably 'sticky' over time. If '10' is the prevailing spread, it often remains unchanged for weeks, months or sometimes even years. In that sense, some price components in the FX markets are like matrices, which are 'recalibrated' over time. However, it is not an automatic process. It always involves human behaviour. And humans tend to interact with each other. From the outside, the FX market might seem too large, liquid, efficient and competitive to be of interest to antitrust authorities. Yet many aspects point towards the complete opposite: a market that is concentrated among very few traders who habitually talk to each other.

Why would a group of competing traders voluntarily talk to and trust each other? Apart from the obvious reason that human beings are social animals, I believe an important reason in the FX and money markets in particular relates to 'reciprocity', sometimes referred to as one of the oldest forms of human co-ordination.

The structure of the FX and money markets differs in many ways from that of the stock market. For instance, stocks are traded on an exchange and therefore 'centralised'. The FX and money markets are decentralised, which requires co-ordination to take place in a different way. The stock market has set opening hours and is driven by orders coming into the market. The opening hours of the FX and money markets are more fluid and dependent on market makers' willingness to quote prices. In the stock market, it is easy to work out what a trader's or a bank's inventory or exposure is at all times. It is possible to have zero holdings in Apple shares. A bank cannot, however, have zero exposure to 'money'. In the stock market, investors and traders try to value companies, which is why insiders who can access secret or non-public information might be able to get an advantage over others. In the FX and money markets, it is extremely difficult to define what kind of non-public information could potentially move the market. In fact, the kind of insider information that could fall within this grey zone is also something that makes these markets unique. Importantly, the FX and money markets, despite often symbolising free and unregulated markets, have an inherent link to the state. All money market instruments have a natural anchor in the official central bank interest rate. For example, from 30 January to 21 February 2006, more than half of all panel banks submitted a three-month US dollar LIBOR rate of *precisely* 4.570 per cent on every single day. It could be that these banks had formed a conspiracy and that the actual LIBOR rate should have been different on at least one of those days. However, unless market participants expected that the Federal Reserve would change the official interest rate in the near future, and unless any changes took place with regards to liquidity or credit risk, a more plausible scenario is that banks simply submitted the same rate as the day before. The competing banks did not need to communicate with each other to achieve such price harmonisation. Simply knowing the prevailing central bank rate (which was public information) and being aware of what LIBOR quotes the other banks had submitted the previous day (which also was public information) were enough for this to happen.

Another difference that makes the FX and money markets special relates to secrecy and transparency. As we already know, this was particularly true with LIBOR, where individual prices were neither tradeable nor had to be backed up by evidence of any trading activity taking place at the submitted quote. Prices in FX and money *markets* cannot be compared directly with LIBOR, which is an interest rate *benchmark*. There are, nonetheless, important similarities. As the economists Joseph Stiglitz and Bruce Greenwald point out, 'interest rates are not like conventional prices and the capital market is not like an auction market'.[25] Ultimately, prices in markets involving borrowing and lending depend on judgements around creditworthiness and access to liquidity. Such markets, therefore, become highly dependent on *relationships*. It could be the relationship between a borrower and a lender. It could be the relationship between a bank and a central bank. It could also be the relationship between a bank and another bank, or a trader and another trader.

It is impossible to assess whether the market will go up or down, or whether the other trader or client wants to buy or sell, ahead of every price you quote. You have only a few seconds to think. Often, you have to rely on your instinct, which includes a psychological assessment of the situation at hand. However, it is also impossible to assess what the liquidity will be like a millisecond after you have quoted the price. What if you suddenly end up with a hot potato and, when you try to get rid of it, every single counterparty refuses to quote you a price? What if the market liquidity, to which you and the other market makers are contributing, for some reason suddenly dries up like a desert? There is not enough time to forecast what the liquidity might be like the next second, hour or day. You have to rely on your instincts and, crucially, your assessment of the other market makers' instincts. As a result, the market tends to function as long as market makers are willing to quote each other prices. Banks are market makers and liquidity providers in the FX and money markets. However, in order to be able to be market makers and liquidity providers, banks require *other banks* to also be market makers and liquidity providers. It is a game based on reciprocity and trust.

There are few *written* rules about reciprocity and trust; rather, they are more the widely accepted norms – something that is 'the right thing to do'. The 'run-throughs' I mentioned earlier are a perfect example of such a norm. One of the first things I learned when becoming a market maker in FX swaps was to interpret and trade on, but also *provide*, run-throughs.

A sequence of numbers shouted down the speaker box by a broker first thing in the morning – '115-210-280-510-690-825', say – would indicate a series of FX swap bid prices in a specific currency pair for different maturities that could be dealt on. It meant that another market maker had kicked off that day's market by generously providing an interdealer broker with a set of prices that could be passed on to all their clients, which invariably included all the other market-making banks. The prices were valid for only a few seconds, which meant that, as a trader, you had to be quick if you wanted to trade on any of them. If the broker shouted 'Off, one-month given at 115!' it meant that someone else had been quick and had dealt at 115, after which the prices could no longer be dealt on. The original market maker might then provide a new, perhaps different, run-through. Or maybe another market maker would step in to have a go. There was no *requirement* to provide run-throughs. However, it was a way to support or *make* a market that essentially did not exist until prices were quoted in it. To provide prices – in other words, liquidity – in a market in which the banks were actively involved, without having any guarantee that others would do the same, was seen as the right thing to do. If you didn't do it, why would anyone else?

Reciprocity and trust are endorsed by the trade organisation Forex. The latest version of the ACI Model Code, published in February 2015, states that 'bilateral reciprocal dealing relationships are common in the OTC markets and often extend to unwritten understandings between Dealers to quote firm two-way dealing prices'. Further, the Model Code states that such informal reciprocal dealing relationships are to be 'encouraged' and are 'a logical development in the OTC markets and play an important role in providing support and liquidity'.[26] The trade organisation (whose motto is 'Once a dealer, always a dealer') sees such informal agreements as natural, to be encouraged in order to maintain trust, reciprocity and liquidity in the market place. However, it does not state specifically how these informal agreements ought to be achieved. The logic not only seems to encourage mutual understandings between competitors, it also turns a blind eye to the fact that trust and reciprocity are difficult to obtain unless market makers are allowed to talk to each other. How do you build trust in an environment where you cannot communicate with one another?

The bid–offer spread illustrates this well. In economic theory, a market maker should take into account various costs when quoting a two-way price. A volatile or uncertain market, for instance, should imply a wider spread, as it might be more costly to close out a position in such a market. The same goes for an illiquid market: the more such potential costs are added, the wider the spread should be. At the same time, competition between market makers should force this spread to be as tight as possible at each moment in time.

The question is whether this theory works in *practice*. During the late 1990s, three academics conducted a survey among more than 500 (mostly rather senior) FX dealers in Hong Kong, Singapore, Tokyo and New York, and asked what the main driver was when choosing the interbank spread.[27] Interestingly, fewer than one-third of the respondents argued in favour of 'potential costs', whereas two-thirds went along with the 'market convention'. The main reason for following the market convention appears to have been to maintain an 'equitable and reciprocal trading relationship'. Other important drivers were 'market image' and 'firm policy'. Fewer than a tenth of the respondents claimed that 'trading profits' were the main driver for following the market convention. Unfortunately, following the FX scandals, it might be difficult to conduct a similar survey today. Nonetheless, the responses demonstrate how FX and money market makers have felt a 'sense of duty' towards the bank and its competitors with regards to liquidity provision. Traders are influenced by the prevailing market practice.

Indeed, the number sequence '115-210-280-510-690-825' in the example above contained only bid prices. Often, but not always, the prevailing bid–offer spread was presumed to be known. The broker might even add 'with standard bid–offer spreads', confirming that the bank which had provided the prices assumed that all competitors knew which spreads were to be applied. A bid price of 115 might mean an offer price of 120, assuming the bid–offer spread was 5; '5' had become a convention that was supposed to last until, for some reason, it broke down.

Violating the market convention, for instance by suddenly quoting a very wide bid–offer spread or not quoting a price at all, would have breached a (mostly unwritten) policy outlined by management to support the market in a certain way. It might simultaneously have tarnished the image of the trader, the desk and the bank. Violating the market convention would also have harmed the relationship with other banks and their traders, and might ultimately have resulted in sanctions or retaliation. Such sanctions could involve more limited access to liquidity in the market. This, in turn, would have led to less profit, less client business and possibly even a withdrawal from the market-making function. Violating the market convention was like shooting yourself in the foot.

Or so I thought. Towards the end of my trading career, a competitor suddenly decided to double, and then quadruple, the spread they quoted me. I did not want to retaliate. But within hours, every other market maker had followed this new 'convention'. As a result of the extraordinarily wide bid–offer spreads, the market virtually died. This was bad news for me, but good news for some of the other market makers who had the opposite position to me. I was furious. But there was, of course, nothing I could do about it. Market conventions were not regulated. And market conventions did not necessarily reflect what would be best for the market as a whole. As with most things in these markets, the conventions were ultimately decided by relatively few, yet powerful, banks.

* * *

When, in 1993, I was taught to trade T-bills and bonds, there was no official rule book on how to call out for Swedish T-bills. The guidelines were more formal than children's playground rules, but the enforcement mechanism if or when you broke them was anything but. A year later, when I quoted my first price in the FX market, I received similar guidelines and instructions from more senior traders. However, there was no involvement by any authority when it came to settling disputes. Instead, this was based on the overriding principle that the game was 'tough' but that the players would keep it 'fair'. A player quoting slow or wide prices could expect slow and wide prices back. A player refusing to quote amounts agreed by everybody else could expect to find it difficult to close large positions in the future. Invariably, a player not adhering to the social norms could expect to receive less valuable information, be treated with less consideration and occasionally even be excluded from social events. The enforcement mechanism was based on retaliation – or, more precisely, the *fear* of retaliation.

'Individuals may participate in social norms in part because of an expectation that others will also participate,' Dean Harley wrote in the *California Law Review*.[28] Richard McAdams, also with a law background, defines social norms as 'informal social regularities that individuals feel obligated to follow because of an internalized sense of duty, because of a fear of external non-legal sanctions, or both'.[29]

There is nothing inherently 'wrong' with social norms – think of shaking hands, bowing, saying sorry, please and thank you. Just as there is nothing wrong in theory with a market maker calling a competitor for a price in an 11-month foreign exchange swap either. It is just that, for most currency pairs, you are *supposed to* stick only to certain maturities, the closest in this case being nine months or 12 months.

Similarly, there is nothing wrong with a London-based market maker calling a London-based competitor for a price after 4 p.m. It is just that you are *supposed to* respect local opening hours (the London close, the New York open, etc.) even if the market trades 24/7.

Nor is there anything wrong with a market maker calling a competitor for a price in Swiss francs against US dollars. It is just that you are *supposed to* ask the other way round: US dollars against Swiss francs.

There are many more such social norms and market conventions that, for example, govern how fast you are *supposed to* quote, the language you are *supposed to* use, how often you are *supposed to* restrict yourself from calling other market makers, how you are *supposed to* treat interdealer brokers or how large each trade ticket is *supposed to* be. With few formal rules and regulations, and the constant uncertainty in financial markets, such *conventions* become extremely important. Market conventions act to settle disputes quickly and prevent anarchy in an environment that otherwise would be very susceptible to collapse. Market conventions also allow expectations about the future to be harmonised and to become somewhat orderly – at least to a degree. However, it would be a misunderstanding to think that the sheer size of the FX market, or indeed the LIBOR-indexed derivatives market, automatically means that it is competitive. It would also be a misunderstanding to believe that the *whole* market has been involved in shaping its social norms, informal rules and practices over the years. Banks have always been in the driving seat. Market conventions might, of course, change at any time. However, if they become attached to the daily trading routine, or part of the glue that binds the industry together, participants in the market become increasingly confident that they are relevant and valid.[30] They become part of the 'culture', to borrow a term from the UBS press release following the revelation of the bank's involvement in the FX scandal.

A common theme with the markets and benchmarks that have been the subject of scandals in recent years is that they have largely been unregulated and lacked transparency. This, however, does not mean that they have lacked 'rules'. It is just that many of the social practices and conventions have evolved without intrusion by governments or regulators.

When I was having the previously mentioned conversation with the managing director about the possible ramifications of uncovering the truth of the FX market, he continued by saying: 'On the other hand, the biggest manipulators of all are the central banks. They bully the market all the time.'

The fact that central banks, which are ultimately responsible for printing a country's money, could use their foreign exchange reserves to intervene in the market, argue in favour of capital controls to prevent FX trading from taking place, or influence exchange rates by changing the interest rates or issuing biased press releases, he saw as evidence that the market would never be subject to a thorough investigation. If the banks were to be found guilty of putting grains of sand into the machinery of the free markets, surely the central banks should take some blame? If this ended up being classified as a conspiracy, surely it would go all the way to the top? The central banks might not have had a vote in deciding how the market conventions evolved, but given their importance as stakeholders in the markets relating to the concept of money, they were often invited as 'observers'.

Whenever I was asked to fill out a survey or questionnaire by a central bank, or if a central banker called me directly to ask my opinion about the market, I felt special. Being selected to 'help the state' because of my position as a market maker engendered a sense of pride and duty. Whatever I was doing as a job, it was of great importance. Despite the fact that the vast majority of trading was driven by speculation, it served as a reminder that my role as a market maker actually meant something. The state wanted, even *needed*, people who provided liquidity to the markets.

* * *

Although banks have received very large fines for their traders' behavioural failings in the unregulated FX market, it seems like such behaviour was widespread. The conspiracy did not involve just one or two banks, but a group of banks controlling more than half of the global FX market. The conspiracy did not involve only junior and inexperienced traders, but senior traders, chief dealers and global heads of FX trading. More than any other market, the FX and money markets are quite literally about money. Banks, dominant in these markets, are also secretive by nature. Money, secrecy and traders are three ingredients that, when mixed together, can end up in a conspiracy.

Very few people (academics, regulators or others) bothered to look into the FX trading culture before the scandal broke. This might seem strange, given how large and important the market is. On the other hand, I think one reason it received so little attention was precisely *because* it was so large. From the outside, it seemed too global, too competitive, too efficient – simply too perfect to have space for something that could be referred to as a 'culture'. As in the case of LIBOR, this perception was false.

'People of the same trade seldom meet together, even for merriment and diversion, but the conversation ends in a conspiracy against the public, or in some contrivance to raise prices,'[31] Adam Smith wrote more than 200 years ago. The contours of a conspiracy, however, do not need to take shape in a smoke-filled cigar club or an electronic chatroom. Conventions, whether they later are classified as conspiracies or not, can also evolve on the desk, during a dinner, a seminar, a cigarette break or perhaps even in a classroom.

CHAPTER 7

ROTTEN APPLES

When the journalist asked me whether I recognised myself in characters that feature in *Wall Street*, *American Psycho* or *Cosmopolis*, I gave an evasive answer.

'The books and films you mention are bestsellers and blockbusters, even Oscar winners. Although, like many such films, they tend to over-dramatise life as a trader, of course there are some truths in them,' I said.

'Many people, not only traders, can relate to the drama and characters in these stories, otherwise they would not be such universally popular films. They deal with power, guilt, humanity and morality, as in much of literature – in Dostoyevsky, Kafka ... or in Heinrich Böll's books, to mention one of my favourite German writers.' To me, asking traders or rogue traders whether they identified themselves with Bud Fox or Gordon Gekko was like asking a policewoman whether she identified herself with Sarah Lund in *The Killing* or a policeman with Kurt Wallander in one of Henning Mankell's crime novels.

The interview never made it to print.

I could have elaborated much more in my answer to the question, which was cleverly phrased to prompt me into explaining what really goes on in the mind of a rogue trader. Who do rogue traders see as their mentors, sources of inspiration and role models? I had not seen the film *Cosmopolis*, nor read the book it was based on, but I did like *Wall Street* a lot. I also thought Bret Easton Ellis's *American Psycho* was an excellent novel. Patrick Bateman, the anti-hero, was exactly that: a psycho who happened to be American. But as to whether any of these films and books held any fundamental truths about traders, I was dubious. Even so, I decided not to tell the journalist that, a very long time ago, I used to book squash courts under the pseudonym Pat Bateman.

I believe that perceptions, or rather misperceptions, about LIBOR, foreign exchange and other closely linked markets and benchmarks were a key factor in enabling various forms of wrongdoing to go on for such a long time – without governments, regulators, academics, the media or members of the public taking notice. In a way, there was an omnipresent view of how things worked, or ought to work, in the dealing rooms, with few people bothering to question whether this view was actually correct. In hindsight, it is clear that some banks profited from the status quo established by this perception, and only seriously began to alter their practices once it became obvious that their house of cards was on the verge of falling apart.

Even though banks have been punished for staging the arena in which manipulative behaviour took place, much of the blame has fallen on relatively few individuals working in the dealing rooms of these banks. Banks have paid fines, settled lawsuits, sorted out what they often refer to as 'legacy issues' and, albeit under much more scrutiny, moved on with business. Meanwhile, a small number of employees whose conduct has been classified as 'unacceptable', to use the words of UBS in relation to the FX scandal, have been disciplined, sacked, banned from the industry or even criminally charged. Despite often being highly paid employees, these 'rotten apples' have tended to be relatively lowly in the hierarchy. However, rotten apples, particularly in the glamorous world of finance, make juicy headlines.

But do the pre-existing (and often understandably) negative stereotypes of rotten apples in finance that dominate the popular imagination get in the way of understanding how traders *really* think and operate? Does it matter?

I believe it does, although I can only speak from my own experience. To me, some perceptions about traders – and in particular about rotten apples such as 'rogue traders' – are often completely misguided, no matter how convenient they might be. The industry is not stuffed with Patrick Batemans – it would certainly be easier to deal with if it were true. But such a perception, like misperceptions about the market more broadly, obscures the true, pernicious nature of the system. Portraying the problem as being just a few rotten apples enables people to give the tree a clean bill of health.

* * *

In January 2015, I was invited to give a talk to business students from the University of Iowa. My spontaneous reaction to delivering a lecture about my rogue trading history was always going to be a 'No thanks'. Talking about my case, even privately, had not been a positive experience. So why do it in front of a large group of people who did not know me? But I could see that the professor had honest, constructive and refreshing intentions behind his proposal. I accepted, knowing that I was not going to be able to hide my nervousness, but hopeful that I could put together a lecture that might be different.

I decided to use the journalist's question as an anecdote in my presentation, because, for me, it captured an important point about how the financial markets tend to be perceived. Although I felt there was no real point in challenging the common view of what life on the trading floor was like – the reality often manages to trump the portrait depicted in fictional stories or by the media – I wanted to show how a stereotype can be constructed, how perceptions can turn into misperceptions, and what the consequences of this are. For instance, the fact that I, an ex-rogue trader, used to book squash courts under the pseudonym of a fictional Wall Street psychopath could be seen as hugely revealing. It might trigger a reader to think about the connection, to seek out causes and motives that led me to turn rogue. They might assume that I chose it because I admired Bateman in some way. In the end, the students laughed, and understood the point I was trying to make. The truth behind the squash court bookings, as I will go on to explain, was rather more prosaic.

A year later, a journalist visited my class when I was planning to give a lecture on a similar topic. Having reported on the LIBOR scandal for the *Wall Street Journal*, and being in the process of writing a book about Tom Hayes, he was very familiar with traders in trouble. For a moment, I contemplated not including the same anecdote. Although I largely trusted him, I also knew he wanted to sell newspapers. Then I thought, perhaps over-optimistically: 'If I mention I used to book squash courts under the name of Pat Bateman, then also say I could never reveal this to journalists, surely he must not only feel privileged to hear the background to why I did it, but also be uneasy about including it without explaining the whole story.'

The real story behind my squash court alias is rather uninspiring. Looking back, both Jeppe (my squash partner back in the 1990s) and I agree that there were three reasons for using the fictional name when booking a court. First: boredom. We grew up in a small town in Finland, as far away from Wall Street as you could imagine. There was only one native English-speaking person around, an Australian named Paul Wilson who owned a record shop. English names stood out, so we used the pseudonym to prompt a reaction, or perhaps the opposite: a non-reaction to a name that so clearly could not exist in the place where we grew up. Nobody else we knew had read *American Psycho*, and it was a way of placing ourselves completely outside our own, somewhat dull, reality at the time. Moreover, we belonged to the Swedish-speaking minority, which made up less than 6 per cent of the tiny population. Claiming to have a name that belonged neither to the majority nor the minority felt like a statement in a country that had few ethnic outsiders at the time. Second: weariness at hearing yourself calling the sports centre over and over again using the same name. We played a lot, and, as it happened, my friend's surname was rather similar to mine. Third: in *American Psycho*, Patrick Bateman frequently used pseudonyms himself when booking restaurants. I guess that was the real inspiration, rather than any admiration or empathy for the character. The truth is that Pat Bateman the squash player was not a psycho, nor anything close. Regardless of whether my friend or I had booked the court, he always turned up and paid for the session, and left no corpses behind.

'In college, he booked squash courts under the name "Patrick Bateman", the fictional investment banker and serial killer in the book *American Psycho*,' the article in the *Wall Street Journal* read.[1] Although the interview portrayed me as a much more multifaceted rotten apple than any previous article mentioning me, the back story behind my rationale for using Patrick Bateman as an alter ego was not mentioned. Although initially I was frustrated, I went on to reflect that perhaps it only confirms my suspicion about how difficult it can be to break down stereotypical perceptions of traders. A boring or complicated truth can interfere with well-established prejudices or theories. The reason why I brought it up during the lecture was that, to my mind, it illustrated how difficult it can be to change perceptions not only of rogue traders but also of those LIBOR and FX manipulators who had begun to receive a lot of publicity in recent years. These are not psychos (as far as I know), but real people acting according to rationales that make sense in the context in which they are working, sometimes with the implicit encouragement of the banks they work for. The problem isn't simply one of a few vilified rotten apples working against the banking industry; rather, it is symptomatic of a system that has supported, even rewarded, such behaviour.

Many people seem to think that rogue traders were rogue individuals who ended up as traders – rather than traders who ended up going rogue. Many people also seem to analyse the FX and LIBOR manipulators in terms of them being manipulators who happened to be involved in the trading of FX and LIBOR derivatives, rather than the other way round. In the years after the events of 2009, I had come to learn that I would always be judged in relation to those events and the media coverage that followed. Revealing my unusual choice of pseudonym would only serve to strengthen the perception that rogue, rather than trader, came first. It was like an anchor that had got stuck on the bottom of the sea. Every time I tried to pull it up, the currents worked against me.

When, following the *New York Times* article, the media storm hit, it lasted about 48 hours. I have since learned that two or three days are standard. The paparazzi disappear after that, and newspapers find other interesting events to write about. While 48 hours is a relatively short period, it did not feel like that at the time. A roller coaster ride rarely lasts for more than 60 seconds, but this felt as if it were a ride that would last forever and whose only direction was down. But when the ride eventually came to a halt, I did not feel happy that it was finished. Instead, it was as if I were unable to get off, with no way of judging when or whether the ride would start moving again. Those 48 hours made me see the people around me in a different way, and often it was not a pretty sight. At the same time, I could see how people now looked at me, bewildered, and mostly not liking what they saw either. Surprisingly few said anything to my face. Instead, Maria was used as a go-between. 'You stood by him throughout the good times, now you need to stand by him during the bad times,' she was advised by a neighbour after having dropped off our daughters at school. 'Now you will learn how other people live their lives,' a friend told her, as if she had been wearing rose-tinted spectacles throughout my career in banking. Others were less direct, asking in hushed tones whether I was 'OK' when I was out of hearing range or had left the room.

Examples of fraudulent behaviour were often brought up in dinner conversations. 'My cousin fiddles with his taxes,' someone could remark out of the blue. 'A friend of mine lost £25,000 on a dodgy investment scheme,' someone else added. I think many of such comments were well intentioned, told in order to break the ice somehow. They were desperate for me to deliver *the whole story*, and up until then they would tiptoe around me, and around the subject itself. Perhaps they also wanted to level the playing field, by stressing how many rogue people there were out there, that I wasn't alone. During one dinner party, though, I got tired of the glances and the never-ending anecdotes of unsuccessful criminals or lousy investors. 'If you haven't lost 100 million, you don't know what it feels like,' I suddenly interrupted. Everyone fell silent. Then, a few seconds later, they burst out laughing – looking relieved that I had finally delivered the confession they wanted to hear: that I was actually the person they now thought I was.

Someone told me a local newspaper in Finland had claimed I had been instrumental in causing the global financial crisis. Although I had been closer to the epicentre than most people, the statement was absurd. However, what kind of counterclaim could I possibly have come up with? Who, in March 2009, knew the true causes behind the crisis and whose fault it was? I certainly did not. My close friends in Finland were both supportive and concerned, but they were not approached by the media. What, really, could they have said, having no experience of the market at all? What is more, I was following Merrill Lynch's instructions to keep my mouth shut, so there was little I could say to provide comfort to those whom I trusted without disclosing too many details.

People who had been nowhere near the Merrill Lynch dealing room demanded retribution. It was as if they felt a right to define what kind of guilt I should feel. 'I will not pay back your deposit, because your media storm caused my wife to have a nervous breakdown,' our landlord told me after my wife and I moved out of the flat we had lived in during the time it all happened. Less than a month after the article in the *New York Times* was published, I received an email stating: 'Due to being door stepped by various people including the press as a result of you being investigated by the FSA, I have suffered loss of rental income which has also exacerbated my financial situation due to bankruptcy.' In effect, he argued that the episode had affected him personally, and demanded compensation in cash. Although I felt exploited, I had bigger problems to deal with. We ended up settling out of court, and for a couple of thousand pounds I was relieved of my guilt towards him and his wife.

But not all comments related to money, at least not directly. 'One day, I will put a bullet through your head,' was the most extreme response I received. I had never received a death threat before, and it was frightening to hear it over the phone from someone I knew. But, as with the multitude of accusations and comments I had got used to, it also felt predictable somehow. I had grown accustomed to people looking at me suspiciously, to the degree that I would start a conversation by exclaiming 'Google me!' to avoid the awkward moment the next time we met and they *had* Googled me. If they wanted to do some 'research' on their own, I might as well make it clear that I was not trying to hide my Google history from them – and this included all the anonymous comments below the numerous online articles arguing that I deserved, at least, to be put in jail.

Others were afraid that, because of my past, I might cause them trouble in the future – or that, because of my past, I might be perceived *by others* as a person who could be a source of trouble for them in the future. Although I did not want to accept such thinking, I could see their logic. A job offer from a university was withdrawn when some faculty members had second thoughts about me delivering lectures on economics and finance to students who they thought were more susceptible to influence than they were. Although they did not necessarily perceive a direct risk in me teaching students how to 'turn rogue', it was quite plausible that fee-paying parents might do so. A sympathetic professor suggested that I should reapply if and when the FCA lifted my five-year ban from working in the financial industry. I found the idea daunting that the FCA had the power to decide who was fit and proper to work not only in the City but also on university campuses all around England. The regulator had no legal jurisdiction in academia, of course, but that did not seem to matter in my case. However, I did not know of any other ex-rogue traders applying for positions at academic institutions, so there was not much support in terms of a suitable precedent.

A vice chancellor at another university keen on hiring me was more supportive, but at the last minute called me on my mobile. The university wanted further assurances that I had now, beyond any doubt, come clean. I was told I needed to meet with the university's board members in order to demonstrate that I was of good character and that they had nothing to fear by having me roam unmonitored around the campus. I could sense that he knew how disappointed I was, and he told me to think about it for a couple of days. Although I was confident I could provide sufficiently comforting answers in a boardroom, by this stage I had grown exhausted of conforming to criteria that seemed to change every time I tried to move on. So I politely declined the opportunity to seek redemption in my new job – before I had even signed on the dotted line.

While I tried to appear calm and patient to others, inside it was a different story. Many of the comments above made me angry, upset and afraid. The continuing suspicion towards me planted seeds of doubt as to whether there would be a time when I would be able to look back and say: 'It is finally over.'

When I met my friend, the broker, in Borough Market in 2011, I was certain he would end up feeling misunderstood in the years to come. Probably, like me, he would also be angry, upset and afraid. I was not only thinking about the upcoming and extremely complex LIBOR problem he had become embroiled in. I was also wondering whether perceptions about him personally would change if and when more information about LIBOR was made public. Since then, I have also thought a lot about all the other traders and brokers involved in or closely connected to the LIBOR and FX scandals – many of whom have made headlines, many of whom I know. I doubt whether any of them had spent much time reflecting on the consequences of 'getting caught', for lack of a better expression. Having operated within an environment where their behaviour (which today is classified as unacceptable or even criminal) merely resulted in retaliation by other market participants or, at most, a quiet exit from the bank or brokerage firm, there were few warning signs.

It would be only natural to want to distance yourself from them as much as possible, particularly if you had been a colleague or manager or had done business with them in the past. But it doesn't stop there. The disorientation truly kicks in once you realise how neighbours, former classmates, taxi drivers and other 'ordinary' people have suddenly changed their perception of you. This sense of isolation is difficult to describe. 'Imagine being a house, and that people find out that you have been contaminated with asbestos,' I might say to those who ask. It is the closest image I can come up with.

But people still tend to find asbestos, nuclear waste and human outcasts interesting – at least for research purposes. They are fascinating, and the rarer they are, the more fascinating they become. Considering how many people work in banking, the number of traders is very small. Trading is a peculiar job, and strong bonds are often forged between traders working together – or even against each other. Within this small group of traders, a few go rogue at some point in their career. Among these, a tiny fraction do so on such a spectacular scale that rumours turn into reality, and secrecy into public knowledge. It is rare to be a rogue trader, LIBOR manipulator, FX cartel member or some other rotten apple from the trading community. Considering the glamour attached to the dealing room environment, it is not surprising that it is an intriguing subject.

* * *

Towards the end of my PhD studies, I had a coffee in Russell Square with a researcher from Cambridge who was investigating the sociology of rotten apples, rogue traders, whistle-blowers and other outcasts in the financial industry. As I, according to her, belonged to this group, she asked whether I believed there ought to be a network for 'people like us'. Given that we had all gone through psychological ordeals – 'deservedly or undeservedly', she added – our isolation could perhaps be broken by forming a group where we could exchange ideas and express sympathy towards each other. I was so surprised by the idea that my response was to smile and mumble something incomprehensible. I found the proposition absurd. To me, I had absolutely nothing in common with the others in the group she referred to. If anything, being associated with one another in a formal setting would only serve to strengthen the negative perception of who and what we were. Rather I, and I suspect the others too, wanted the exact opposite – to feel *less* associated with 'people like us'. The idea of an AA for rogue traders was a complete non-starter to my mind.

Moreover, up until then I had never considered myself a rogue trader, simply because I did not fit the definition of what it represented.

I had been a trader, and it could be said that I had 'gone rogue', but the combination of the two words meant crossing a line. Rogue trading was generally associated with criminality, and I had never been subject to a criminal investigation. To me, the term was as charged as 'terrorist' or 'rapist'. There was a stigma attached to it.

'Nobody reads my blog anyway,' the Channel 4 newsreader Jon Snow replied to Maria, years after he had written about me on his blog. Maria had bumped into him in a pub and immediately told him: 'I believe you owe my husband an apology.' He wasn't even able to recall who I was, or why he had written about me in a sarcastic way. Presumably, because he could not remember, and claimed he had few blog readers, the content was of little importance in the great scheme of things. Few cared, and even fewer would remember. But I remembered. My family remembered.

When I found out that I had been classified as a rogue trader in a chapter in an academic book, my heart rate increased. The chapter, called 'From Dishonesty to Disaster: The Reasons and Consequences of Rogue Traders' Fraudulent Behavior' made a connection between rogue trading, dishonesty and white-collar crime, stating that 'rogue, or unauthorized, trading takes place when a trader is buying or selling financial instruments in amounts beyond the organizational risk limits and conceals his/her activities'. The authors then included a list, complied by themselves, of the 'most noticeable cases of rogue trading in 1991–2011'. Among the 17 names listed, my name appeared alongside the bank, the nominal loss, the financial instruments involved and the year the trading took place.

How could two academics, let alone a serious publishing company, suddenly claim I was a rogue trader? Doubting that many of the other 16 individuals were avid readers of the academic book, I took it upon myself to write to the publisher:

> As a fellow academic, I do not object to the overall content, to the definitions or to the theoretical link drawn between rogue trading, dishonesty and white-collar crime. I do, however, seriously object to the inclusion and the publication of my name in Table 2 and in this context – on these grounds: my case (Merrill Lynch/2009) did not involve any unauthorized trading. As such, the term 'rogue trader' is not applicable, my case did not involve a criminal investigation and my case (see Final Notice from the FSA attached) did crucially not involve the word 'dishonest'.

I received a lengthy email back, arguing that I was wrong on all three counts. First, they argued that since the term 'rogue trader' had entered the public domain, various definitions could be used. The consultancy firm Accenture defined it slightly differently: 'rogue trading refers to traders engaging in fraudulent practices, while trading on behalf of their institutions with a view of deliberately violating an institution's trading related rules or mandates'. Moreover, the authors stated that the names had been selected on the basis of the losses the banks incurred as a result or the amount of publicity they had received (whether such coverage was accurate or not). To support their argument, the authors provided references to *The Guardian*, *The Times*, *The Evening Standard*, *Forbes*, Sky News, *The Huffington Post*, Reuters and other outlets where my name had appeared in the context of rogue trading or as a rogue trader. Second, there had been no *direct* inference or suggestion that I was subject to a criminal investigation. Third, they argued that the term 'dishonesty' was an incredibly subjective one, and that the definition provided by the Merriam-Webster dictionary defined it as a 'lack of honesty or integrity: disposition to defraud or deceive'. Despite the fact that the FSA crucially had omitted the word from my Final Notice, the publisher argued that my behaviour could be 'construed as dishonest conduct'. Dishonesty was subjective, and according to the Merriam-Webster dictionary, people's perception about me as a dishonest person wasn't incorrect. Therefore, because of the size of my losses, the media coverage, and a slightly different linguistic definition of what it meant, I could be perceived as a rogue trader.

It seemed pointless to waste more time and energy on this. But it made me realise that the real disappointment I felt related not so much to how the publisher defended the authors, but,

249

to my mind, to the sneaky way in which the authors had gone about writing it. They had never met me. They had never even attempted to talk to me. It followed a familiar pattern. There were plenty of journalists writing about rogue traders and there were plenty of academics spending time in libraries researching rogue traders. Some clearly disliked the rotten apples in the financial industry, but others wrote more sympathetically about Nick Leeson, Kweku Adoboli, Jérôme Kerviel or the others who featured on the shortlist I was now very familiar with. Few, however, seemed to have met any of them, whether in person or electronically. Yet, new theories about how traders behave or why traders sometimes go rogue were continuously proposed based on knowledge in the public domain.

The stage had already been set. Scripts with new inter-pretations were written. As for those playing the leading roles, it was only about selecting the right costumes for the drama.

* * *

All the 17 people on the rogue trader ranking list had lost a phenomenal amount of money because of trading. Patrick Bateman in *American Psycho*, Bud Fox in *Wall Street* and Eric Packer in *Cosmopolis* were all incredibly wealthy because of the jobs they did in finance. Money, finance and rogue behaviour linked them together.

However, rogue trading is not predominantly about money and glamorous dealing rooms. Rogue trading is about *risk*. The publisher was correct in pointing out that rogue trading could be defined in various ways, such as 'violating an institution's trading related rules or mandates'. Another definition describes rogue trading as 'when a trader is buying or selling financial instruments in amounts beyond the organizational risk limits and conceals his/her activities'. Whichever definition we use, we are referring to traders taking risk. First, the trader takes a risk. Then, the trader takes too much risk, breaking the rules of the institution they work for (typically a bank). The activity is covered up, but is then uncovered. As a result, the trader becomes a rogue trader. It is tempting to presume that everything relates to just money and greed. However, if we really want to understand how traders and rogue traders behave, we cannot ignore the aspect of risk.

Although other people in the market probably saw me as a big risk taker, I didn't spend much time thinking about it – at least not until it was too late. The reflection came later. Many people I've never met got to know me when I was inducted into the rogue traders' hall of fame in the media. Perhaps my infamy can be compared to a sports personality caught taking anabolic steroids, though with two important caveats. First, sport is associated with popularity and fame, whereas trading and banking are secretive. Second, the public tends to admire sports personalities for their achievements, whereas traders are mostly disliked for their profession. Cheating athletes not only lose their medals, world records and sponsorship contracts, they are also seen as having brought disgrace upon the whole 'ethos' of the sport. When it comes to rogue traders, it is debatable whether 'clean' (non-cheating) traders are regarded as contributing to society in a similar way to 'clean' athletes. Admittedly, there *are* some people who idolise particular investors or traders as if they were athletes. 'What do I need to do to become like Warren Buffett?' I often get asked, as if I not only held the secret to Mr Buffett's phenomenally successful long-term investment track record, but also believed it could be taught. This admiration, however, quickly fades if the legendary investor or trader loses an awful lot of money. Past performances are suddenly erased. This downfall, of course, is steeper for rogue traders. Almost overnight, their identities as anonymous traders are replaced by the identities of disgraced traders in the public domain.

I had never really thought about fame before I received the text message from one of my brokers in March 2009 saying 'You're famous now!' He could just as well have written 'You're no longer anonymous!' I had been anonymous, but I didn't know the value of it until suddenly it was gone.

Also, sporting achievements are easily measurable in seconds, minutes, metres, kilograms, goals, points and so on. Because professional athletes want to win, the logic behind using forbidden substances is easy to grasp – cheating increases the likelihood of winning. Trading involves money, which is also easily measurable, and traders, it is often believed, are *only* driven by a desire to make money. This approach is consistent with standard economic theories on incentive structures (carrots and sticks, basically) in banking. Banks are profit-maximising institutions, and risk taking can be said to be fundamental to their existence. Banks therefore need professional risk takers (traders). Banks use incentives (bonuses) in order to induce traders to *actively* take risk. Otherwise, so the thinking goes, traders might just as well play solitaire all day long and pretend that they are thinking about a clever trading strategy or waiting for the right moment to buy or sell. Because of competition, banks constantly need to provide more lucrative incentive structures (bigger bonuses) than their peers. Otherwise, the talented and hard-working traders will go elsewhere, leaving behind those who prefer to play solitaire all day long.

However, traders sometimes win, but they also regularly lose. Too much risk taking can result in a catastrophe, and even the most experienced traders can make sloppy mistakes. It can happen that a buy order is inputted as a sell order, or the '0' key is pressed one too many times, causing the amount to be multiplied by ten. 'Fat fingers' such as these can be expensive. Likewise, a calculation error stemming from having used the wrong day count convention, or even from forgetting whether Christmas Eve is a business day or a holiday in a particular country or currency, is often a costly affair.

The risk-taking activity therefore needs to be managed, supervised and controlled, which is why traders face a number of hurdles that are deliberately put in place to keep them in check. The contract of employment sets out what they are supposed to do, and how they might be rewarded. Managers set yearly targets. People in the back office, middle office, financial control, valuation and product control check that traders trade only those financial instruments they are allowed to trade, and that they are booked and valued correctly. The credit department makes sure that traders do not trade with institutions that might go bust. The compliance department ensures that traders read internal policy manuals on codes of conduct, complete training courses, know what they should do if there is a fire in the dealing room or an earthquake. Risk managers make sure that risk taking is kept within defined and reasonable boundaries. Beyond that, central banks and financial regulators set limits on how much risk a bank can take as a whole.

In sum, it is generally assumed that traders act rationally and that the primary motivation for risk-taking behaviour is the anticipated *reward*. To tame excessive risk-taking behaviour among traders, therefore, banks and regulators ought not only to have proper controls in place (to prevent rogue trader scandals happening), but also to fine-tune the incentive structures. For instance, rather than be paid out in cash, bonuses could be paid out in shares at some point in the distant future in order to align the traders' interests with those of the shareholders. This, in effect, is the logic behind a number of banking reforms that have been implemented since the financial crisis of 2007–08. Banks had tolerated, even encouraged, risk-taking behaviour that had almost brought the global financial system to its knees. Now it was time to change the system of carrots and sticks.

Gary Becker, an economist and also a Nobel laureate, wrote an article outlining how it was possible to model optimal policing and punishments using similar mainstream economic thinking. This is my interpretation of the model. Every individual is rational and strives to maximise their utility. Their utility is measured in money, and there are two ways in which money can be obtained: work or *crime*. The expected utility of any individual at any moment in time, therefore, is a purely mathematical function of the money obtained through honest work and the money obtained from committing a crime. However, there is a catch. When committing a crime, you also need to take into account that there is a risk that you might get caught. And if you get caught, there is a risk that you might be prosecuted and, ultimately, punished. The idea is that policy makers and law enforcement agencies can use this model to figure out how much they should spend on policing the streets (to increase the risk of getting caught) and how much they should spend on the justice system (to increase the risk of getting prosecuted, being fined, sent to prison, etc.). Human beings, it is thought, just want money, and risk is something they take to increase their chances of getting their hands on that money. In standard economics textbooks, the world is portrayed almost as cynically as in the book and film series *The Hunger Games*. In the latter, the players know the rules of the game: they kill each other until there is only one person left. The players maximise their utility: the time they have left to live. Players collaborate only if it increases the likelihood of surviving a little bit longer. In the end, however, even friends will, quite literally, stab each other in the back. For those who have read all the books in *The Hunger Games* series and are on the lookout for their next dystopian bestseller, ask a librarian to find you a textbook in economics or finance.

It is true that money and greed may cause people to take risk. But the reality is more complicated than that. As the behavioural finance professor Daniel Kahneman notes: 'Utility cannot be divorced from emotion.'[2] Most people do not like playing roulette or games in which you have to guess whether the next person crossing the street is male or female. Even if the odds are exactly even, the frustration of losing a thousand dollars *feels* more powerful than the joy of winning a thousand. As a trader, I always felt more like a loser following a day when I had lost $10,000 or $100,000 than I felt like a 'winner' when I had made the same amount. The fact that losses loom larger than gains is called 'loss aversion'. Nobody likes losing, of course, but a potential loss (or 'negative' reward) changes the way we approach risk taking.

Another bias that complicates standard economics and finance theory is called 'mental accounting'.[3] In a nutshell, it refers to the way in which we often segregate different gambles into different accounts, and in so doing use very different criteria to assess how we utilise the various accounts. The brain acts like a chest of drawers, with different types of problems sorted into different compartments. For instance, we might count the pennies when shopping for groceries, but when celebrating a birthday or a special occasion we are often less sensitive to the shockingly high price of a bottle of champagne. Likewise, an individual might speculate on a volatile stock market yet be extremely careful when saving for a future retirement. Traders also do a lot of mental accounting. An FX trader watches every minuscule currency movement in the dealing room during the day, yet when on holiday in Spain will withdraw euros from the nearest ATM, oblivious to the outrageous bank fees and commissions.

A standard question I used to be asked when being interviewed by another bank was to describe my trading style. How much of your trading revenue comes from market making to other banks? How much is generated from customer flows (i.e. from the bank having a customer franchise in the currencies and financial instruments I traded)? How much do you make from arbitrage activities? How much is derived from fundamental analysis, macroeconomic views and proprietary trading (effectively placing bets using the bank's money)? My answers to such questions might provide clues as to whether I took my own initiatives or largely relied on my current employer's customer base. They therefore also hint at my *risk appetite*. Proprietary trading often involves more active risk taking, whereas customer flows less. However, the main question also involves a form of psychological self-assessment on the part of the interviewee, essentially asking: 'What kind of mental accounting do you perform within your environment?' A trader might do hundreds of deals during the day in an attempt to profit from tiny short-term price movements and customer deals. Depending on the market in which the trader is active, there might also be arbitrage opportunities from which to profit. At the same time, however, the same trader might have positions that are deliberately left untouched for days, weeks or even months – reflecting a very different, more long-term view of the market. Being able to combine both, sometimes conflicting, approaches often requires considerable recourse to mental accounting. It is not a straightforward process to assess the individual contribution of such 'accounts'. Market making was what I had been trained to do from the start, while arbitrage and various mathematical strategies were areas where I felt very comfortable. Growing the customer franchise and increasing the market share was something that spurred me on. Proprietary trading interested me. My answer therefore tended to be 'a bit of everything', which generally seemed to be regarded as a good answer.

Thus, different traders might have different attitudes to risk. More fundamentally, even a single trader might have very different attitudes to different types of risk. One of the strongest (and most dangerous) emotions is what we used to call 'getting married to your position'. Sometimes it was possible to get so closely attached to a trading strategy or position that, regardless of how much the market consensus disagreed with you, you continued to fight tooth and nail to convince yourself that you were right. 'The central bank will never cut rates,' someone could say, certain that it was impossible for LIBOR to go any lower. 'What could possibly go wrong?' someone else might try to persuade themselves after having put an elaborate trading strategy into action. At times, traders could almost sound as if they were preaching to a group of new disciples, desperately wanting them to believe in the gospel they were delivering with absolute conviction. I am not referring to FX sales people trying to get clients to trade (that would simply have been classified as excellent sales skills), but about traders so fanatically obsessed with a trading idea that they *had* to be right. The global financial crisis was full of such behaviour. An endless list of traders refused to realise, for too long, how serious matters were – and how this would affect their trading positions. Others, like me, continued to believe in the apocalypse for too long. It is a classic mistake. In behavioural finance, it tends to be referred to as the 'disposition effect': traders often refuse to take stop-losses in time and therefore hold on to losers for too long – i.e. they become irrationally convinced that they will be able to turn their position around, just as gamblers on a losing streak don't know when to walk away. It could also mean the opposite: that profits on brilliant long-term positions are closed out too early. Regret, or *fear* of regret at some point in the future, is an emotion that is common in dealing rooms as well.

* * *

All the theories outlined above have also been used to explain the behaviour of traders going rogue. A common feature of many major rogue trader scandals is that a very large amount of money has been lost, and that this process has, to some degree, been concealed from others. A rogue trader might deceive not only in order to be paid a larger bonus or be promoted, but due to guilt and to avoid losing face with their boss, family or colleagues. Losses might be allowed to escalate, and covered up even further, in the hope of a sudden turnaround in the market. It is convenient to think that traders, because of the job they do (buying and selling money), the things they make (money-related instruments) and the environment they work in (dealing rooms), make for perfect case studies relating to theories that deal with the ways in which people constantly juggle risk and reward. Rogue traders and other rotten apples could then be seen as extreme versions of such individuals: misfits who are prepared to put *even more* at risk while obsessively focusing on getting hold of more and more money. Add a few fictional characters at the end of the spectrum, and the extrapolation becomes both logical and hugely interesting.

Based on my own experiences, however, these theories miss two important aspects of trading. First, they are too individualistic – people are perceived to think and act almost in complete isolation from friends and enemies, colleagues and competitors. Second, the (often monetary) reward is always seen as the motivation and end result. Risk taking is then perceived as a necessary evil to increase the likelihood of getting that reward. In reality, however, some people place a higher value on the physical and emotional experience of risk taking than on actually achieving the reward at its end.

Take the example of a skydiver. What is the downside of voluntarily jumping from a plane at a high altitude? Potential injury or death, of course. What is the upside? Certainly not money. What is the downside of climbing Mount Everest?

Frozen toes, perhaps even a devastating avalanche. The upside? Again, not money. In both cases, such activities not only cost a considerable amount of money, but sooner or later they run the risk of at least one minor accident. Car racing is also an extremely dangerous activity, and unless you belong to a select group of Formula One drivers, it is unlikely ever to bring in huge monetary rewards.

'There is a percentage of people who want to be a little bit outside their comfort zone and I am one of them,' Alain Robert, the 'French Spider-Man' famous for climbing skyscrapers without equipment or safety nets, once said. Cynical economists might argue that he repeatedly risks his life in order to earn sponsorship deals and make money from motivational speaking engagements, but that would be to miss the point. There are a number of people, both within and outside sports, who enjoy – or even love – taking risks. Sociologists sometimes mention professions such as undercover police officers, but also traders. Banks are in the business of taking risk in order to make money. However, not all bankers like taking risk. Banks, therefore, need to hire professionals who are willing to actively take risk. These people are called *traders*.

Around the time of the 1997 Asian financial crisis, there was one chaotic Friday I will never forget. People were panicking and as a result were trading frenetically. As soon as I had traded with someone, or someone had traded with me, the Reuters Dealing screen and the switchboard lit up like a Christmas tree with incoming calls from banks, brokers and sales people requesting, even demanding, prices. The pace was relentless, and I did not have time to book one trade before the next one was done. Because I knew my overall position was good, I managed to keep calm. The market was heading towards chaos, which suited my trading book. However, I also knew that it was heading there too fast for me to be able to keep track of my position. The risk that I would make a calculation error and end up with a losing hand by the weekend (which was only a few hours away) was overwhelming. My manager saw what was going on and calmly sat down on the closest seat that happened to be vacant. He switched on the computer systems, tracked every conversation I was having and began to input the trades one by one – monotonously, quietly, as if he was working on a factory floor, completely unfazed by the several levels of seniority that separated us. On that day, I made more money than I was targeted to do throughout the whole year.

On that Friday afternoon, however, I had begun to believe that the 'trend had become my friend'. I did not close my positions. Instead, I hoped that Monday would deliver more of the same. But I was wrong. Instead, the market quickly swung all the way back to where it had started on Friday morning and more than 90 per cent of my profits were erased within a matter of a few hours. I was angry with myself and felt like a fool for not having been able to foresee the dangers in sticking to my risky positions. For a brief moment of time, I had begun to feel invincible, with a hubristic sense of self-confidence taking control of my actions.

Most traders I know, or have known, are attracted to something that most people avoid like the plague: risk. Although they enjoy monetary rewards, they are often equally smitten by the buzz on the trading floor and simply playing 'the game'. I don't think greed was the only, or even the main, reason why I became so self-confident that Friday. It was something else:

an incredibly strong desire to master something extremely difficult, to be proven right against almost impossible odds. Likewise, I never felt that my manager had taken on the boring work from me that day so I could make more money, which would in turn increase his own bonus at a later stage – a trading boss tends to receive a bonus based not only on their own trading performance but also on that of everyone below them in the trading room hierarchy. Rather, I knew that he had previously been in a similar situation, respected what I was doing, and was doing everything he could to enable me to make the right decision with regard to my own risk taking. It was *my* job and not his. In the end, I made the wrong decision, of course, and that decision was mine. But this was also a fundamental and integral part of trading. Risk taking is very individualistic. Ultimately, fear is an emotion and a very personal feeling.

One problem with voluntary risk taking (or 'edgeworking', as sociologists refer to it[4]), whether it be in extreme sports or extreme trading, is that it is highly addictive. If you get hooked, you want to do more of it. Alpine skiers, rock climbers and scuba divers I know or have met often talk about the importance of being able to 'test your own limits'. Once a certain level of skill has been achieved, the ski slope or mountain needs to be steeper or the ocean floor less visible to even be worth exploring. Unfortunately, the same thing could be said about risk taking in financial markets. Doing the same thing day in and day out gets boring after a while. After all, you are paid to actively trade – *paid to take risk* – not the other way round. However, increasingly risky undertakings often involve accidents, stress, sleep deprivation and other physical or mental injuries. Trading might not seem like a physically dangerous job, but these are two sentences I wrote back in 2009: 'I was exhausted' and 'The repetitive strain injury is better now, but I still suffer from stomach pain.' Mentally, as I mentioned before, I was a wreck. However, even though such risks can naturally be seen as self-inflicted, or as something that 'comes with the job', risk takers often claim that it is those 'who don't know what they're doing' who are at risk. When, back in the late 1990s, I was told by one of my managers 'Your position is massive', I knew I had put on a risky bet. However, I *had* repressed the thought that I was betting against very experienced traders who knew what they were doing. I did not feel I was at risk; rather, I thought that *they* were the ones at risk. Such thinking can seem absurd coming from risk takers. Nonetheless, in my experience, it was surprisingly common for even the biggest traders to try to calm risk managers by saying that it was 'the others' in the bank or the financial markets who had no clue about assessing how risky a particular trade was.

Risk taking often involves fear, and voluntary risk taking requires that to some degree you are comfortable with being afraid now and then – sometimes very afraid. However, you cannot ever become paralysed by fear. The riskier the jump from the plane, the more vertical the impossible ski slope or the deeper the ocean, the calmer you have to be in order not to panic. Traders need to develop an ability to maintain self-control in situations that verge on chaos.

* * *

On the morning of 11 September 2001, like most other traders in London, I was in the middle of trading. When the events in New York unfolded on the TV screens above the FX options desk around the time of the opening of the US market, most of us stood up and watched. It looked as if a missile had targeted the World Trade Center. But somehow it seemed too slow for a missile. I knew that Maria and our seven-month-old daughter were having lunch with an American friend she had got to know when we lived in Tokyo. I called and told her that a plane had hit one of the towers. 'What kind of plane?' she asked. 'A small private plane making a terrible flight error,' I told her.

A few minutes later I dialled her number again, now with a very different message. It was clear that it was a commercial airliner that had hit the first tower and another aircraft had just hit the other tower. Simultaneously, Maria's friend received a phone call from her husband who was a broker at Cantor Fitzgerald in London. I could only imagine what kind of distress he and his colleagues must have felt. I had visited Cantor's head office once, and knew how high up their trading floor was located in the World Trade Center. 'Why would anyone want to hurt us?' I could hear Maria's friend asking in the background.

Around me, I could hear my own colleagues talking to their family members, telling them to switch on the TV. Others were frantically trying to get through to their brokers in New York, especially those at Carr Futures, the derivatives broking arm of our bank, which was located on the ninety-second floor of the North Tower. At the time, nobody had any idea who or what was under attack, let alone who or what the attacker was. But I remember feeling a sense of threat, wondering about the essential things that would be required if the financial system – or even our whole society – broke down. Cash and water, I thought.

'Buy water and go home,' I told Maria.

There were so many rumours flying around in the market, each one more frightening than the last. I think most of us felt personally secure, but also that the City of London was unsafe. Being located next to the building site for the Gherkin skyscraper made it all the scarier.

As there were no circuit breakers in the FX and money markets, trading continued. However, this was not business as usual. Trading-wise it was a blank sheet where traders tried to either eliminate risk or take advantage of the situation. Quite a few were trying to put bets on an imminent rate cut by the Federal Reserve. Eurodollar futures were being bought in the anticipation that LIBOR would collapse the next day. Soon, traders came to the realisation that this strategy was rather risky. If people were hoarding bottles of water or cans of food in New York or London, they would also hoard *cash*. And the cash everybody wanted during times of crisis was the world reserve currency: the US dollar. It was safer to bet on the *fear* in the market than on banks lending to each other at lower interest rates once the Federal Reserve had managed to cut the official central bank rate. That fear tended to result in a rush towards assets that were considered safe: US dollar cash. The focus quickly shifted to the FX swap market, where banks were able to borrow US dollar cash as long as they lent some other currency in return.

The frenzied trading went on unabated until a senior manager stood up and announced that the trading had to stop. I think people higher up in the bank, not directly involved in the activities on the trading floor, had found it inappropriate considering the events that were unfolding. As a result, a hitherto unheard-of decision to halt the market making was taken. We were sent home. I switched off my computer screens, noting that not all traders in the market had received the same instructions. Some banks were still calling, desperate to trade no matter what.

Not many hours were devoted to mourning and reflection. Within a couple of days, more or less normal trading had resumed. The fear, however, remained for weeks, months, even years. In the beginning, not a day went by without a rumour flying around that a suspect package had been found at Liverpool Street station, that a plane had gone missing or that George W. Bush had been assassinated. Unfounded statements, such as 'Credit Suisse has been evacuated!' or 'The Bank of England is on fire!', could quickly be verified by traders in London simply by looking out of the window. Sometimes, it was even possible to profit from others' fear of an imminent attack, as traders in smaller and safer financial centres in other parts of the world regularly overreacted to such hearsay. In a way, it was better to be closer to the source of the fear, because then you could see or feel the reality on which it was based. Trades were also put on that would pay out in case of an attack, particularly ahead of weekends and holidays. In theory, there was a higher probability of an attack during any given weekend than, say, on any randomly chosen Tuesday.

Looking back at this tragic historical event, I cannot help wondering how a 'rational' trader ought to have behaved on that day in September 2001. Tried to remain calm and simply follow the written and unwritten rules in trading and banking? If there was one moment when traders *needed* to put their emotions aside, this was it. Although I think that most traders managed to remain remarkably calm and controlled throughout the chaos that unfolded (nobody walked out of the dealing room in tears, which probably would have been a normal emotional reaction), I don't think they were completely ruthless or inconsiderate either. Many of the victims were work colleagues, competitors or otherwise closely connected to the industry. Rather, it revealed how ugly the world could become if traders, having been programmed to take risk in order to make money for the banks, simply followed instructions. It was a day when rationality was at war with humanity.

* * *

Like competitive sports, trading is intrinsically very competitive. It is no surprise that a common expression for trading better than the average of everyone else is referred to as 'beating the market'. Trading is a job where employers allow, encourage or pressure employees to be competitive on a daily basis. The average is not good enough, so traders want to trade better than others, which, of course, improves the average with which you are compared. The average can be an abstract benchmark of some sort, such as an index. However, it can also be peers at other competing banks. Competing market makers can almost act as opponents. As a trader, you do not necessarily play in the same league or compete against each other all the time, but even so you often score points at the expense of an opponent – or the other way round.

Although many traders and risk takers dislike each other personally (perhaps a rather natural outcome of such competition), they often show each other much more respect than they do people who do not take risk. This is why a derivatives trader might *respect* an FX spot trader, but not an equity analyst or sales person. Analysts and sales people are not risk takers. Risk managers, compliance officers, brokers and back office staff are not risk takers either. This, perhaps, could be a reason why traders are often perceived as being extremely arrogant and egocentric. I remember myself delivering monologues with a complete lack of self-doubt to colleagues, competitors, brokers and sales people. Often, the substance involved little of interest to people not working on the trading floors – although indirectly they were naturally affected by those thoughts and arguments should they evolve into actions in the financial markets.

The feeling associated with extreme risk taking can be almost impossible to describe. Studies have been conducted on skydivers in order to explain their experiences. Responses range from 'It is a waste of time to even begin to describe what I felt' to 'I felt alive'. This is often how I felt at the time, and is where the *feeling* of risk taking might seem contradictory.

On the one hand, some of the trades that I did were so large they were almost surreal. On the other hand, it was precisely those trades that made me feel that the market was 'real' – almost as if I could touch it.

On the one hand, some exceptionally volatile or chaotic moments in the financial markets in reality lasted only seconds or minutes. On the other hand, it was precisely those moments that felt to me like an eternity.

When the market had been quiet for a long period of time, I longed for the moments of extreme pressure. Long-term thinking (beyond a year, say) might be a good strategy for investments, but the explosive nature of trading rarely caters to such behaviour. The ability to share and describe those brief moments of utter exuberance or nightmarish gloom requires an audience that truly understands how they feel. Invariably, other traders who have been through similar experiences make up that crowd. This sentiment has nothing to do with which bank you happen to be employed by, which is why I am not surprised by the nicknames of some of the foreign exchange chatrooms revealed in recent years. If a name such as 'The Cartel' or 'The Mafia' is chosen for a group of colluding FX traders, it shows how much the members respect each other – even though they officially play for different teams (or banks).

When, on 11 December 2012, Tom Hayes was presented with an arrest warrant, accused of LIBOR manipulation, he corrected the police officer's pronunciation. 'You mean LIE-BOR' (rather than LEE-BOR), Tom said before being driven to his cell.[5] When, back in the 1990s, our FX chief dealer exclaimed that 'The Governor has never made a two-way price in his life!', all the traders agreed that it did not matter how powerful or closely connected you are to the foreign exchange market, unless you had 'been there and done that' as a trader, you would never understand what it was like. Such a self-perception creates a kind of exclusivity. What might be regarded as snobbery or arrogance by others adds to the glue that binds traders together. The more difficult it is to explain the situation to other people, the more natural it becomes to seek understanding among like-minded individuals in the trading community. A club mentality is a natural consequence of this.

Regulators and lawmakers have uncovered an almost endless list of comments and remarks made by traders that in any other situation would be regarded as outrageous or scandalous in relation to the LIBOR and FX manipulation cases. While many of these should undoubtedly be seen as indefensible, and they hardly portray traders in a sympathetic light, they also provide a rather one-dimensional view of how traders think.

'You interacted with these guys and lived this life and I'd love to get your perspective,' a Bloomberg journalist asked me when doing his background research on traders and brokers who had been actively involved in the LIBOR derivatives market. I have to admit that I was initially taken aback by the journalist's casual claim that I had lived that 'life', implicitly suggesting that I was like them. However, he was probably correct in his assessment. There were not many other people who could relate the 'life' they had lived before they were labelled rotten apples – let alone afterwards.

* * *

It would be tempting to classify voluntary risk takers, and traders among them, simply as gamblers and thrill-seeking hamsters. Nothing, however, could be further from the truth. Rolling a dice or spinning a roulette wheel does not involve any skill, only luck. Going on a roller coaster ride in an amusement park certainly provides a thrill, but your fate is completely in someone else's hands (the builders or the engineers). The same applies to turbulence when flying. Even though I know the risk of crashing is minimal, the knowledge that I have to rely on the pilot and Mother Nature makes me feel uncomfortable, rather than excited, when hitting turbulence.

Traders, in my experience, want to have some control over the situation even though the reality – which is often unpredictable, volatile or even dangerous – appears to make this impossible. That is not to say that traders do not like going to Las Vegas, Monte Carlo or amusement parks. Some I have met enjoyed participating in 'Fight Clubs', amateur boxing events where they almost certainly ended up taking an almighty beating. Others like racing cars, knowing that the risk of a fine or temporarily losing their driver's licence is a constant threat. I remember a trader once showing a large black-and-white photograph of his Porsche and the speed at which it was going, sent by the authorities as evidence against him. He held up the photo as if it were a trophy or diploma for others to admire. Most experienced traders are also aware of the culture of alcohol, drugs, betting and bizarre sex games that have been witnessed by numerous storytellers about the City or Wall Street. I have no intention of adding to this growing literature, because addictions in various forms are common throughout society. In my experience, traders who are involved in such activities are not doing so to complement the professional risk taking done during the day. Rather, given the constant stress of the dealing room, they are a form of relaxation that can become obsessive – a bit like my own running or interest in music. However, no matter how extreme – and, in some people's cases, also risky – such hobbies might be, this should not be confused with the buzz of trading. Some might see it as a luxury add-on, others as a price you have to pay to survive being at the top of your game.

Trading is very addictive. Once you get hooked on the adrenaline rush, other things in life can begin to feel less and less interesting – and less and less important. Problematically, this change is not easy to spot yourself. I never thought about how many of my friends and acquaintances worked in the financial markets until March 2009, when I was required to freeze my communication. I was shocked by how short my contact list had suddenly become. In fairness, I was so out of touch with reality that a profit or loss of $100 million almost felt 'ordinary'.

Merrill Lynch, together with its four US investment banking peers – Bear Stearns, Goldman Sachs, Lehman Brothers and Morgan Stanley – was an aggressive risk-taking institution by almost any measure. The profitability of these institutions (and subsequent disaster for some of them) was a direct result of their appetite for, and ability to warehouse, risk. As traders, we were regularly fed updates on how well the other four investment banks were doing in terms of profitability. Information also slipped through in rumours and gossip. Over the years, discussions gradually gravitated from 'How much have you made?' or 'How much are you making?' to 'How much *can* you make?' The amounts became more abstract and the capacity to take risk began to seem limitless. Up until 2009, this change appealed to me. It was a development that suited who I was as a person, or perhaps who I had become. However, what is now well documented is that the global financial crisis did not immediately alter the direction of these banks as risk-loving institutions. In some respects, and particularly considering how risky the environment had become, the banks became even more aggressive in their endeavours to explore new planets in this galaxy – in other words, to make more money.

* * *

'Alexis is on fire!' a senior manager strolling past my desk shouted once, the day after what had been a very profitable trading day. His voice was loud enough for me to feel an immense sense of pride, but perhaps it was also intended as a warning to those who were having a 'bad run'.

'Is there anything you need?' he asked.

Perplexed by this sudden attention from someone high up in the hierarchy, I simply mumbled: 'Well, my computer is a bit slow.'

When I came in the next morning I was met by engineers and IT staff who were crawling under my desk to upgrade my hardware. Ignoring any potential envy from others, I could only be thankful for such a completely non-bureaucratic act of generosity. I had asked for a few extra milliseconds of computer speed, and this was exactly what I had got. But there was another side of the coin, of course – I would not be able to complain about computer speed again. I had been given extra fuel to trade more and faster, and that advantage came with an expectation to deliver accordingly. I was beginning to feel like an astronaut sent further and further into space – enthusiastic about the mission, but increasingly unsure whether I would ever return.

Trading requires you to stretch yourself to the limits of your ability and test the boundaries of these limits. The stress can be difficult, of course, but at the same time there is a certain logic and predictability to it – you know exactly where the pressure is coming from. There is also a great deal of uncertainty involved, things that are beyond your control. But you are not really seeking these dangers when you are a trader. It is more like volunteering to serve in a war zone while constantly trying to avoid the fatal bullet. Banks need professionals who want to serve in these 'war zones' but who also have a natural survival instinct. Bonuses often form a significant part of a trader's compensation, as a key incentive, even though they tend to be paid out 'only' once a year. Although it could be argued that an aggressive bonus culture can result in reckless risk taking, more significant in my opinion is that the risk taking *itself* can lead

BAROMETER OF FEAR

to sensations of achievement and thrill impossible to achieve otherwise. Daily, or even intra-daily, swings in profits and losses quickly become intertwined with the confidence, self-esteem, ego or arrogance of a trader. A potential bonus payment after 365 days is of less immediate importance on an individual level, although it serves to confirm that risk taking is of institutional importance – whether the risk is taken because you are allowed to, encouraged to or pressured to. I was never *forced* to become a trader, and never *forced* to take risk. I did so voluntarily.

Rogue trading is, among other things, about risk and about breaking risk limits. I didn't break any risk limits that were imposed upon me, or that I was made aware of. That, however, does not make me innocent. Likewise, many traders caught up in the FX and LIBOR scandals might not have broken any written rules or existing laws while working for their banks. Some of them might even have followed instructions from more senior staff.

Guilty or not guilty, however, a different choice could always have been made along the way.

CHAPTER 8

THE PERFECT STORM

In 2009, I went through a phase when I believed I had not only thrown away a promising career, but also that I had wasted 15 years of my life on something that was completely useless. I could have chosen a different path, but instead I became a trader. I could, at any moment during those 15 years, have walked out the door. But instead, I stayed. I sailed on.

When people I meet today ask how I look back on 2009, what I learned from the experience, if I have any top tips on how to become a trader, or what I think should be done about trading and banking in general, I say there are no easy answers to any of those questions.

In many ways, I got caught up in the perfect storm. I was the wrong person in the wrong place at the wrong time. But so did many traders involved in LIBOR and FX. The financial crisis was never the true cause of anything that happened to me or anything else mentioned in this book. The crisis, however, acted as a trigger by laying many things bare, including some of the dark sides of the world of finance.

When thinking about a good way to respond, I sometimes wonder what you would tell a person wishing to learn how to sail and explore the oceans. What do you tell him or her? What kind of guarantees can you give that it will be safe? The seas can be dangerous, so you need to learn a variety of things related to sailing: rules, licences, engineering, meteorology, navigation, how to use a barometer and so on. Many of these things can be learned from textbooks and further knowledge can be obtained from sailors who have successfully navigated both calm and rough seas.

But there will always be some things that cannot be taught. If you end up in a perfect storm, the boat has sunk and you suddenly have a fear of drowning, you just have to trust your instinct. As difficult as it is to teach someone to become a trader (or warn someone off becoming one), it is necessary in order to make the world of trading safe for those involved in it and those affected by it.

* * *

I sometimes have to pinch myself when I think about how much the perception of the markets in which I was actively trading for 15 years has changed in recent years. They used to be seen as virtually flawless – how could manipulative, abusive and collusive practices exist in such immensely competitive, efficient and liquid markets? Now, they are symbolic of banking and trading behaviour gone very wrong. Yes, the markets could be volatile, but the diabolical waves weren't seen to be caused by the huge cargo ships cruising the ocean. The largest market on the planet was infected by malpractice. The most important benchmark in the world was rigged. Other markets, benchmarks on markets, derivatives on benchmarks on markets, or even benchmarks on derivatives on benchmarks on markets (such as the so-called ISDAfix), were subject to manipulation or conspiratorial behaviour.

It could be argued that only 'sophisticated' traders, investors, fund managers and multinational corporations that traded financial derivatives or foreign exchange contracts on a daily basis were really impacted. After all, the vast majority of turnover in these markets takes place between banks, or between banks and large institutions. They were the ones opting to go to sea.

But because the prices and numbers affected had a direct link to money and banks, and because money and banks are such an integral part of our society, the list of people affected is longer than one might initially think. Mortgages and bonds held by pension funds have been affected, as have student loans and credit card debt. Indirectly, it goes even further. It has affected valuation methods relating to accounting and trading portfolios, tax, risk management and central bank policy. The level of interest rates and the value of currencies affect us all, not least given how interconnected the international financial system has become. That is why the issue has had consequences far beyond the few dozen traders and banks directly involved in the scandals. The waves have grown larger and larger, reaching those on land – most of whom were completely unaware of what was going on out at sea, let alone inside the vessels causing the tsunami.

As a direct consequence of the LIBOR and FX scandals, regulators and policy makers have attempted to establish 'correctness' in the way important financial benchmarks are generated. Although, as we know, benchmarks are not and cannot be markets in themselves, some of them have been made to 'look' more like markets. For instance, the time window for calculating the WM/Reuters 4 p.m. London closing spot rate has been widened from one to five minutes. By including more trade and order data, the fixing not only becomes more difficult to manipulate, but it also captures more of what is actually going on in the market during any particular day.[1] The widely used FX benchmark is still not a market per se, but is seemingly a better reflection of a market.

Not all benchmarks are based on actual transactions, with LIBOR being the prime example. According to new rules, however, *if* there is an underlying market out there, such data shall be used 'if available and appropriate'.[2] Banks are still very reluctant to lend to each other for longer maturities, or indeed to the wider economy. Acknowledging that the underlying market might be illiquid or even non-existent, provisions have instead been made that allow LIBOR banks to base their submissions not only on traditional borrowing and lending activities between banks, but also upon financial contracts in related markets, such as interest rate futures, interest rates swaps, forward rate agreements, FX swaps and OISs.[3] In a worst-case scenario, such as during periods of 'market turmoil and inactivity when inter-bank offers are absent', banks may even use their so-called 'expert judgement' when submitting their LIBOR quotes.[4] Several currencies and maturities have also been removed from the LIBOR fixing mechanism altogether.[5] For instance, there is no nine-month US dollar LIBOR any longer. Nor are there any LIBORs linked to the Canadian dollar or the Swedish krona, which, instead, have kept their domestic benchmarks (CDOR and STIBOR).

In sum, these benchmarks have been made to *appear* more market-like, but no change has been made to the definition of what they *are*. The LIBOR definition remains exactly the same as it used to be, and the new rules hardly challenge its existence. On the contrary, making the process more formal and robust will probably only serve to justify and encourage its further use. In a sense, LIBOR, like the large banks that are part of the panels setting it, has been deemed 'too big to fail'. Overall, these measures should be seen as steps in the right direction – but only as long as the process is moving towards greater transparency. A pair of 3D glasses might make a film more realistic. However, it will not make it real.

* * *

The perception of the industry has also changed at a more micro level. LIBOR and FX manipulation, rogue trading and other scandals have been used as illustrations of how the banking culture has changed, increasingly becoming fertile soil for 'rotten apples'. Some argue that it is simply a matter of cutting off the diseased branches of a tree. After all, it sometimes appears as if junior traders and bank employees have almost single-handedly caused tremendous damage to the banks and to faith in the financial system. Others argue that the true problems lie in the soil, that breaking the law, bending the rules or taking excessive risk is something that relates to the environment in which traders work. That it is all about perverse incentive structures, the lack of regulation and controls, managers' desire to push traders to the limit, or the erosion of a decent 'culture' in the City or Wall Street.

Since the financial crisis of 2007–08, a number of reforms have been introduced with the aim of not only preventing future crises, but also steering bankers and traders away from risky behaviour and a culture of short-term thinking. 'Remuneration policies which lead to risk–reward imbalances, short-termism and excessive risk-taking undermine confidence in the financial sector,' the CEO of the UK's Prudential Regulation Authority

(PRA), Andrew Bailey, said in 2016. Stricter rules on the form in which bonuses are paid out, and even clauses allowing banks to claw back bonuses should things go wrong, are thought to align the interests of traders more closely with those of the shareholders of the bank. The logic is familiar, the idea being that traders think short term and take excessive risk almost by default if a potential reward is offered to them personally. Change the reward structure, and traders will behave differently.

While this certainly might trigger some traders to leave trading (many already have) and discourage new generations from entering the banking sector in search of easy money, I am less convinced about its effectiveness in preventing risk taking more generally. Bonuses had no direct influence on my mismarking episode at Merrill Lynch during those six weeks in early 2009. The next potential bonus payment was at least ten months away, and I couldn't see that far ahead. In fact, in late 2008 I felt that there was nothing the bank could do to compensate me for what I was going through. However, being paid well for what I did probably made me believe that I was very good at it, and that what I was doing was of some greater importance, whatever that might be. Bonuses, whether small or large, tend to be paid once a year. This might be considered as short term to shareholders or to society as a whole. However, 365 days is an eternity in the foreign exchange and money markets. A minute or a day can be long. Curbing bonuses is not, in itself, going to solve all the problems. Irrespective of potential monetary rewards, some people will always be attracted to unpredictable and dangerous seas.

Trading and risk taking go hand in hand. Even by the standards of Merrill Lynch, I was a very aggressive risk taker.

When the Irish Financial Regulator fined the bank after my scandal, it argued that Merrill had failed to 'manage effectively market risk limits in respect of the trader's activities'. Strangely, to date, I cannot recall a single moment when I was emailed or told formally, or even informally, what, if any, my risk limits were. All other banks I had worked for, or heard of, set clear limits on how much risk a trader was allowed to take. Sometimes, traders (myself included) would argue for bigger limits, in which case they might be increased. Merrill Lynch was different. Nowhere else, I thought, were traders given so much trust and power at the outset – and were then encouraged and motivated to maximise a seemingly limitless potential. For me, it was like being in heaven. It was an environment I thrived in, like giving Viagra to a sex addict or inviting an alcoholic to a free bar. The flipside, of course, was that it was also like driving a Formula One car without a helmet or skydiving without a back-up parachute.

In the run-up to the financial crisis, many banks took a great deal of risk. Because of the chaos that followed, regulators have since made it much more difficult for banks to speculate as freely as they did before. This ought to not only make banks safer for the public again, but also make banks safer from potential rogue trading scandals in the future. Risk taking, however, is inherent in banking, and banks will continue to take risks in the financial markets regardless of what any future regulation looks like. I think it is important to remember that the risk-taking activity itself is delegated to relatively few individuals within the banks. In order to understand what banks do, how markets work or what risk is about, it is not enough to have a thorough knowledge of 'banks', 'markets' and 'risk'. It is also necessary to understand how traders think, talk, behave and interact.

Another set of reforms, or reform proposals, have aimed to achieve greater 'formalisation and professionalism'.[6] For instance, from having been an unregulated activity (or, to be more precise, a self-regulated activity among the panel banks themselves in conjunction with the BBA), LIBOR is now regulated by the FCA. A similar shift has taken place with IBORs in other jurisdictions. A specific code of conduct ('the LIBOR Code') sets out standards that LIBOR panel banks are expected to follow. These changes are logical given the string of fines imposed on banks for having manipulated, or having attempted to manipulate, the benchmark.

'Rabobank's misconduct is among the most serious we have identified on LIBOR. Traders and submitters treated LIBOR submissions as a potential way to make money, with no regard for the integrity of the market. This is unacceptable,' said Tracey McDermott, the FCA's Director of Enforcement and Financial Crime, after the UK regulator had fined the Dutch bank £105 million in October 2013.[7]

Benchmark manipulation has also been made a criminal offence, and, following the first guilty verdict of an individual involved, the Hon. Mr Justice Cooke said: 'The conduct involved here is to be marked out as dishonest and wrong, and a message sent to the world of banking accordingly. The reputation of Libor is important to the City, as a financial sector, and the banking institutions of this City.'[8] All in all, the reforms following the scandals have strived to eliminate – or at least greatly reduce – the *incentives* for manipulation, abuse or collusive practices. Considering the threatened punishments, neither banks nor individual traders would likely see them as activities worth doing.

Revelations about how some traders have thought, talked, behaved and interacted have made spectacular headlines in recent years. No matter how awful some of these conversations might seem, however, it is important not to see them in isolation when shaping new theories, rules or laws.

* * *

Banks themselves have also attempted to change, introducing stricter rules, controls and training requirements. For reputational, regulatory or legal reasons, no bank would want to find such behaviour going on inside their dealing room. Furthermore, no bank would be willing to defend dealing room behaviour on the basis that it was following conventions that were based on 'what everyone else in the market had been doing for years'.

Banks have also substantially increased the number of compliance officers scrutinising what the traders are up to. Numerous dealing room conventions have been banned, or have become subject to internal monitoring and oversight (such as the use of mobile phones and multi-bank electronic chatrooms), in order to limit the possibilities for improper communication between traders and their competitors, interdealer brokers and clients. However, as two Bloomberg journalists pointed out, 'while banks can limit access to details about client orders on their computer systems, they can't keep employees from talking to one another'.[9] Communication via Snapchat, in the restroom or in the smokers' corner is difficult to monitor. Reportedly, some banks have even gone as far as hiring experts from the military or the CIA to study the behavioural patterns of traders, and so to identify the next possible market manipulator or rogue trader.[10] An underlying assumption here is that traders in these markets have often manipulated, colluded or gone rogue as a result of having the means and opportunities to do so. By reducing and monitoring human communication, society (and the banks themselves) can thus be reassured that the markets are fair. Everyone, in theory, should feel safer.

Whereas boosting the support functions within banks and allowing compliance officers and risk managers to do their jobs more independently of traders are a good thing, this also poses new questions about trading and banking more generally. Trust and reciprocity remain central to banking, as well as to trading in the FX, money and derivatives markets. If informal norms and conventions in the market are deliberately broken down, how will this affect liquidity, what kind of rules will follow, and how will the enforcement mechanism work?

Senior bankers have been vocal too. 'Banks must undergo a wholesale change in their culture and refocus their behaviour on meeting the needs of customers to restore trust in the industry,' Stephen Hester, then CEO of RBS, said in 2012. Marcus Agius, then Chairman of Barclays, argued in 2010 that: 'The leaders of industry must collectively procure a visible and substantive change in the culture of our institutions, so as fundamentally to convince the world once again that they are businesses which can be relied on.' Banks, so they claim, want to change their culture in order to gain the public's trust again. Regulators and policy makers, meanwhile, want the moral code of banking to be more in line with the morality of society as a whole. Traders and bankers, it is argued, need to know the difference between right and wrong and start behaving accordingly. And banks, therefore, need to have clear principles with regard to what is 'right' and 'wrong' trading and banking.

These might just be nice words. Regardless of the political view one might have, however, they are also the core of the issue. Banks need to change, and they need to do so voluntarily. What is clear is that the structure should not be seen as one in which 'a small number of employees' have been able to cheat the system. Rather, banks created this system – and then took advantage of having contributed to, and sustained, a great illusion of what the world truly looked like.

* * *

On 16 March 2015, I was watching the FCA website like a hawk. I kept on reloading the page, checking whether they had removed me from their list of 'prohibited individuals'. It was five years to the day since I had received my five-year ban, and more than six years since I had last set foot in the Merrill Lynch dealing room. I wasn't desperate to go out to sea again. I was desperate for some kind of closure.

Nothing happened. I was still a prohibited individual. Nothing happened the next day either, or the day after that.

I contacted the FCA, but nobody I spoke to knew how the process worked. There seemed to be a process in place for adding rotten apples to the prohibited individuals list, but not for removing them.

After a couple of weeks, I finally got hold of the right person, who told me I had to make an application to get the prohibition order revoked – effectively demonstrating that I had rehabilitated myself. I wrote a long letter, and waited.

Then, more than a month later, I finally got the reply. My ban had been revoked. Although I hadn't been given a licence to trade, I was no longer prohibited from applying, should I wish to do so.

Should I ever wish to go through it all again.

Should I ever wish to put myself in a position where I *had* to go through it again ...

GLOSSARY

Arbitrage: A trading strategy that takes advantage of two or more financial instruments being mispriced relative to each other.

Banging the close: Aggressively buying or selling a financial instrument in order to influence the price level at a specific time during the day.

Base rate: The interest rate that the Bank of England charges banks for secured overnight lending.

Behavioural finance: The study of the influence of psychology on the behaviour of participants in the financial markets.

Bid: The price that a market maker is prepared to pay for an asset or a financial instrument.

Bid–offer spread: The difference between the price at which a market maker is willing to buy an asset or a financial instrument and the price at which it is willing to sell.

Book: The portfolio of financial instruments held by a trader.

Brokerage firm: A financial institution that facilitates the buying and selling of financial instruments between a buyer and a seller.

Call-out: A co-ordinated action to simultaneously request prices in a particular financial instrument from multiple market makers.

Cap: An interest rate cap, or simply a 'cap', is a derivative that pays out when a specified interest rate benchmark (such as LIBOR) is above a certain level.

Collateralised debt obligation (CDO): A derivative whose income payments and principal repayments are dependent on a pool of different financial instruments which themselves are loans and are due to pay interest and ultimately be repaid.[1]

Covered interest parity: The covered interest parity states that the interest rate differential between two currencies in the money markets should equal the differential between the FX forward and FX spot rates. If this is not the case, arbitrage would be possible.

Credit default swap (CDS): A derivative designed to provide protection against the risk of a credit event (e.g. bankruptcy) relating to a particular company or country.

Cross-currency basis swap (CRS): A derivative where two counterparties effectively borrow from each other in two different currencies. The counterparties exchange principals at both the start and the maturity of the swap, as well as regular floating interest rate payments, which generally are indexed to LIBOR or equivalent benchmarks.

Derivative: A financial contract whose value is dependent on (i.e. derived from) the value of an underlying asset, index or measurement.

Discount window: A credit facility in which eligible financial institutions can borrow from the central bank.

Eurodollar market: The birth of the Eurodollar market occurred in 1957, when banks created a market in Europe in which US dollar deposits were re-lent to European institutions instead of being reinvested in the United States. Eurodollars thereby came to be defined as deposits denominated in US dollars in banks outside the US. These kinds of deposits were later denominated in other currencies, and these 'Eurocurrencies' in general (Eurodeutschmarks, Euroyen, Eurosterling and so on) came to represent borrowing and lending outside the jurisdiction of the central bank issuing the currency in question.

Federal Reserve: The central bank of the United States.

Floor: An interest rate floor, or simply a 'floor', is a derivative that pays out when a specified interest rate benchmark (such as LIBOR) is below a certain level.

Forward rate agreement (FRA): An OTC derivatives contract on the future level of interest rates (typically LIBOR).

FX forward: An agreement to exchange sums of currency at an agreed exchange rate on a value date that is in more than two bank business days' time.

FX spot: An agreement to exchange sums of currency at an agreed exchange rate on a value date that is usually in two bank business days' time.

FX swap: A combination of an FX spot transaction plus an FX forward done simultaneously, but in the opposite direction.

Government bond: A debt security issued by a government, typically with a term of one year or more.

Hedge: A trade, often involving the use of derivatives, designed to reduce risk.

Interbank money market: The market where banks borrow from and lend to each other.

Interdealer broker: A brokerage firm that acts as an intermediary between major dealers (typically banks) to facilitate trades.

Interest rate swap (IRS): A derivative where two counter-parties agree to exchange periodic interest payments based on a specified notional amount. Typically, interest rate swaps involve the exchange a fixed interest rate for a floating rate (e.g. LIBOR), or vice versa.

Layering: Submitting a series of manipulative buy (or sell) orders with the intention of selling rather than buying (or buying rather than selling). The manipulative orders are intended to trick other market participants by creating the false impression of heavy buying or selling pressure.

LIBOR fixing: The LIBOR fixing is calculated using a trimmed arithmetic mean of the individually submitted rates from the LIBOR panel banks.

LIBOR panel bank: A bank participating in the LIBOR fixing mechanism.

Liquidity: A term used to describe the ease and speed with which an asset can be turned into cash.

Low-balling: Reducing a LIBOR submission in order to avoid the stigma of being perceived by others (market participants, media, etc.) as having a high cost of borrowing.

Mark to market: To adjust the value of a financial instrument or portfolio to reflect its current market value (usually the daily closing price).

Market maker: A market participant who facilitates trading in a financial instrument by supplying (tradeable) buy and sell quotes.

Mismark: To wrongly adjust the value of a financial instrument or portfolio to reflect its current market value.

Monetary transmission mechanism: The process by which monetary policy decisions taken by a central bank affect prices, interest rates, credit and ultimately agents' behaviour and decision making in the wider economy.

Money market risk premium: The difference between the interest rate at which banks borrow from each other for a specific maturity and the 'risk-free' interest rate for the same maturity.

Mortgage bond: A debt security issued by a financial institution that is collateralised by one or several mortgaged properties.

Offer: The price at which a market maker offers to sell an asset or a financial instrument.

Option: A financial contract that gives the buyer the right, but not the obligation, to buy or sell an underlying instrument at a predetermined price in the future.

Over the counter (OTC): Used to describe transactions that are bilaterally negotiated between two market participants.

Overnight index swap (OIS): An interest rate swap where the floating rate is an overnight rate (or overnight index rate), compounded over a specified term.

Position: The amount of a financial instrument held by a trader and generally a term for how sensitive the trader's book is to different price movements in the market. The holder of a long position will profit if the price of the financial instrument goes up, whereas the holder of a short position will profit if the price goes down.

Repo: A repurchase agreement, or 'repo', is a form of asset-backed borrowing, usually for the short term. The borrower sells securities (such as bonds) and simultaneously agrees to buy them back at a predetermined price at a later date.

Run-through: A sequence of prices or price indications provided by an interdealer broker to its clients.

Spoofing: Submitting a manipulative buy (or sell) order with the intention of selling rather than buying (or buying rather than selling).

Stop-loss order: An order that is triggered when a reference price reaches a certain predetermined level. A stop-loss order is designed to limit the loss on a position in a financial instrument in the event of an unfavourable price move.

Syndicated loans: Credits granted by a group of banks to a borrower.

Take-profit order: An order that is triggered when a reference price reaches a certain predetermined level. A take-profit order is designed to lock in profits on a position in a financial instrument in the event of a favourable price move.

T-bill: A short-term debt security issued by a government, typically with a term of one year or less.

Term Auction Facility (TAF): Established in December 2007, the TAF enabled banks to borrow from the Federal Reserve without using the discount window.

Tomnext: Financial contracts with a start date tomorrow and an end date the day after tomorrow.

Wash trade: A sale or purchase of a financial instrument where there is no change in beneficial interest or market risk, or where the transfer of beneficial interest or market risk is only between parties acting in concert or collusion.[2]

White hat: An ethical computer hacker.

NOTES

Introduction
1   Central Bank of Ireland (2009).
2   Unless specifically mentioned, I use the term 'LIBOR' in this book also when referring to other 'IBORs', such as EURIBOR, TIBOR, STIBOR, NIBOR, etc.
3   Stenfors (2013).
4   Story and Dash (2009).
5   Dominiczak (2009).
6   On 21 December 2015, the sentence was reduced to 11 years. Royal Courts of Justice (2015).
7   *The Telegraph* (2015).
8   Berkshire Hathaway Inc. (2002).
9   Thornton (2009).

1. The barometer of fear
1   Spiegel (2001).
2   Bank of England (1999).
3   For a good overview of liquidity risk, see Kyle (1985) and Brunnermeier (2009).
4   Brunnermeier (2009); Khandani and Lo (2007).
5   Thornton (2009).
6   Bank of England (2007).

2. 'Why did you do it?'
1   Feist (2012).
2   Sandel (2012).

3. Superheroes and beauty pageants
1   Financial Services Authority (2012a).
2   BBA (2012a).
3   JBA (2012).

4   Gyntelberg and Wooldridge (2008). The authors acknowledge
    that LIBOR panel banks, in theory, could act strategically in their
    fixing, but that the trimming process acts as a hindering factor.
5   Financial Services Authority (2012b).
6   UBS (2012).
7   Financial Services Authority (2012c).
8   Treanor (2015).
9   Financial Services Authority (2013a).
10 Financial Conduct Authority (2015).
11 Financial Services Authority (2012d).
12 Vaughan (2015c).
13 Fortado (2015).
14 Vaughan (2015b).
15 Davies (2015); Campbell (2015).
16 Financial Services Authority (2012b).
17 Mollenkamp and Whitehouse (2008).
18 Financial Services Agency (2011a; 2011b; 2011c).
19 Stenfors (2014a).
20 Keynes (1936).
21 Duffy and Nagel (1997); Ho et al. (1998); Nagel (1995; 1999);
    Nagel et al. (2002).
22 Güth et al. (2002).
23 Financial Services Authority (2012b).

4. The LIBOR illusion

1   BBA (2008b).
2   Stenfors (2014a).
3   This chapter draws extensively from Stenfors and Lindo (2016).
4   ECB (2016).
5   Sarver (1990).
6   World Trade Organization (2016).
7   Higonnet (1985).
8   Higonnet (1985).
9   Einzing (1970).
10 Clendenning (1970).
11 United States Department of Justice (2012); Eaglesham and Perez
    (2012).

12 MacKenzie (2007).
13 Sarver (1990).
14 Financial Services Authority (2013b).
15 Arrow and Debreu (1954); Copeland and Weston (1988); Ross (1976).
16 Financial Services Authority (2009).
17 CME (2006).
18 Mollenkamp et al. (2012).
19 Futures Industry Association (2012).
20 CME (2006).
21 BIS (1986; 1999; 2013a).
22 BIS (2014).
23 Camacho and Nieto (2009).
24 Statistisk Sentralbyrå (2016).
25 Statistisk Sentralbyrå (2014).
26 Hodges (2016).
27 Hodges (2016).
28 ECB (2016).
29 BIS (2010a).
30 Hull (1991).
31 See, for instance, Bank of England (2007), McAndrews et al. (2008) and Soultanaeva and Strömqvist (2009).
32 SNB (2015).
33 Stenfors (2014b).
34 Stenfors (2014a).
35 United States District Court Southern District of New York (2012).
36 Vaughan (2015a).

5. The value of secrets
1 Simmel (1906).
2 CFTC (2016a).
3 State of New York Office of the Attorney General (2009b); McCool (2009); Kollewe (2009).
4 Board of Governors of the Federal Reserve System (2009).
5 Clark (2009).
6 Story and Dash (2009).

7   State of New York Office of the Attorney General (2009a).

8   Central Bank of Ireland (2009).

9   Strange (1986).

10 *Euromoney* (2012a; 2012b).

11 Goodhart (1989).

12 Vaughan and Finch (2013).

13 Financial Stability Board (2011).

14 BBA (2012b).

15 European Banking Federation (2012a).

16 BBA (2008b).

17 BBA (2008a).

18 ACI (2008a; 2008b).

19 Mollenkamp and Whitehouse (2008).

20 CFTC (2016a).

21 CFTC (2014a).

22 Financial Conduct Authority (2015).

23 BBA (2013); European Banking Federation (2012b); FNO
    (2011); JBA (2012).

24 Lukes (1974).

6. Conventions and conspiracies

1   CFTC (2014b).

2   BBC News (2014).

3   Chon et al. (2015).

4   BIS (2016).

5   *Euromoney* (2012b).

6   BIS (2010b).

7   Barber and Odean (2001).

8   Financial Conduct Authority (2014b).

9   New York State Department of Financial Services (2015).

10 Financial Conduct Authority (2014b).

11 Financial Conduct Authority (2014b).

12 *Business Wire* (2015).

13 BIS (2016).

14 Aitken et al. (1996); Mitchell (2001); Goodhart and Curcio
    (1991); Grossman et al. (1997).

15 Yule (1927); Tversky and Kahneman (1974).

16 Ball et al. (1985).

17 New York State Department of Financial Services (2015).

18 Christie and Schultz (1994a; 1994b).

19 SEC (1996a).

20 SEC (1996b).

21 SEC (1996b).

22 European Commission (2014).

23 FEMR (2015).

24 United States District Court Southern District of New York (2015).

25 Stiglitz and Greenwald (2003), p. 26.

26 ACI (2015), pp. 103–4.

27 Cheung and Chinn (2001); Cheung and Wong (2000).

28 Harley (2006), p. 781.

29 McAdams (1997).

30 See, for instance, Carvalho (1983–84) and Lawson (1985).

31 Smith (1991 [1776]).

7. Rotten apples

1 Enrich (2016).

2 Kahneman (2011).

3 Thaler (1985).

4 See, in particular, Lyng (1990).

5 See http://graphics.wsj.com/libor-unraveling-tom-hayes/1.

8. The perfect storm

1 FEMR (2015).

2 European Council (2015), p. 79.

3 ICE (2016).

4 IBA (2014).

5 HM Treasury (2012).

6 IBA (2014).

7 Financial Conduct Authority (2013).

8 Hickey and Grierson (2015).

9 Verlaine and Finch (2014).

10 Finch et al. (2016).

Glossary

1 http://lexicon.ft.com/Term?term=Collateralised-debt-obligation-CDO.

2 https://www.handbook.fca.org.uk/handbook/MAR/1/6.html?date=2016-06-30.

BIBLIOGRAPHY

ACI (2008a) 'Euribor ACI recommendation to BBA on Libor fixing issue'. Letter to Angela Knight, 6 June. Available from: http://www.aciforex.org/docs/misc/20080606_Euribor_ACI_recommendation_to_BBA_on_Libor_Fixing_issue.pdf [accessed 1 September 2012].

ACI (2008b) 'Euribor ACI final recommendation to BBA on Libor fixing issue'. Letter to Angela Knight, 8 July. Available from: http://www.aciforex.org/docs/misc/20080708_Euribor_ACI_final_recommendation_to_BBA_on_Libor_Fixing_issue.pdf [accessed 1 September 2012].

ACI (2015) *The Model Code: The International Code of Conduct & Practice for the Financial Markets.* February 2015 edition. Paris: ACI.

Aitken, M., Brown, P., Buckland, C., Izan, H. Y. and Walter, T. (1996) 'Price clustering on the Australian Stock Exchange'. *Pacific-Basin Finance Journal*, 4, 297–314.

Arrow, K. J. and Debreu, G. (1954) 'Existence of an equilibrium for a competitive economy'. *Econometrica*, 22, 265–90.

Ball, C. A., Torous, W. A. and Tschoegl, A. E. (1985) 'The degree of price resolution: the case of the gold market'. *Journal of Futures Markets*, 5, 29–43.

Bank of England (1999) *The Transmission Mechanism of Monetary Policy*. London: Monetary Policy Publications, Bank of England.

Bank of England (2007) 'An indicative decomposition of Libor spreads'. *Bank of England Quarterly Bulletin*, 47 (4), 498–9.

Barber, B. and Odean, T. (2001) 'Boys will be boys: gender, overconfidence, and common stock investment'. *Quarterly Journal of Economics*, 116, 261–92.

BBA (2008a) 'BBA LIBOR consultation: feedback statement, 5th August 2008'. London: British Bankers' Association (BBA). Available from: http://hb.betterregulation.com/external/BBA%20Libor%20Con.pdf [accessed 1 September 2012].

BBA (2008b) 'LIBOR gets enhanced governance and scrutiny procedures'. Press release, 18 December. London: British Bankers' Association (BBA). Available from: http://www. bbalibor.com/news-releases/libor-gets-enhanced-governance-andscrutiny-procedures [accessed 1 September 2012].

BBA (2012a) 'BBALIBOR explained'. British Bankers' Association (BBA) website. Available from: http://www.bbalibor.com/ bbalibor-explained/the-basics [accessed 1 September 2012].

BBA (2012b) 'About us'. British Bankers' Association (BBA) website. Available from: http://www.bba.org.uk/about-us [accessed 1 September 2012].

BBA (2013) 'Panels'. British Bankers' Association (BBA) website. Available from: http://www.bbalibor.com/panels [accessed 1 May 2013].

BBC News (2014) 'Six banks fined £2.6bn by regulators over forex failings'. BBC News, 12 November. Available from: http://www. bbc.co.uk/news/business-30016007 [accessed 21 December 2016].

Berkshire Hathaway Inc. (2002) 2002 Annual Report. Omaha NE: Berkshire Hathaway Inc. Available from: http://www. berkshirehathaway.com/2002ar/2002ar.pdf [accessed 21 December 2016].

BIS (1986) Recent Innovations in International Banking. CGFS Publications No. 1 (April). Basel: Bank for International Settlements (BIS).

BIS (1999) Central Bank Survey of Foreign Exchange and Derivatives Market Activity 1998. Basel: Bank for International Settlements (BIS).

BIS (2010a) Triennial Central Bank Survey: Foreign exchange and derivatives market activity in April 2010. Preliminary results. Basel: Bank for International Settlements (BIS). Available from: http:// www.bis.org/publ/rpfx10.pdf [accessed 21 December 2016].

BIS (2010b) Triennial Central Bank Survey: Report on global foreign exchange market activity in 2010. Basel: Bank for International Settlements (BIS). Available from: http://www.bis.org/publ/ rpfxf10t.pdf [accessed 21 December 2016].

BIS (2013a) Triennial Central Bank Survey: OTC interest rate derivatives turnover in April 2013. Preliminary global results. Basel:

Bank for International Settlements (BIS). Available from: http://
www.bis.org/publ/rpfxf13irt.pdf [accessed 21 December 2016].

BIS (2013b) *Triennial Central Bank Survey. Foreign exchange
turnover in April 2013. Preliminary global results.* Basel: Bank for
International Settlements (BIS). Available from: http://www.bis.
org/publ/rpfx13fx.pdf [accessed 21 December 2016].

BIS (2014) 'International banking and financial market
developments'. *BIS Quarterly Review*, December.

BIS (2016) *Triennial Central Bank Survey. Global foreign exchange
market turnover in 2016.* Basel: Bank for International Settlements
(BIS). Available from: http://www.bis.org/publ/rpfxf16fxt.pdf
[accessed 21 December 2016].

Board of Governors of the Federal Reserve System (2009) 'Treasury,
Federal Reserve, and the FDIC provide assistance to Bank of
America'. Press release, 16 January. Washington DC: Board of
Governors. Available from: https://www.federalreserve.gov/
newsevents/press/bcreg/20090116a.htm [accessed 21 December
2016].

Brunnermeier, M. K. (2009) 'Deciphering the liquidity and credit
crunch 2007–2008'. *Journal of Economic Perspectives*, 23 (1),
77–100.

Business Wire (2015) 'UBS participates in resolutions of industry-wide
FX matter'. *Business Wire*, 20 May. Available from: http://www.
businesswire.com/news/home/20150519007252/en/UBS-AG-
UK-Regulatory-Announcement-UBS-Participates [accessed 21
December 2016].

Camacho, C. M. and Nieto, J. A. R. (2009) 'The globalization of
financial capital, 1997–2008'. Research on Money and Finance
Discussion Papers No. 6. London: Department of Economics,
SOAS, University of London.

Campbell, A. (2015) 'Libor trial hears of "bribe" wash trades as
Lehman failed: bank's collapse hampered ¥400 billion wash
trade'. Risk.net, 12 June. Available from: http://www.risk.net/
operational-risk-and-regulation/news/2412989/lIBOR-trial-
hears-of-bribe-wash-trades-as-lehman-failed [accessed 21
December 2016].

Carvalho, F. J. C. (1983–84) 'On the concept of time in Shacklean
and Sraffian economics'. *Journal of Post Keynesian Economics*, 6
(2), 265–80.

Central Bank of Ireland (2009) 'Settlement agreement between the
    Financial Regulator and Merrill Lynch International Bank Lim-
    ited'. Press release, 23 October. Dublin: Central Bank of Ireland.
    Available from: http://www.centralbank.ie/press-area/press-re-
    leases/Pages/SettlementAgreementbetweenFinancialRegulato-
    randMerrillLynchInternationalBankLimited.aspx [accessed 21
    December 2016].

CFTC (2014a) 'In the matter of: Lloyds Banking Group
    plc and Lloyds Bank plc'. CFTC Docket No. 14-18.
    Washington DC: Commodity Futures Trading Commission
    (CFTC). Available from: http://www.cftc.gov/idc/groups/
    public/@lrenforcementactions/documents/legalpleading/
    enflloydsorderdf072814.pdf [accessed 1 June 2011].

CFTC (2014b) 'CFTC orders five banks to pay over $1.4 billion
    in penalties for attempted manipulation of foreign exchange
    benchmark rates'. Press release, 12 November. Washington DC:
    Commodity Futures Trading Commission (CFTC). Available
    from: http://www.cftc.gov/PressRoom/PressReleases/pr7056-14
    [accessed 21 December 2016].

CFTC (2016a) 'In the matter of: Citibank, N.A.; Citibank Japan
    Ltd.; and Citigroup Global Markets Japan Inc.'. CFTF Docket
    No. 16-17. Washington DC: Commodity Futures Trading
    Commission (CFTC). Available from: http://www.cftc.gov/idc/
    groups/public/@lrenforcementactions/documents/legalpleading/
    enfcitibanklibororder052516.pdf [accessed 21 December 2016].

CFTC (2016b) 'Examples of misconduct from written and oral
    communications by Citibank, N.A. (Citi) and its affiliates,
    Citibank Japan Ltd. (CJL) and Citigroup Global Markets
    Japan Inc. (CGMJ)'. Washington DC: Commodity Futures
    Trading Commission (CFTC). Available from: http://www.
    cftc.gov/idc/groups/public/@newsroom/documents/file/
    libormisconduct052516.pdf [accessed 21 December 2016].

Cheung, Y.-W. and Chinn, M. D. (2001) 'Currency traders and
    exchange rate dynamics: a survey of the US market'. *Journal of
    International Money and Finance*, 20, 439–71.

Cheung, Y.-W. and Wong, C. Y.-P. (2000) 'A survey of market
    practitioners' views on exchange rate dynamics'. *Journal of
    International Economics*, 51, 401–19.

BIBLIOGRAPHY

Chon, G., Binham, C. and Noonan, L. (2015) 'Six banks fined $5.6bn over rigging of foreign exchange markets'. *Financial Times*, 20 May. Available from: http://www.ft.com/cms/s/0/23fa681c-fe73-11e4-be9f-00144feabdc0.html#slide0 [accessed 21 December 2016].

Christie, W. and Schultz, P. (1994a) 'Why did NASDAQ market makers avoid odd-eight quotes?' *Journal of Finance*, 49, 1813–40.

Christie, W. and Schultz, P. (1994b) 'Why did NASDAQ market makers stop avoiding odd-eight quotes?' *Journal of Finance*, 49, 1841–60.

Clark, A. (2009) 'John Thain gets subpoena over Merrill Lynch bonuses'. *The Guardian*, 27 January. Available from: https://www.theguardian.com/business/2009/jan/27/john-thain-subpoenaed-over-bonuses [accessed 21 December 2016].

Clendenning, E. W. (1970) *The Euro-Dollar Market*. Oxford: Clarendon Press.

CME (2006) 'CME celebrates 25th anniversary of benchmark CME Eurodollar futures contract'. Note to shareholders. Available from: http://files.shareholder.com/downloads/CME/0x0x114640/01d03c80-55a0-4741-a374-9531675830/220929.pdf [accessed 1 June 2011].

Copeland, T. E. and Weston, J. F. (1988) *Financial Theory and Corporate Policy*. Reading MA: Addison-Wesley Publishing Company, Inc.

Davies, A. (2015) 'Hayes promised fees to brokers through "wash" trades, court hears'. Reuters, 12 June. Available from: http://www.reuters.com/article/2015/06/12/trial-llBOR-idUSL5N0YY2O120150612#4fdrR5iPe8GMgBS7.97 [accessed 21 December 2016].

Dominiczak, P. (2009) '£85m rogue trader: it's a misunderstanding'. *The Evening Standard*, 12 March. Available from: http://www.standard.co.uk/news/85m-rogue-trader-its-a-misunderstanding-6831492.html [accessed 21 December 2016].

Duffy, J. and Nagel, R. (1997) 'On the robustness of behaviour in experimental beauty contest games'. *Economic Journal*, 107 (445), 1684–700.

Eaglesham, J. and Perez, E. (2012) 'U.S. charges star trader'. *The Wall Street Journal*, 19 December. Available from: http://www.wsj.

com/articles/SB10001424127887324731304578189752666144398 [accessed 21 December 2016].

ECB (2016) 'MMS – Money Market Survey'. Statistical Data Warehouse website. Available from: https://sdw.ecb.europa.eu/browseExplanation.do?node=9689706 [accessed 21 May 2016].

Einzing, P. (1970) *The Euro-Dollar System: Practice and theory of international interest rates*, 4th edition. London: Macmillan.

Enrich, D. (2016) 'A disgraced trader's struggle for redemption'. *The Wall Street Journal*, 29 April.

Euromoney (2012a) 'Euromoney rates survey 2012'. *Euromoney*, 43, 515 (March).

Euromoney (2012b) 'Euromoney FX survey 2012'. *Euromoney*, 43, 517 (May).

European Banking Federation (2012a) 'Mission statement'. EBF website. Available from: http://www.ebf-fbe.eu/index.php?page=mission-statement [accessed 4 September 2012].

European Banking Federation (2012b) *Euribor Code of Conduct*. Brussels: European Money Markets Institute. Available from: http://www.euribor-ebf.eu/assets/files/Euribor_code_conduct.pdf [accessed 4 September 2012].

European Commission (2014) 'Antitrust: Commission settles cartel on bid–ask spreads charged on Swiss franc interest rate derivatives; fines four major banks €32.3 million'. Press release, 21 October. Available from: http://europa.eu/rapid/press-release_IP-14-1190_en.htm [accessed 21 December 2016].

European Council (2015) 'Proposal for a regulation of the European Parliament and of the Council on indices used as benchmarks in financial instruments and financial contracts. Approval of the final compromise text, 14985/15'. Brussels: Council of the European Union. Available from: http://data.consilium.europa.eu/doc/document/ST-14985-2015-INIT/en/pdf [accessed 24 February 2016].

Feist, P. (2012) *The Winter War and a Winter Warrior. The Redwood Stumper 2010: the newsletter of the Redwood Gun Club*. Arcata CA: Redwood Gun Club.

FEMR (2015) *Fair and Effective Markets Review: Final Report, June 2015*. London: Bank of England.

Financial Conduct Authority (2013) 'The FCA fines Rabobank £105 million for serious LIBOR-related misconduct'. Press release, 29 October. London: Financial Conduct Authority. Available from: https://www.fca.org.uk/news/the-fca-fines-rabobank-105-million-for-serious-libor-related-misconduct [accessed 21 December 2016].

Financial Conduct Authority (2014a) 'Final notice 2014: Lloyds Bank plc, Bank of Scotland plc, 28 July 2014'. London: Financial Conduct Authority. Available from: https://www.fca.org.uk/static/documents/final-notices/lloyds-bank-of-scotland.pdf [accessed 21 December 2016].

Financial Conduct Authority (2014b) 'Final notice 2014: HSBC Bank plc, 11 November'. London: Financial Conduct Authority. Available from: https://www.fca.org.uk/static/documents/final-notices/final-notice-hsbc.pdf [accessed 21 December 2016].

Financial Conduct Authority (2015) 'Final notice 2015: Deutsche Bank AG, 23 April'. London: Financial Conduct Authority. Available from: https://www.fca.org.uk/static/documents/final-notices/deutsche-bank-ag-2015.pdf [accessed 21 December 2016].

Financial Services Agency (2011a) 'Administrative actions against Citibank Japan Ltd'. Press release, 16 December. Tokyo: Financial Services Agency. Available from: http://www.fsa.go.jp/en/news/2011/20111216-1.html [accessed 21 December 2016].

Financial Services Agency (2011b) 'Administrative action on Citigroup Global Markets Japan Inc.' Press release, 16 December. Tokyo: Financial Services Agency. Available from: http://www.fsa.go.jp/en/news/2011/20111216-2.html [accessed 21 December 2016].

Financial Services Agency (2011c) 'Administrative actions against UBS Securities Japan Ltd and UBS AG, Japan branches'. Press release, 16 December. Tokyo: Financial Services Agency. Available from: http://www.fsa.go.jp/en/news/2011/20111216-3.html [accessed 21 December 2016].

Financial Services Authority (2009) 'Speech by Adair Turner, Chairman, FSA, The City Banquet, The Mansion House, London, 22 September'. FSA website. Available from: http://www.fsa.gov.uk/pages/Library/Communication/Speeches/2009/0922_at.shtml [accessed 21 December 2016].

Financial Services Authority (2012a) 'Barclays fined £59.5 million for significant failings in relation to LIBOR and EURIBOR'. Press release, 27 June. London: Financial Services Authority. Available from: http://www.fsa.gov.uk/library/communication/pr/2012/070.shtml [accessed 21 December 2016].

Financial Services Authority (2012b) 'Final notice 2012: Barclays Bank Plc, 27 June'. London: Financial Services Authority. Available from: http://www.fca.org.uk/static/documents/final-notices/barclays-jun12.pdf [accessed 21 December 2016].

Financial Services Authority (2012c) 'UBS fined £160 million for significant failings in relation to LIBOR and EURIBOR'. Press release, 19 December. London: Financial Services Authority. Available from: http://www.fsa.gov.uk/library/communication/pr/2012/116.shtml [accessed 21 December 2016].

Financial Services Authority (2012d) 'Final notice 2012: UBS AG, 19 December'. London: Financial Services Authority. Available from: http://www.fca.org.uk/static/documents/final-notices/ubs.pdf [accessed 21 December 2016].

Financial Services Authority (2013a) 'Final notice 2013: The Royal Bank of Scotland plc, 6 February'. London: Financial Services Authority. Available from: http://www.fca.org.uk/static/fca/documents/final-notices/rbs.pdf [accessed 21 December 2016].

Financial Services Authority (2013b) 'The regulation and supervision of benchmarks'. Policy Statement PS13/6 (March). London: Financial Services Authority. Available from: http://www.fsa.gov.uk/static/pubs/policy/ps13-06.pdf [accessed 21 December 2016].

Financial Stability Board (2011) 'Policy measures to address systemically important financial institutions, 4 November'. Basel: Financial Stability Board. Available from: http://www.financialstabilityboard.org/publications/r_111104bb.pdf [accessed 21 December 2016].

Finch, G., Detrixhe, J. and Choudhury, A. (2016) 'Spies who chased terrorists join banks to hunt for rogue traders'. Bloomberg, 16 February. Available from: http://www.bloomberg.com/news/articles/2016-02-16/spies-who-chased-terrorists-join-banks-to-hunt-for-rogue-traders [accessed 21 December 2016].

FNO (2011) 'Rules for the calculation and publication of Norwegian money market rates – NIBOR'. Oslo: Finans Norge (FNO). Available from: http://www.fno.no/no/Hoved/Markets/NIBOR---the-Norwegian-Interbank-Offered-Rate/ [accessed 1 May 2013].

Fortado, L. (2015) 'Former ICAP broker Darrell Read denies helping rig Libor'. *Financial Times*, 17 May. Available from: http://www.ft.com/cms/s/0/cfac6d1c-8d35-11e5-a549-b89a1dfede9b.html#axzz4IdxxeWso [accessed 21 December 2016].

Futures Industry Association (2012) 'Annual volume survey 2011'. *Futures Industry*. Available from: http://www.futuresindustry.org/files/css/magazineArticles/article-1383.pdf [accessed 21 December 2016].

Goodhart, C. A. E. (1989) *Money, Information and Uncertainty*, 2nd edition. London: Macmillan.

Goodhart, C. and Curcio, R. (1991) 'The clustering of bid/ask prices and the spread in the foreign exchange market'. LSE Financial Markets Group Discussion Paper No. 110. London: London School of Economics and Political Science (LSE).

Grossman, S. J., Miller, M. H., Cone, K. R., Fischel, D. R. and Ross, D. J. (1997) 'Clustering and competition in asset markets'. *Journal of Law and Economics*, 40 (1), 23–60.

Güth, W., Kocher, M. and Sutter, M. (2002) 'Experimental "beauty contests" with homogeneous and heterogeneous players and with interior and boundary equilibria'. *Economics Letters*, 74, 219–28.

Gyntelberg, J. and Wooldridge, P. (2008) 'Interbank fixings during the recent turmoil'. *BIS Quarterly Review*, March, 47–72.

Harley, D. (2006) 'Anticompetitive social norms as antitrust violations'. *California Law Review*, 94 (3), 769–92.

Hickey, S. and Grierson, J. (2015) 'Former City trader Tom Hayes given 14-year sentence for Libor rigging'. *The Guardian*, 3 August. Available from: https://www.theguardian.com/uk-news/2015/aug/03/former-city-trader-tom-hayes-convicted-of-libor-rigging [accessed 21 December 2016].

Higonnet, R. P. (1985) 'Eurobanks, Eurodollars and international debt' in Savona, P. and Sutija, G. (eds) *Eurodollars and International Banking*. Basingstoke: Macmillan.

HM Treasury (2012) *The Wheatley Review of LIBOR: Final report*. London: HM Treasury. Available from: http://cdn.hm-treasury.

gov.uk/wheatley_review_libor_finalreport_280912.pdf [accessed 21 December 2016].

Ho, T.-H., Camerer, C. and Weigelt, K. (1998) 'Iterated dominance and iterated best response in experimental "p-beauty contests"'. *American Economic Review*, 88 (4), 947–69.

Hodges, J. (2016) 'U.K. trader's "blind ambition" led to Libor fixing, SFO says'. Bloomberg, 17 May. Available from: http://www.bloomberg.com/news/articles/2016-05-17/libor-asks-by-barclays-big-dogs-were-tough-to-ignore-sfo-says [accessed 21 December 2016].

Hull, J. (1991) *Introduction to Futures and Options Markets.* Englewood Cliffs NJ: Prentice Hall.

IBA (2014) 'Libor Code of Conduct: contributing banks. issue 2: 3 February 2014'. London: ICE Benchmark Administration Limited. Available from: https://www.theice.com/publicdocs/IBA_Code_of_Conduct.pdf [accessed 15 March 2015].

ICE (2016) *Roadmap for ICE LIBOR: 18th March 2016.* London: ICE Benchmark Administration. Available from: https://www.theice.com/publicdocs/ICE_LIBOR_Roadmap0316.pdf [accessed 21 December 2016].

JBA (2012) *JBA TIBOR Publications Rules.* Tokyo: Japanese Bankers Association. Available from: http://www.zenginkyo.or.jp/en/tibor/publication_rules/index/publication_rulesE.pdf [accessed 1 September 2012].

Kahneman, D. (2011) *Thinking, Fast and Slow.* New York NY: Farrar, Straus & Giroux.

Keynes, J. M. (1936) *The General Theory of Employment, Interest and Money.* London: Macmillan.

Khandani, A. E. and Lo, A. W. (2007) 'What happened to the quants in August 2007?' *Journal of Investment Management*, 5 (4), 5–54.

Kollewe, J. (2009) 'Merrill Lynch reports record fourth-quarter loss'. *The Guardian*, 16 January. Available from: https://www.theguardian.com/business/2009/jan/16/merrilllynch-citigroup [accessed 21 December 2016].

Kyle, S. A. (1985) 'Continuous auctions and insider trading'. *Econometrica*, 53 (6), 1315–35.

Lawson, T. (1985) 'Uncertainty and economic analysis'. *Economic Journal*, 95 (380), 909–27.

Lukes, S. (1974) *Power: A radical view.* London: Macmillan.

Lyng, S. (1990) 'Edgework: a social psychological analysis of voluntary risk taking'. *American Journal of Sociology*, 95 (4), 851–86.

MacKenzie, D. (2007) 'The material production of virtuality: innovation, cultural geography and facticity in derivatives markets'. *Economy and Society*, 36 (3), 355–76.

McAdams, R. H. (1997) 'The origin, development, and regulation of norms'. *Michigan Law Review*, 96, 338–433.

McAndrews, J., Sarkar, A. and Wang, Z. (2008) 'The effect of the term auction facility on the London Interbank Offered Rate'. *Federal Reserve Bank of New York Staff Reports*, 335.

McCool, G. (2009) 'Merrill bonus names are not secret: NY judge'. Reuters, 18 March. Available from: http://www. reuters.com/article/us-bankofamerica-merrill-bonuses-idUSTRE52H7BT20090318 [accessed 21 December 2016].

Mitchell, J. D. (2001) 'Clustering and psychological barriers: the importance of numbers'. *Journal of Futures Markets*, 21 (5), 395–428.

Mollenkamp, C. and Whitehouse, M. (2008) 'Study casts doubt on key rate'. *The Wall Street Journal*, 29 May. Available from: http://www.wsj.com/articles/SB121200703762027135 [accessed 21 December 2016].

Mollenkamp, C., Ablan, J. and Goldstein, M. (2012) 'How gaming Libor became business as usual'. *International Financing Review*, 20 November. Available from: http://www.ifre.com/special-reporthow-gaming-libor-became-business-as-usual/21053916. article [accessed 21 December 2016].

Nagel, R. (1995) 'Unravelling in guessing games: an experimental study'. *American Economic Review*, 85, 1313–26.

Nagel, R. (1999) 'A survey of experimental beauty contest games: bounded rationality and learning' in Budescu, D., Erev, I. and Zwick, R. (eds) *Games and Human Behavior: Essays in honor of Amnon Rapoport*. Mahwah NJ: Lawrence Erlbaum.

Nagel, R., Bosch-Domènech, A., Montalvo, J. G. and Satorra, A. (2002) 'One, two, (three), infinity, …: newspaper and lab beauty-contest experiments'. *American Economic Review*, 92, 1687–701.

New York State Department of Financial Services (2015) 'In the matter of Barclays Bank plc, Barclays Bank plc, New York Branch, consent order under New York Banking Law §§ 44 and 44-a'. New York

NY: New York State Department of Financial Services. Available from: http://im.ft-static.com/content/images/ee8b6f40-fef5-11e4-84b2-00144feabdc0.pdf [accessed 21 December 2016].

Porter, T. (2005) *Globalization and Finance.* Cambridge: Polity Press.

Ross, S. A. (1976) 'Options and efficiency'. *Quarterly Journal of Economics*, 90, 75–89.

Royal Courts of Justice (2015) 'EWCA Crim 1944, Case No: 201504027 C3'. London: Royal Courts of Justice. Available from: https://www.judiciary.gov.uk/wp-content/uploads/2015/12/r_-v_tom_alexander_william_hayes_redacted_approved.pdf [accessed 21 December 2016].

Sandel, M. J. (2012) *What Money Can't Buy: The moral limits of markets.* New York NY: Farrar, Straus & Giroux.

Sarver, E. (1990) *The Eurocurrency Market Handbook*, 2nd edition. New York NY: New York Institute of Finance.

SEC (1996a) 'Order execution obligations, 17 CFR Part 240'. Washington DC: Securities and Exchange Commission (SEC). Available from: https://www.sec.gov/rules/final/37619a.txt [accessed 21 December 2016].

SEC (1996b) 'Report pursuant to section 21(a) of the Securities Exchange Act of 1934 regarding the NASD and the Nasdaq stock market'. Washington DC: Securities and Exchange Commission (SEC). Available from: https://www.sec.gov/litigation/investreport/nd21a-report.txt [accessed 21 December 2016].

Simmel, G. (1906) 'The sociology of secrecy and secret societies'. *American Journal of Sociology*, 11 (4), 441–98.

Smith, A. (1991 [1776]) *The Wealth of Nations.* London: Everyman's Library.

SNB (2015) 'Monetary policy strategy'. Swiss National Bank (SNB) website. Available from: http://www.snb.ch/en/iabout/monpol/id/monpol_strat#t7 [accessed 21 December 2016].

Soultanaeva, A. and Strömqvist, M. (2009) 'The Swedish money market risk premium: experiences from the crisis'. *Sveriges Riksbank Economic Review*, 3, 5–25.

Spiegel, M. (2001) 'The return of the "Japan premium": trouble ahead for Japanese banks?' *FRBSF [Federal Reserve Bank of San Francisco] Economic Letter*, 2001-06.

State of New York Office of the Attorney General (2009a) 'Attorney General's memorandum in opposition to motion to intervene and

petition to quash or modify subpoena, index no.: 400381109, 11
March'. New York NY: State of New York Office of the Attorney
General. Available from: http://www.wsj.com/public/resources/
documents/MemInOpp20090311.pdf [accessed 21 December
2016].

State of New York Office of the Attorney General (2009b) 'Re:
Bank of America – Merrill Lynch merger investigation. Letter
from Andrew M. Cuomo, 23 April'. New York NY: State of New
York Office of the Attorney General. Available from: http://
www.wsj.com/public/resources/documents/BofAmergLetter-
Cuomo4232009.pdf [accessed 21 December 2016].

Statistisk Sentralbyrå (2014) *Kulturstatistikk 2014*. Oslo: Statistics
Norway. Available from: https://www.ssb.no/en/kultur-
og-fritid/artikler-og-publikasjoner/_attachment/250101?_
ts=152cab395e8 [accessed 21 December 2016].

Statistisk Sentralbyrå (2016) 'Norwegian exports of weapons 2011–
2015: exports of arms rose in 2015. Press release, 15 January.
Oslo: Statistics Norway. Available from: https://www.ssb.no/en/
utenriksokonomi/artikler-og-publikasjoner/exports-of-arms-
rose-in-2015 [accessed 21 December 2016].

Stenfors, A. (2013) 'Determining the LIBOR: a study of power and
deception'. PhD thesis, SOAS, University of London.

Stenfors, A. (2014a) 'LIBOR as a Keynesian beauty contest: a process
of endogenous deception'. *Review of Political Economy*, 26 (3),
392–407.

Stenfors, A. (2014b) 'LIBOR deception and central bank forward
(mis-)guidance: evidence from Norway during 2007–2011'.
Journal of International Financial Markets, Institutions and Money,
32, 452–72.

Stenfors, A. and Lindo, D. (2016) 'The LIBOR eclipse: political
economy of a benchmark'. Research on Money and Finance
Discussion Papers No. 47. London: Department of Economics,
SOAS, University of London.

Stiglitz, J. and Greenwald, B. (2003) *Towards a New Paradigm in
Monetary Economics*. Cambridge: Cambridge University Press.

Story, L. and Dash, E. (2009) 'Undisclosed losses at Merrill Lynch
lead to a trading inquiry'. *The New York Times*, 5 March. Available
from: http://www.nytimes.com/2009/03/06/business/06wall.

html?n=Top%2fReference%2fTimes%20Topics%2fSubjects%2fF%2fFinances [accessed 21 December 2016].

Strange, S. (1986) *Casino Capitalism*. Oxford: Basil Blackwell.

Thaler, R. (1985) 'Mental accounting and consumer choice'. *Marketing Science*, 4 (3), 199–214.

The Telegraph (2015) 'Tom Hayes LIBOR trial: the top quotes'. *The Telegraph*, 4 August. Available from: http://www.telegraph.co.uk/finance/financial-crime/11780670/Tom-Hayes-LIBOR-trial-the-top-quotes.html [accessed 21 December 2016].

Thornton, D. L. (2009) 'What the Libor–OIS spread says'. Economic Synopses No. 24. St. Louis MO: Federal Reserve Bank of St. Louis.

Treanor, J. (2015) 'Libor-rigging fines: a timeline'. *The Guardian*, 23 April. Available from: http://www.theguardian.com/business/2015/apr/23/libor-rigging-fines-a-timeline [accessed 21 December 2016].

Tversky, A. and Kahneman, D. (1974) 'Judgement under uncertainty: heuristics and biases'. *Science*, 185 (4157), 1124–31.

UBS (2012) 'UBS Board of Directors authorizes settlements of LIBOR-related claims with US and UK authorities; Swiss regulator to issue order'. Press release, 19 December. Zurich: UBS. Available from: https://www.ubs.com/global/en/about_ubs/media/global/releases/news_display_media_global.html/en/2012/12/19/20121219a.html [accessed 21 December 2016].

United States Department of Justice (2012) 'United States of America v. Tom Alexander William Hayes and Roger Darin, 12 MAG 3229'. Washington DC: United States Department of Justice. Available from: https://www.justice.gov/sites/default/files/ag/legacy/2012/12/19/Hayes-Tom-and-Darin-Roger-Complaint.pdf [accessed 28 December 2016].

United States District Court Southern District of New York (2012) 'In re LIBOR-based financial instruments antitrust litigation, case no. 12 CV 1025 (NRB)'. New York NY: US District Court.

United States District Court Southern District of New York (2015) 'In re foreign exchange benchmark rates antitrust litigation, case no. 1-13-CV-07789'. New York NY: US District Court.

Vaughan, L. (2015a) '"I've got my wizards hat on:" What broker said about Libor moves'. Bloomberg, 23 October. Available from: http://www.bloomberg.com/news/articles/2015-10-23/-i-ve-got-my-wizards-hat-on-what-broker-said-about-libor-moves [accessed 21 December 2016].

Vaughan, L. (2015b) 'Ex-Tullett broker said he lied to Hayes about Libor to save job'. Bloomberg, 12 November. Available from: http://www.bloomberg.com/news/articles/2015-11-12/ex-tullett-broker-said-he-lied-to-hayes-about-libor-to-save-job [accessed 21 December 2016].

Vaughan, L. (2015c) '"Barrow boy" brokers were ignored by bankers on Libor, Read says'. Bloomberg, 17 November. Available from: http://www.bloomberg.com/news/articles/2015-11-17/-barrow-boy-brokers-were-ignored-by-bankers-on-libor-read-says [accessed 21 December 2016].

Vaughan, L. and Finch, G. (2013) 'Libor lies revealed in rigging of $300 trillion benchmark'. Bloomberg, 6 February. Available from: http://www.bloomberg.com/news/articles/2013-01-28/libor-lies-revealed-in-rigging-of-300-trillion-benchmark [accessed 21 December 2016].

Vaughan, L. and Finch, G. (2015) 'Was Tom Hayes running the biggest financial conspiracy in history? Or just taking the fall for one?' Bloomberg, 14 September. Available from: http://www.bloomberg.com/news/articles/2015-09-14/was-tom-hayes-running-the-biggest-financial-conspiracy-in-history- [accessed 21 December 2016].

Verlaine, J. and Finch, G. (2014) 'Biggest banks said to overhaul FX trading after scandals'. Bloomberg, 16 September. Available from: http://www.bloomberg.com/news/articles/2014-09-15/biggest-banks-said-to-overhaul-fx-trading-after-scandals [accessed 21 December 2016].

World Trade Organization (2016) 'Time series on international trade'. WTO website. Available from: http://stat.wto.org/StatisticalProgram/WSDBViewData.aspx?Language=E [accessed 20 September 2016].

Wu, T. (2008) 'On the effectiveness of the Federal Reserve's new liquidity facilities'. Working Paper No. 0808. Dallas TX: Federal Reserve Bank of Dallas Research Department.

Yule, G. U. (1927) 'On a reading scale'. *Journal of the Royal Statistical Society*, 90 (3), 570–9.

INDEX

314

ABOUT THE AUTHOR

Alexis Stenfors spent 15 years as a foreign exchange and interest rate derivatives trader at HSBC, Citi, Crédit Agricole and Merrill Lynch. In 2009, he found himself at the centre of a 'mismarking' scandal that would eventually result in him being described as one of the 'world's most infamous rogue traders'. Returning to academia the same year, he completed his doctoral thesis with the title 'Determining the LIBOR: A Study of Power and Deception' in 2013. Alexis holds a civilekonom degree and an MSc in financial economics from the Stockholm School of Economics, a CEMS master's degree from the Community of European Management Schools, and a PhD in economics from SOAS, University of London. He is currently senior lecturer in economics and finance at Portsmouth Business School.

Edwards Brothers Malloy
Ann Arbor MI. USA
July 17, 2017